Drive Around

Languedoc
and Southwest France

YOUR GUIDE TO GREAT DRIVES

Titles in this series include:

- **Andalucía and the Costa del Sol**
- **Bavaria and the Austrian Tyrol**
- **Brittany and Normandy**
- **Burgundy and the Rhône Valley**
- **California**
- **Catalonia and the Spanish Pyrenees**
- **Dordogne and Western France**
- **England and Wales**
- **Florida**
- **Ireland**
- **Italian Lakes and Mountains with Venice and Florence**
- **Languedoc and Southwest France**
- **Loire Valley**
- **Provence and the Côte d'Azur**
- **Scotland**
- **Tuscany and Umbria**
- **Vancouver and British Columbia**
  and

- **Selected Bed and Breakfast in France** (annual edition)

For further information about these and other Thomas Cook publications, write to Thomas Cook Publishing, PO Box 227, The Thomas Cook Business Park, 15–16 Coningsby Road, Peterborough PE3 8SB, United Kingdom.

Drive Around

Languedoc
and Southwest France

The best of Languedoc's diverse and unspoilt landscapes, from the beaches of the coastal resorts to the wild and remote mountain plateaux, including Cathar country, the Cévennes and the Pyrenees, and the Tarn and Gard regions.

Gillian Thomas and John Harrison

Thomas Cook
Publishing

www.thomascookpublishing.com

Published by Thomas Cook Publishing,
a division of Thomas Cook Tour Operations Limited
PO Box 227
The Thomas Cook Business Park
15–16 Coningsby Road
Peterborough PE3 8SB
United Kingdom

Telephone: +44 (0)1733 416477
Fax: +44 (0)1733 416688
E-mail: books@thomascook.com

For further information about
Thomas Cook Publishing, visit our website
www.thomascookpublishing.com

ISBN 1-841574-69-4

Text: © 2005 Thomas Cook Publishing
Maps and diagrams:
Road maps supplied and designed by Lovell Johns Ltd, OX8 8LH
Road maps generated from Collins Bartholomew Digital Database
© Collins Bartholomew Ltd, 1999
City maps prepared by RJS Associates, © Thomas Cook Publishing

Head of Publishing: Chris Young
Series Editor: Charlotte Christensen
Production/DTP Editor: Steven Collins
Project Administrator: Michelle Warrington

Written and researched by: Gillian Thomas and
John Harris
Update research by: David Brown
Driving information: Michael Hafferty

About the authors

Gillian Thomas and **John Harrison**, husband-and-wife authors of this book, are both members of the British Guild of Travel Writers. They live in Ealing, West London.

After graduating in French and German at Birmingham University, Gillian joined the BBC. She first combined travel with writing while working in the Paris news office. Returning to the UK she became a freelance journalist, mainly covering women's and educational topics. Later she moved into travel writing, initially by describing family holidays in France with their three young children.

John's first steps in journalism were on Cherwell, the undergraduate newspaper at Oxford which he edited. He then spent 31 years with the BBC where his jobs ranged from radio announcer to TV science programmes organiser; he also set up the British Forces TV service in Germany. Having spent many hours as his wife's unpaid assistant, he joined her in full-time travel writing when he left the BBC.

Below
Château de Peyrepertuse

They have been visiting the Languedoc on holiday for many years, attracted initially by its long sandy beaches. Both had happy memories of their own childhood holidays in England but wanted to be sure of sunshine and warm sea for their small children as well as good sand for buckets and spades.

With the bonus of French food and wine and the area's wide choice of campsites, it proved an ideal formula. They all enjoyed the area's colourful markets, driving through its dramatic gorges, trips on its scenic railways, clambering around lofty rugged castles and venturing into the awe-inspiring caves. The scenery was a continuous delight too, embellished at dusk by magnificent sunsets.

Gillian and John would like to thank Ann Noon and Marie-Thérèse Smith of the French Tourist Office in London, Peter Mills of Rail Europe in London and Patricia de Pouzilhac of the Languedoc-Roussillon CRT for the help they gave them during their research for this book.

Contents

About Drive Around Guides

Thomas Cook's Drive Around Guides are designed to provide you with a comprehensive but flexible reference source to guide you as you tour a country or region by car. This guide divides The Languedoc and Southwest France into touring areas – one per chapter. Major cultural centres or cities form chapters in their own right. Each chapter contains enough attractions to provide at least a day's worth of activities – often more.

Star ratings

To make it easier for you to plan your time and decide what to see, every sight and attraction is given a star rating. A three-star rating indicates an outstanding sight or major attraction. Often these can be worth at least half a day of your time. A two-star attraction is worth an hour or so of your time, and a one-star attraction indicates a site that is good, but often of specialist interest. To help you further, individual attractions within towns or theme parks are also graded, so that travellers with limited time can quickly find the most rewarding sights.

Chapter contents

Every chapter has an introduction summing up the main attractions of the area, and a ratings box, which will highlight the area's strengths and weaknesses – some areas may be more attractive to families travelling with children, others to wine-lovers or people interested in finding castles, churches, or good beaches.

Each chapter is then divided into an alphabetical gazetteer, and a suggested tour. You can select whether you just want to visit a particular sight or attraction, choosing from those described in the gazetteer, or whether you want to tour the area comprehensively. If the latter, you can construct your own itinerary, or follow the author's suggested tour, which comes at the end of every area chapter.

The gazetteer

The gazetteer section describes all the major attractions in the area – the villages, towns, historic sites, nature reserves, parks or museums that you are most likely to want to see. Maps of the area highlight all the places mentioned in the text. Using this comprehensive overview of the area, you may choose just to visit one or two sights.

One way to use the guide is simply to find individual sights that interest you, using the index, overview map or star ratings, and read what our authors have to say about them. This will help you decide whether to visit the sight. If you do, you will find plenty of practical

Symbol Key

- ❶ Tourist Information Centre
- ❷ Advice on arriving or departing
- ❷ Parking locations
- ❷ Advice on getting around
- ❷ Directions
- ❶ Sights and attractions
- ❶ Accommodation
- ❶ Eating
- ❷ Shopping
- ❷ Sport
- ❷ Entertainment

Practical information

The practical information in the page margins, or sidebar, will help you locate the services you need as an independent traveller – including the tourist information centre, car parks and public transport facilities. You will also find the opening times of sights, museums, churches and other attractions, as well as useful tips on shopping, market days, cultural events, entertainment, festivals and sports facilities.

information, such as the street address, the telephone number for enquiries and opening times.

Alternatively, you can choose a hotel, perhaps with the help of the accommodation recommendations contained in this guide. You can then turn to the overall map on page 10 to help you work out which chapters in the book describe those cities and regions that lie closest to your chosen touring base.

Driving tours

The suggested tour is just that – a suggestion, with plenty of optional detours and one or two ideas for making your own discoveries, under the heading *Also worth exploring*. The routes are designed to link the attractions described in the gazetteer section, and to cover outstandingly scenic coastal, mountain and rural landscapes. The total distance is given for each tour, as is the time it will take you to drive the complete route, but bear in mind that this indication is just for the driving time: you will need to add on extra time for visiting attractions along the way.

Many of the routes are circular, so that you can join them at any point. Where the nature of the terrain dictates that the route has to be linear, the route can either be followed out and back, or you can use it as a link route, to get from one area in the book to another.

As you follow the route descriptions, you will find names picked out in bold capital letters – this means that the place is described fully in the gazetteer. Other names picked out in bold indicate additional villages or attractions worth a brief stop along the route.

Accommodation and food

In every chapter you will find lodging and eating recommend-ations for individual towns, or for the area as a whole. These are designed to cover a range of price brackets and concentrate on more characterful small or individualistic hotels and restaurants. In addition, you will find information in the *Travel facts* chapter on chain hotels, with an address to which you can write for a guide, map or directory. The price indications used in the guide have the following meanings:

€   budget level
€€   typical/average prices
€€€   de luxe.

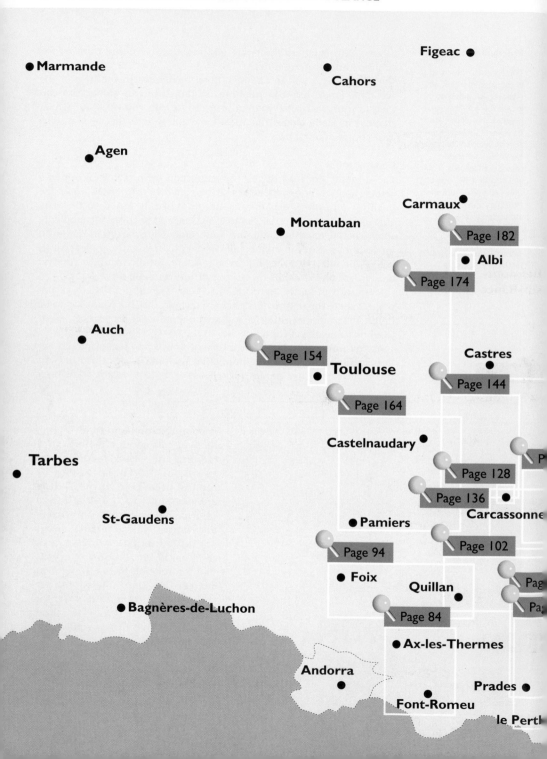

Figeac ●

● Marmande

Cahors

Agen ●

Carmaux ●

Page 182

Montauban ●

● Albi

Page 174

Auch ●

Page 154

Castres ●

Toulouse

Page 144

Page 164

Castelnaudary ●

Tarbes ●

Page 128

Page 136

St-Gaudens ●

Carcassonne ●

● Pamiers

Page 94

Page 102

● Foix

Quillan ●

Pag

● Bagnères-de-Luchon

Pa

Page 84

● Ax-les-Thermes

Andorra ●

Prades ●

Font-Romeu ●

le Perth

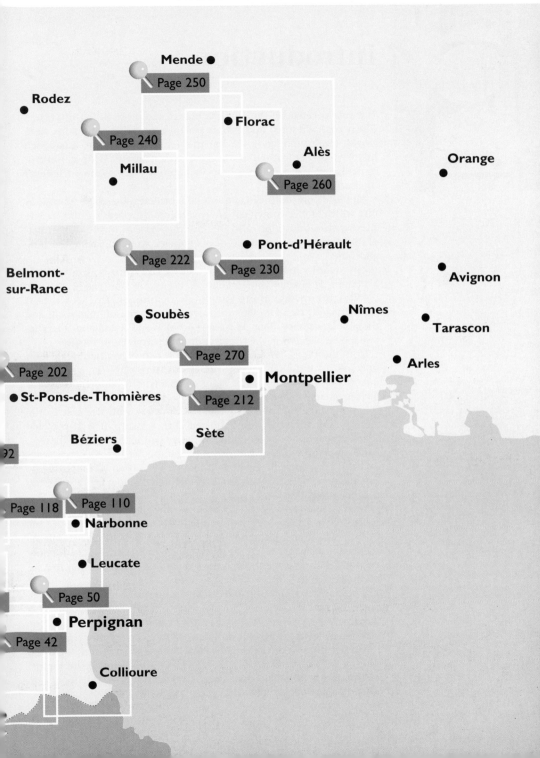

Mende ●
Page 250

Rodez ●

● Florac

Page 240

Alès
Page 260

Orange ●

Millau ●

● Pont-d'Hérault

Page 222

Page 230

Belmont-
sur-Rance

Avignon ●

● Soubès

Nîmes ●

Tarascon

Page 270

Arles ●

Page 202

● Montpellier

St-Pons-de-Thomières ●

Page 212

Sète ●

Béziers ●

92

Page 118   Page 110

● Narbonne

● Leucate

Page 50

● Perpignan

Page 42

● Collioure

Introduction

The area covered by this book is one of the most varied in France. Glossy coastal resorts, wild remote plateaux, towering mountains, deep gorges, forests and caves – it has them all in abundance. Add a rich history, castles, cathedrals and an exceptionally wide variety of museums and it provides plenty to interest every visitor, whatever their particular taste.

All five *départements* of Languedoc-Roussillon (one of the 22 regions into which France is divided) are covered: Aude, Gard, Hérault, Lozère and Pyrénées-Roussillon; also the four *départements* in the eastern half of the Midi-Pyrénées region: Ariège-Pyrénées, Aveyron, Haute-Garonne and Tarn.

The major cities featured are Albi, Carcassonne, Montpellier, Narbonne, Perpignan and Toulouse.

Though crowded along the coast in summer, the area is still predominantly rural. It offers the traveller the bonus of quiet roads and unspoilt landscapes – but be warned – hotels and restaurants are often few and far between in the countryside, and petrol stations scarce.

Until the 1960s, few people went to this part of southern France for holidays. In those days too its vineyards were better known for the quantity of their wines rather than the quality. The anonymous *vins de table* invariably hailed from the area.

Today Languedoc and its wines are up there with the best in the world – and the coastline is dotted with a string of well-planned resorts, the result of a far-sighted initiative by the French government. Furthermore, the building of marinas, apartments and villa complexes – some of the most imaginative in Europe – has been accompanied by careful conservation of the fragile dunes and shallow lagoons behind the long sandy beaches.

Driving inland you are very soon surrounded by vineyards. They cover the flat Languedoc plain and stretch up the sunny slopes of the Corbières hills and the Montagne Noire. The fact that an increasing number of the wines reach the *appellation contrôlée* standard is not only good news for everyone who enjoys them but is also helping to raise the area's profile.

Mountains frame both ends of the region, the Cévennes in the northeast and the Pyrenees in the south, making it one of the most varied in France. Jagged ridges, deep river canyons and rocky limestone plateaux (with vast caves beneath) make it one of the most scenic too.

Not surprisingly, the mountains have become as popular as the coast, though without the crowds. Canoeists enjoy shooting the rapids, walkers and horse riders have miles of waymarked trails to explore and, when the snow arrives in winter, skiers flock to the Pyrenees.

Though so many of the buildings along the coast are modern, the area has plenty to show for over 2000 years of history. Discoveries in a cave near the tiny village of Tautavel in the Corbières have revealed that people settled the area 700,000 years ago.

More recently – around the first century AD – the Romans left plenty of traces of their occupation, when Narbonne was capital of Gaul. A section of their Via Domitia highway, revealed during recent excavations and now the centrepiece of the city's main square, is just one of many relics from that remarkable era.

Touring the area today, you soon become aware of the havoc caused by religious and political conflicts over the centuries. The ruined castles which cling precariously to hilltops played a leading role in the struggles between Cathars and Catholics at the beginning of the 13th century. Others guarded the volatile border with Spain.

Whole communities were wiped out during the merciless campaigns to rid the area of the Cathar 'heretics' and later when Protestants fought for religious freedom. Many magnificent churches have survived, often fortress-like with a single nave designed to enable huge numbers to worship together and so be left in no doubt about the power of the clergy. Albi Cathedral is the most outstanding of all.

Happier times and prosperity arrived when blue became the fashionable colour – woad, from which blue dye was produced, grew in profusion in the 'golden triangle' between Toulouse, Albi and Carcassonne. Local merchants were quick to capitalise on its availability and sold it around Europe. Their profits enabled them to build grand mansions which still grace the streets of Toulouse and other towns, some now converted into museums.

More than most areas of France, Languedoc changes with the seasons. In summer the vineyards are a mass of vivid green leaves, yet come winter they are cut back to bare stumps that look more dead than alive. Each plant is neatly clipped by hand, a true labour of love. In autumn those same vines transform the countryside once more when the leaves turn orange, maroon and purple.

The appearance of the mountains varies dramatically too. Autumn is the most beautiful time as the hillsides are patched with vivid yellows, reds and browns thanks to the beech and chestnut trees. In winter, snow covers the meadows and pine-covered slopes around the Cerdagne plateau in the Pyrenees, and also the highest parts of the Cévennes.

Despite having so much historic and scenic diversity to offer, the Languedoc has still to catch up with its neighbour, Provence, as an instantly recognisable tourist region. Holidaying on the coast in summer, it's pleasing to find more than enough room on the beach to spread out your towel. And there is certainly some way to go yet before the beaches begin to feel overcrowded. In high season, however, the coastal roads can become unpleasantly busy; but how delightful that so many places in the Languedoc and the Southwest are still off the beaten track. Visit and you will discover the best of the area and its diverse secrets.

Travel facts

Accommodation

The area's hotels range from basic to luxurious, though most are in the small and reasonably priced category. They tend to be in the cities and towns rather than in the countryside and many close out of season (usually Nov–Mar).

To help offset the summer heat, bedrooms are usually uncarpeted, and have shutters on the windows; they also help keep out the winter wind. If you don't like the look of the bolster on the bed, softer pillows (and extra blankets) can invariably be found in the wardrobe. Tea/coffee-making facilities are rarely provided.

Few hotels are part of international chains, except in the cities (particularly Toulouse and Montpellier). Chains represented include the modern 4-star Sofitel and Holiday Inn Crowne Plaza, 3-star Mercure and Novotel and 2-star Campanile, Climat, Comfort Inn and Ibis.

Many of the smaller ones are members of the Logis de France association of privately-owned hotels whose owners have signed a quality charter guaranteeing modern comforts and friendly service. These are marked by a distinctive yellow and green chimney sign outside. Their prices are always reasonable and the restaurants invariably feature home cooking with an emphasis on regional specialities. Many Logis hotels are in interesting old buildings and most are family-run, with the owners in residence to provide a homely welcome. The Logis directory, *Le Guide des 3000 hôtels-restaurants de France*, is available free from the French Tourist Office shop at *178 Piccadilly, London W1J 9AL (tel: 0906 824 4123 (premium rates apply))*. Reservations tel: *(00 33 outside France) 01 45 84 83 84; www.logis-de-france.fr*

Gîtes

For self-catering, *Gîtes de France* are country properties, often part of a farm, whose owners have refurbished them for holiday accommodation (under a government grant scheme). Standards vary – from basic upwards. To book a gîte, go to **Gîtes de France**: *tel: 01 49 70 75 75; www.gites-de-france.fr.* **Brittany Ferries** *(tel: 08705 360360)* also deals with enquiries about gîtes and other self-catering accommodation which are featured in its 'French Collection Holidays' brochure; *tel: 08705 143 537; www.brittanyferries.co.uk.* A selection of country cottages, apartments and houses is also available through Interhome: *tel: 020 8891 1294; www.interhome.ch* or through local tourist offices and agencies *(see page 31)*. Another large selection,

Hotel chains

Accor (includes Ibis, Mercure, Novotel, Sofitel, Formule-1). *Central reservation number: UK tel: 0870 609 0961; USA tel: 1800 221 4542; www.accorhotels.com*

Best Western *UK tel: 01904 695495; USA tel: 1800 528 1234; www.bestwestern.com*

Campanile (includes Climat) *UK tel: 020 8569 6969; www.envergure.fr*

Choice Hotels (includes Comfort and Quality Inns) *France tel: 0800 12 12 12; UK tel: 0800 44 44 44; USA tel: 1800 4-CHOICE; www.choicehotels.com*

Holiday Inn Crowne Plaza *UK tel: 0800 40 50 60; USA/Canada tel: 1 800 465 4329; www. intercontinentalhotelgroup. com*

Relais et Châteaux
UK tel: 020 7924 5834;
USA tel: 1 877 334 6464;
www.relaischateaux.com

bookable direct with the owners, appears in the 'Owners in France' brochure: *tel: 08709 013 400; www.ownersinfrance.com*

Bed and Breakfast

'Le B&B' is an internationally recognised term for accommodation in guestrooms in private homes, whether it's in a simple farmhouse, a town house or a grand chateau. The French also call it *chambres d'hôtes*. Thomas Cook Publishing, in co-operation with Bed & Breakfast (France), publish an annual directory *Bed & Breakfast France* (price £12.99 plus p&p), available from **Thomas Cook Publishing**, *PO Box 227, The Thomas Cook Business Park, 15–16 Coningsby Road, Peterborough PE3 8SB, UK; tel: 01733 416477*. **Bed & Breakfast (France)** has a website at *www.bedbreak.com*. You can book your bed & breakfast on the website or by phone; *tel: 020 8956 2390*.

Camping

Campsites are graded from one to four stars. Facilities and standards in the top category can be very impressive, including hot showers, supermarkets, takeaway restaurants and extensive sports amenities. Some have caravans (mobile homes) and chalets for hire (but not camper vans); pre-erected tents and caravans can also be booked, including travel, through several UK tour operators (*see page 31*). The Camping France website at *www.campingfrance.com* handles online bookings for a range of owners covering more than one thousand campsites in southern France.

Airports

Montpellier and Toulouse have international airports serving cities around Europe, including London and Paris. Low-cost flights from the UK go to Carcassonne and Perpignan. The only direct service to the area from North America is between Montreal and Toulouse; other transatlantic services go to Paris but there are frequent internal flights or you can continue your journey by train or car. All the major car rental companies have desks at Toulouse airport. Toulouse airport *www.toulouse.aeroport.fr*; Montpellier-Méditerranée airport *www.montpellier.aeroport.fr*. Other regional airports, including Nîmes, Pau, Bordeaux and Biarritz-Bayonne, are linked to Toulouse and Perpignan by *autoroute*.

Children

The sandy beaches along the Languedoc-Roussillon coast make its resorts very popular with families. The larger ones have children's beach clubs during the school holidays in summer (July and August). There are

Customs regulations

When you arrive from another country within the European Union, there are no customs formalities. However, tax-free tobacco and alcohol are restricted to personal use; 10 litres of spirits; 20 litres of wine; 110 litres of beer; 400 cigarettes; 200 cigars; 1kg of tobacco.

Limits are lower for arrivals from outside the EU and also cover coffee, tea and perfumes.

Non-EU residents can claim the TVA (VAT) back on goods purchased in France when they spend a large sum in the same shop (though not all shops offer this facility).

Electricity

Plugs have either two or three round pins. As this is not a standard European design, you are likely to need an adaptor. The voltage is 220 (50 MHz).

Aqualand water parks with slides in St-Cyprien-Plage (*see page 59*) and Cap d'Agde (*see page 273*), and a safari park, Réserve Africaine de Sigean (*see page 121*), south of Narbonne. Inland the area is short of man-made attractions but its many caves, hilltop castles and tortuous mountain roads can provide plenty of excitement for young visitors.

Climate

The area enjoys some of the best weather in France with plenty of clear, dry days. During July and August, temperatures along the coast average around 28°C (82°F), dropping to 11°C (52°F) in February. Perpignan is one of the warmest places in France. However, the coast can also be windy due to the *Tramontane* which frequently blows across the Corbières hills from the northwest, for three, six or nine days continuously. Another famous wind, the warm gusty *Autan*, blows from the sea. 'It drives you mad', they say in Toulouse and Albi. In the mountains the weather is always a little cooler. The higher areas in the Pyrenees have enough snow for skiing, and the Cévennes can also get a smattering of snow.

On doors and shutters of houses throughout the Causses you will often see a dried *chardon du causse* (thistle) hanging. When rain is imminent, the thistle closes up, but in good weather it stays open; thus it acts as a natural barometer.

Currency

The unit of currency, the euro (€), is divided into 100 cents. When sums are written, a comma rather than a decimal point is used to separate euros from cents. Payments can be made in euro notes and coins from any of the countries in the Eurozone. Airports and banks, as well as some shopping centres and tourist offices, have bureaux de change. Cash points (ATMs) are widespread. Payments can be made in euros by credit cards or traveller's cheques.

Drinking

Languedoc-Roussillon is one of the most prolific wine-producing regions in France. In the vineyard areas on the plains just inland from the coast, there are frequent opportunities for a *dégustation* (sampling) at co-operative cellars and roadside stalls, as well as at the *domaines* (wine-producing estates) themselves. The red, white and rosé *vins de pays* (table wines) are inexpensive, though an increasing number of high-quality *appellation d'origine contrôlleé* vintages are being produced.

If in doubt about what to drink with a meal, ask the waiter for advice. They are invariably knowledgeable and willing to help. The cheapest option is to have open wine which comes in a *pichet* (litre

Regional specialities

A strong Arabic influence is noticable in Catalan cakes which ooze with honey and are flavoured with nuts and spices. *Crème Catalan* is a vanilla custard topped with crisp caramel, but lighter than *crème brûlée*.

The cherries which grow around Céret are the earliest variety in France and are followed by a succession of other fruits, particularly peaches, apricots, pears and apples. Seasonal fruit is used in flans for dessert.

Several towns have their own special cakes, including *petits pâtés* in Pézanas, *Glorias* and *Alleluias* in Castelnaudary and *jeannots* in Albi.

jug) or *demi-pichet*. If you ask for a beer – *une pression* or *une bière* – you automatically get a *demi* (½-litre) unless you specify more. Beer, pastis, kir (wine and cassis), Floc de Gascogne (sweet wine), whisky, fruit juice and mineral water are the accepted aperitifs – or sparkling wine. These are usually served with an *amuse gueule* (cocktail snack) such as olives or small pastries. Note, however, that your food will not be served until the glasses are empty!

It is safe to drink tap water; indeed restaurants invariably place a carafe on the table. It is not 'done' for men to drink only water with dinner in the evening, though driving or work are acceptable excuses for having soft drinks only. Mineral water can be more expensive than wine.

Café prices vary depending whether you are served at the bar, at a table inside or at a table on the terrace, but price lists must be displayed both outside and inside. The staff are required to give bills for orders over 13 euros; for lower amounts, they must give you one if you ask for it.

Eating out

The larger towns offer an interestingly varied choice of restaurants, including many good ones in hotels. All are legally required to offer a set menu. Brasseries are less formal, stay open longer and offer snacks as well as two or three set menus. Sunday lunchtime is invariably busy everywhere (so it pays to make a reservation). Some restaurants are closed on Sunday evening and also on a weekday, often Monday. Many shut for a month or so in winter.

In the evening, restaurant menus (served from around 1900) are more expensive and elaborate than at lunchtime (1200–1400) when it is perfectly acceptable to order one dish and no alcohol. Bread is served automatically.

In restaurants, always wait to be shown to a table as it is 'not done' to choose one yourself. If you don't like it, you can then ask to be seated elsewhere. The bill (*l'addition*) will be brought to the table for payment.

Hotels and restaurants affiliated to the Logis de France association can be relied on to serve home cooking and regional specialities. In the countryside, you can also eat at *fermes-auberges* (farm restaurants) where the farmer's wife invariably provides a robust country meal using local seasonal ingredients. You usually need to book a day in advance and probably won't be offered a choice.

Entry formalities

Visas are not required by EU nationals or visitors from the United States, Canada and New Zealand staying not more than three months. Visitors from most other countries, including Australia

Conversion tables

Distances

Metric	Imperial
1m	3ft 3in
5m	16ft 6in
10m	33ft
50m	164ft
100m	330ft
1km	0.75 mile
2km	1.5 miles
5km	3 miles
10km	6 miles
20km	12.5 miles
50km	31 miles
100km	62 miles

Weight

Kg	Lbs
1	2
2	4.5
5	11
10	22
20	45
50	110
75	165
100	220

Fluid measures

Litres	Imperial gallon
5	1.1
10	2.2
20	4.4
50	11

Area

1 hectare = 2.471 acres
1 acre = 0.4 hectares

and South Africa need one, obtainable from their local French consulate.

Festivals

Every town and village seems to have its own festival during the summer months, often with a bonfire and fireworks, processions, street entertainment and barbecues. No matter how small, they are an occasion not to miss and visitors are always welcome to join in. Bastille Day (14 July) is celebrated in great style.

Mid-summer is also a time for street parties. Les Feux de la St-Jean takes place on 23 June, particularly around the Canigou mountain. Torches lit from bonfires on the mountain are carried down to more bonfires in the villages and towns below. When the embers begin to die down, everyone starts jumping over them. Many people join the grand procession into Perpignan.

Music festivals include sacred music in Perpignan (Holy Week), jazz in the open air in Albi (May and June), dance in Montpellier (June) and riverside concerts in Toulouse (June); also a medieval festival in Narbonne (August).

Food

Cassoulet, a sustaining meat stew with white beans, is one of the area's most famous dishes. Originally designed for hearty appetites, it features on menus in and around Toulouse and Carcassonne. Several kinds of fish stew are available on the coast, including *brandade de morue*, made from salt cod with milk and garlic. Bouziques oysters are cultivated in the Bassin de Thau; anchovies are a speciality in Collioure; and plump mussels are served stuffed with a herb and tomato sauce in Sète. Inland you find mainly freshwater fish, particularly trout.

The area's most famous cheese is the creamy blue-veined Roquefort. Made from ewes' milk, it is produced in rounds and matured for up to six months. Bleu des Causses is a also a blue cheese, but made from cow's milk. Pélaradon des Cévennes is a small, round, mountain cheese made with goat's milk; it can be eaten fresh while soft, or left to mature and harden.

Information

Most towns and some villages have a tourist office, though some are only open in high season. In smaller places it is called the Syndicat d'Initiative (SI) and in larger ones the Office de Tourisme (OT). Many have an accommodation booking service, usually free. All have free local maps and accommodation lists.

Unfortunately many close at lunchtime, around 1200–1400, even at the height of summer. A solution is to seek out a café with a Bonjour sign. This means it stocks local tourist information.

To get information on a particular area, bear in mind that France is divided into 22 regions. The regions in turn are split into *départements*. Do not expect an office to provide information about other *départements*.

The Languedoc-Roussillon Tourist Board – Comité Régionale du Tourisme (CRT) – is based at *20 rue de la République, 34000 Montpellier; tel: 04 67 22 81 00; www.sunfrance.com*. The Comitées Départementaux du Tourisme (CDTs) in Languedoc-Roussillon are: Aude: *11855 Carcassonne; tel: 04 68 11 66 00; www.audetourisme.com*; Gard: *3 place des Arènes, 30010 Nîmes; tel: 04 66 36 96 30; www.cdt-gard.fr*; Hérault: *avenue des Moulins, 34184 Montpellier; tel: 04 67 67 71 71; www.herault-en-languedoc.com*; Lozère: *14 boulevard Henri Bourrillo, 48001 Mende; tel: 04 66 65 60 00; www.france48.com*; Pyrénées-Orientales: *16 avenue des Palmiers, 66005 Perpignan; tel: 04 68 51 52 53; www.cdt66.com*. For Midi-Pyrénées the CRT is at *54 boulevard de l'Embouchure, 31022 Toulouse; tel: 05 61 13 55 12; www.tourism.midi-pyrenees.org*. The relevant CDTs in Midi-Pyrénées are Ariège-Pyrénées: *31 bis avenue du Général du Gaulle, 09004 Foix; tel: 05 61 02 30 70; www.ariege-pyrenees.com*; Aveyron: *17 rue Aristide Brillant, 12008 Rodez; tel: 05 65 75 55 70; www.tourisme-aveyron.com*; Haute-Garonne: *14 rue Bayard, 31015 Toulouse; tel: 05 61 99 44 00; www.tourisme-haute-garonne.com*; Tarn: *Moulin Albigeois, 81006 Albi; tel: 05 63 77 32 10; www.tourisme-tarn.com*. Information about walking tours and hiking can be provided by the National Parc des Pyrénées: *tel: 05 62 44 36 60; www.parc-pyrenees.com*; or the Fédération Française de la Randonnée Pédestre: *14 rue Riquet, 75019 Paris; tel: 01 44 89 93 93; www.ffrp.asso.fr*

French tourist offices abroad are called Maisons de la France: Australia: *25 Bligh Street, Sydney NSW 2000; tel: 29231 5244*; Canada: *1981 avenue MacGill College, Suite 490, Montreal H3A 2W9; tel: 514 876 9881*; Ireland: *30 Upper Merrion Street, Dublin 2; tel: 1560 235 235 (premium rates apply)*; South Africa: *PO Box 41022, 2024 Craighall; tel: 11 880 8062*; United Kingdom: *178 Piccadilly, London W1J 9AL; tel: 09068 244 123 (premium rates apply)*; United States: *444 Madison Avenue, 16th floor, New York NY 10022; tel: 410 286 8310; www.franceguide.com*

Maps

Michelin 1/300,000 (1cm:3km) are a good scale for touring. They come in two series: regional (including Nos 526 Languedoc-Roussillon and 525 Midi-Pyrénées) and local (each covering a smaller area). The local ones for the area covered in this book are Nos 338, 339, 342, 343 and 344.

IGN (Institut Géographique National) publishes a regional 1/250,000 scale Carte-Routière series; No R16 covers Midi-Pyrénées and No R17 covers Languedoc-Roussillon. In its 1/100,000 Green series, the area is covered by Nos 58, 59, 64, 65 and 72. The 1/25,000 Blue series is designed for walkers. Available in the UK direct from

Health

All hotels have a list of doctors and emergency medical services. Pharmacists are qualified to diagnose basic problems and suggest treatments, though you need a doctor's prescription to claim the cost back on insurance. As many people go mushrooming, pharmacists are also trained to identify which ones are poisonous! Pharmacies have a green cross sign outside. They are normally closed on Sundays but display a list of those on duty.

For the emergency medical service, SAMU, dial 15.

Insurance

Non-EU nationals are required to have health insurance. It is highly recommended for EU nationals too, though doctor's fees and basic medical expenses can be reimbursed – eventually – if you have an E111 form (available from UK post offices) with you.

Stanfords, *12–14 Long Acre, London WC2E 9LP; tel: 020 7836 1321; www.stanfords.co.uk*

Regional and departmental tourist boards issue free maps of their areas, marked with tourist attractions and listing useful addresses. Most newsagents and petrol stations sell local maps.

Museums

National museums close all day on Tuesdays and municipal ones on Mondays; also some bank holidays. Privately run attractions normally open daily during high season; many close Oct–Easter. Opening hours vary but are usually from around 0900 or 1000 to 1700 or 1800 (often shorter hours at weekends); many close at lunchtime.

Most charge a small entrance fee with discounts for children. At national museums, under-18s are free and 18–25s and over-60s get a discount. At municipal museums, under-7s and over-60s are free; Sundays are free to everyone.

National and regional parks

The mountainous and sparsely populated Cévennes National Park covers 1000 sq km and rises at Mont Lozère to 1700m. It has large areas of open moorland, known for birds of prey such as eagles, harriers and buzzards as well as butterflies and wild flowers. The park's information centre, Maison du Parc, is in the Château de Florac at Florac; *tel: 04 66 49 53 01; www.cevennes-parcnational.fr*

Haut Languedoc Regional Park, a hilly forested region, is a good place to watch for eagles and other birds of prey, and is also excellent for walking. Information: *place du Foirail, St-Pons-de-Thomières; tel: 04 67 97 38 22; www.parc-haut-languedoc.fr*

Opening times

Banks open from 0800 or 0900 to 1200 and from 1300 or 1400 to 1600 or 1700, but close earlier before a bank holiday. They close Sunday and either Monday or Saturday.

Shops: normal hours are from 0900 or 1000 to 1830 or 1930; smaller ones close between 1300 and 1500 or 1600. Food shops open earlier and hypermarkets stay open later. *Boulangeries* (bakers) and *épiceries* (grocers) open Sunday morning, but other shops are closed, including hypermarkets. Many shops close on Monday, at least in the morning.

Churches: most are open 0800–1900, but usually close between 1145 and 1430. Entry is free. Visitors should not enter during services unless they intend to join the congregation.

Public holidays

1 Jan (New Year), Good Friday, 1 May (Labour Day), 8 May (VE-Day), Ascension Day, Whit Sunday, 14 July (Bastille Day), 15 Aug (Assumption), 1 Nov (All Saints'), 11 Nov (Armistice Day 1918) and 25 Dec (Christmas Day).

Postal services

Post boxes are yellow. Post offices (la Poste) are generally open Mon–Fri 0800–1900, often with a lunchtime break, and until 1200 on Saturdays. There are eight price zones for mail, ranging from postcards and letters up to 20g within the EU to airmail to Australasia. Aerograms are the same for all countries. Stamps (timbres-postes) can also be bought at tobacconists (tabacs).

Reading:

The Cathars by Malcolm Lambert, published by Blackwell.

Travels with a Donkey in the Cévennes by RL Stevenson.

Packing

Swimwear and a sunhat are needed to enjoy the area's beaches (though many have nudist areas). Walking boots or shoes are essential for exploring the mountains on foot. In summer a sweater and/or light jacket is advisable for evenings in case the wind gets up. Clothing requirements in winter depend where you are going, from ski-wear in the Pyrenees to something lighter elsewhere, though the wind can be unexpectedly cold throughout the region.

Public transport

Frequent trains run between the main cities. Typical timings are: Toulouse–Albi 1 hour, Toulouse–Carcassonne 45 minutes, Toulouse–Montpellier 2 hours 10 minutes, Montpellier–Narbonne 1 hour, Narbonne–Perpignan 40 minutes, Narbonne–Carcassonne 55 minutes. Information and bookings; tel: 36 35. Reservations are required on TGV (train à grande vitesse) services which run between Montpellier and Perpignan. Bus services are very patchy. Toulouse has a one-line underground metro and Montpellier a new Tramway.

Right
St-Guilhem-le-Désert

Sport

Rugby, which arrived in the area a hundred years ago, is enthusiastically played and watched. ASB in Béziers is one of France's top teams. Around Carcassonne, rugby league is played too. Football is a particular passion in Toulouse. And in the shade of every dusty square, you are likely to see a game of *pétanque* (boules), played mostly by older men.

Stores

Department stores are few and far between in the area except in Montpellier, Perpignan and Toulouse. Galeries Lafayette are smart fashion stores; Monoprix are middle-range stores selling food, inexpensive fashion, accessories and stationery.

Hypermarkets, which are situated on the outskirts of the largest towns, have a vast selection of food and kitchenware as well as cheap clothes, toys and electrical equipment. These include Auchan, Géant Casino and Leclerc.

Telephones

The regional codes, 04 (Languedoc-Roussillon) and 05 (Midi-Pyrénées), are followed by eight digits; dial the whole number. Cheap rates (50 per cent extra time) are from 1900 (international calls from 2230) to 0800 weekdays and from 1400 on Saturdays and all day Sundays. At most telephone kiosks you will need a *télécarte* (phonecard) obtainable from post offices, *tabacs* and newsagents in 50 or 120 units. Kiosks marked with a blue bell can receive calls.

International calls can be made from most call boxes. To make an international call, lift the receiver, insert a *télécarte*, dial 00 to get an international line, then when the tone changes dial the country code followed by the number (omitting the first 0). International codes: UK 44; US 1.

To dial France from abroad, the international access code is 00 33 followed by the number without the 0 of the local code.

For directory enquiries dial 12.
For the operator dial 13.

Travellers with disabilities

The Hérault *département* has taken a leading role in promoting facilities for the disabled. It publishes a booklet listing adapted accommodation (hotels, campsites and *gîtes*) and special activity

Safety and security

Emergency telephone numbers: Ambulance 15, Police and Fire 18. From a mobile 112.

As in most places, it pays to keep to well-lit streets in towns after dark and to take care of handbags or wallets. When you park your car, hide luggage and valuables, especially cameras.

Shopping

In the southwest of the region, colourful Catalan fabrics are on sale in specialist stores and craft shops, usually made up into household items, as well as skirts and dresses. To the east, potteries abound near the coast, often with attractive terracotta pots and glazed tableware stacked temptingly outside. You are unlikely to leave the region without investing in some wine as there are so many opportunities to buy it – hypermarkets, roadside stalls, *caves coopératives* and the vineyards themselves.

Time

France is one hour ahead of GMT in winter (last Sunday in Oct to last Saturday in Mar) and two hours ahead of it during summer.

Tipping

Service (15 per cent) is included on hotel and restaurant bills, but for particularly good service you may want to give an additional tip of 5–10 per cent; put it on the table as you leave.

It is usual to give taxi drivers, hairdressers and hotel porters a small tip.

Toilets

Restaurants and cafés always have toilets for their customers. Public ones exist in most towns, often French-style (hole in the floor).

holidays and is available from Comité Départemental du Tourisme de l'Hérault, *avenue des Moulins, 34000 Montpellier; tel: 04 67 67 71 71; www.herault-en-languedoc.com*

Wheelchair access is not always available at hotels, though new ones are required to have at least one room adapted for disabled visitors.

Guide Vacances, a guide to accessible accommodation, is published by L'Association des Paralysés de France; *tel: 01 40 78 69 00*. Available by post only from Direction de la Communication, *17 boulevard Auguste Blanqui, 75013 Paris; price €4.70.*

Wine

Languedoc-Roussillon wines are on sale at around 300 officially approved wine cellars, including the vineyards themselves and co-operatives, as well as in supermarkets.

The top *appellation contrôlée* ones are: Coteaux du Languedoc, Clairette du Languedoc, Faugères, St-Chinian, Minervois, Cabardès, Malepère, Crémant de Limoux, Corbières, Fitou, Côtes du Roussillon, Côtes du Roussillon Villages, Collioure and Côtes du Tarn. In addition many excellent Vins de Pays d'Oc are now being produced in the region.

Naturally sweet wines (*vins doux*) to which a little alcohol has been added to stop fermentation, are a speciality of the area. Usually served chilled as an aperitif, they include Banyuls, Maury, Rivesaltes, Grand Roussillon and four muscat wines (produced from a single grape type) – Frontignan, Mireval, Rivesaltes and St-Jean-de-Minervois.

Other local aperitifs include Noilly Prat, which is made from local white wine with added herbs and the stronger Byrrh.

Vin biologique is organically produced wine. No pesticides are used in the cultivation of the grapes, nor preservatives in the production process.

Driver's guide

Members of UK motoring organisations (AA or RAC) can extend their accident insurance and breakdown services to France. Both organisations offer a wide range of information and advice as well as suggesting itineraries and routes. *www.theaa.com* offers a free, turn-by-turn route map of your journey. See also *www.rac.co.uk* *www.viamichelin.co.uk*

Autoroutes

Most of the French autoroutes are toll roads. The commonest system of charging (*péage*) involves taking a ticket from a machine at the start of the toll section, which raises an automatic barrier. On leaving the system, or at an intermediate tollbooth, the ticket is presented and the amount to pay is displayed on an illuminated sign. Payment may be made in euros or by credit card. Signatures are not normally required. Traveller's cheques cannot usually be used for tolls. On autoroutes speed is sometimes automatically computed from time of entry and distance covered on arrival at the tollbooth. If a speeding offence is disclosed you may be prosecuted.

Accidents

You must STOP after any accident. You can be in serious trouble if you don't. Call 15, 17 or 18 to alert the Ambulance, Police or Fire Service as appropriate, or use the EU universal emergency number 112. On an autoroute or main road, use one of the bright orange free SOS emergency roadside telephones located at frequent intervals.

Give whatever aid you are capable of to any person injured or in peril. It is an offence not to do this if it lies within your ability. This applies whether you are driver, passenger or witness. Safeguard against a secondary accident. Hazard lights – warning triangle – signal to other traffic. Exchange details of vehicles, drivers insurance etc. (French cars display insurance details on a windscreen sticker.) Complete a 'European Accident Statement' form – ask your insurers for this before you leave, the French driver will almost certainly have one. This forms a factual record. It is not an admission of fault. Note as many details as you can. Photographs? Witnesses? If someone has been injured, you must inform the police. If you have damaged someone else's vehicle or property and you are unable to give the owner your details, you must inform the police. The police will not usually take details where an accident involves material damage only, unless there is evidence of an offence such as dangerous or drink driving. Inform your insurers as soon as possible.

Breakdowns

If you are on an autoroute, stop your vehicle on the hard shoulder, getting it as far to the right as possible. On ordinary roads, consider using the verge but beware of roadside ditches. Hazard lights on. Place a warning triangle at least 30m from the scene, visible from 100m away. (Remember, it can be very dangerous to walk on the hard shoulder of any motorway.) You and your passengers are probably safer out of the vehicle and well up the verge away from the traffic.

If you need assistance on an autoroute you must use one of the free roadside telephones to connect you with the police. You cannot arrange recovery yourself, even if you are a member of a breakdown service. No garage will send a recovery vehicle onto an autoroute without police permission. There is a fixed scale of charges. (€72 by day, €108 by night.) You may not carry out a DIY tow on an autoroute and you may only do so on an ordinary road for 'a few metres' in an emergency. Makeshift towing is strongly discouraged and usually voids French car insurance.

Documents

Members of EU countries and US citizens only need a valid national driving licence, but an international driving licence is essential for other nationals. Provisional licences are not valid and drivers must be over the age of 18. UK photo card licences are best. Paper licences are lawful but further proof of ID may be required. Registration papers (a logbook) and a letter of authorisation if the car is not registered in your name, insurance papers and Test Certificate (MoT) (originals – photocopies are not valid) and a nationality plate must be carried. The above documents must be produced at the time on request by police. An immediate fine may be imposed if they are not to hand. For UK drivers a 'Green Card' is not required in France for car insurance. Your certificate of insurance issued in Britain conforms to French legal needs. However, this is minimum legal cover. You should ask your insurers to extend your normal, full cover for use abroad for the period of your stay. Continental breakdown insurance is recommended. Should you visit the state of Andorra in the Pyrenees you will require a Green Card. Holders of US insurance must take out a European policy.

Continental breakdown insurance is strongly recommended and one phone call is all it takes to hand the whole problem over to multi-lingual operators who are experts in sorting things out.

Caravans and camper vans (Trailers and RVs)

France is probably the most 'camping and caravanning friendly' country in Europe and there are numerous attractive campsites from economical to de luxe in the area covered by this guide, especially in the most popular locations near the Mediterranean coast and in the Pyrenees. In the latter area, many are open all year to cater for winter sports enthusiasts. There is no need to book ahead, apart from the height of the winter/summer season. Booking ahead is really only necessary in the height of the season. The Alan Rogers' campsite guides are very useful. *Camping sauvage* ('wild' camping) is completely banned. Camping in State Forests or any wooded area is virtually always prohibited because of the serious risk of fire. Overnight parking of motorhomes is frequently permitted (and often free) in the central square of smaller towns and villages where water and toilet facilities are available. There are no campsites in Monaco and whilst you may drive through the Principality on the main roads, parking of caravans or motor homes is not allowed. There are no formalities about bringing a caravan into France if your stay is for less than six months.

Motorhomes and cars towing trailers have to pay a higher toll on autoroutes. Some caravanners use the facilities of the autoroute *aires de repos* (rest areas) for an overnight stop. This is quite lawful, as your autoroute ticket lasts for at least 24 hours. If you do this, you are advised to use common sense and stop in a well-lit spot, in view of passers-by. Thefts and break-ins are, unfortunately, not unknown.

Speed limits for cars towing trailers or caravans are the same as solo vehicles. Occasionally, there may be a reduced speed limit for caravans on long declines. This is to reduce the danger of instability when the caravan is being neither pulled nor braked but is 'floating' behind the towing vehicle.

If you intend driving in the Pyrenees or the Alps (and particularly if you are towing a trailer) you should remember that engine efficiency decreases with altitude, by about 10% per 3000 feet. This can mean that a heavily laden non-turbo car just coping with the additional load at sea level, may not manage the incline as it climbs higher.

Driving in Languedoc

There are three classes of road – motorway (*autoroute* – A); main road (*route nationale* – RN or N); and secondary road (*route départementale* – D).

Autoroutes are of excellent quality with frequent rest and service areas, offering the fastest means of covering long distances by car. The exit slip roads tend to have very tight curves and should be negotiated at much reduced speed, especially if towing a trailer or caravan.

Drinking and driving

The French limit is 50mg of alcohol per 100ml of blood and penalties increase sharply if an 80mg limit is exceeded. There is a determined campaign to reduce incidents of drinking and driving, and penalties are severe, with heavy fines and imprisonment. Random breath tests are common and you should not underestimate the powers of the police or the consequences of failing a test. A large fine may be demanded on the spot and your vehicle may be impounded until it is paid. Any disqualification is immediate. If you are the sole driver, you will be stranded and any 'get-you-home' insurance will be invalidated by reason of you having committed an illegal act.

Essentials

You *must* have a red warning triangle and hazard lights in case of accident, a headlight dip adjusted to the right, a first-aid kit and spare bulbs. You'll also need nationality (GB, IRL, etc.) plates (or a sticker, usually supplied with Channel crossing tickets), a torch, and a petrol container.

Petrol = *Essence*
Unleaded = *Sans plomb 95 and 98 octane*
4-star = *Super*
Diesel = *Gazole, Gasoil or Diesel*
LPG = *GPL*

Routes Nationales and Départementales. As in all France, roads in Languedoc and the Southwest are of a good standard but the closer one gets to the Pyrenees, the more twisting they become and hairpin bends are regular. Care must be taken, especially where black ice (*verglas*) is signed. In winter, snow chains or tyres are compulsory on some sections as indicated by signs and a lay-by is provided for them to be fitted. If skis are carried on a roof rack the points must face to the rear for safety. Any closure of a high altitude pass is signed well in advance. These often sinuous roads may make for slow average speeds but drivers are rewarded by stunning views.

Coastal roads can become very congested in the peak season as the geography of the region funnels all north–south traffic onto them.

Driving rules

Traffic drives on the right in France. A fundamental driving rule is that traffic from the right has priority at junctions. In practice, priority from the right applies mostly in towns and on rural roads. Main roads are clearly signed as such by a yellow and white diamond sign which is repeated every 5km, or the conventional triangle showing a broad vertical black stripe with a narrow horizontal line crossing it (*see page 29*). Junctions marked with a simple X, or not marked at all, are governed by the 'Priority from the Right' rule. Any unmarked junction in a town or village must be treated as subject to this rule.

The rule applies to *junctions* and does not mean giving way to vehicles coming out of lay-bys, driveways, garages, parking spaces, etc. You should, however, give way to buses moving away from a bus stop.

Traffic on roundabouts has priority and drivers entering the system must wait for a safe opportunity. Unfortunately, French drivers are very haphazard about signalling their intentions on roundabouts and care is needed.

Pedestrians have right of way when on marked crossings, but the practice of stopping for a pedestrian waiting to use a crossing is unknown. If you decide to display such courtesy, remember that following drivers may not anticipate your action.

Fuel

Service stations are open all day but are normally closed on Sundays and public holidays. If a public holiday falls on, say, a Thursday, it is common practice to take the Friday off as well, rather than spoil a good weekend. This can mean that petrol stations are closed for four days, especially in the country. In rural areas petrol stations can be few and far between, especially on *départementale* roads.

Fuel is cheapest at big supermarkets in out-of-town retail parks (*Centre Commercial*) and, not surprisingly, most expensive on motorways. Until the changeover of British credit cards to those incorporating a 'chip' is complete, 24-hour automatic pumps which

Fines

The police/*gendarmes* have wide powers to impose on-the-spot fines for a variety of motoring offences. Speed checks are frequent and merciless. Payment must be in cash and should you not be able to pay there and then, for instance if the banks are closed and there is no ATM nearby, your vehicle and your passport may be impounded until you do. The fine is, in fact, a part payment (*amende forfaitaire*) and you may receive notification of a higher penalty later. At present such extra fines cannot be enforced abroad but EU legislation is being contemplated to make this possible.

Speed-trap detection devices are illegal, whether in use or not. The device is invariably seized and a heavy fine imposed.

In practice, if you drive sensibly, you are no more likely to be stopped or prosecuted in France than any other country. It is the *consequences* of such a prosecution that should be considered, especially when you are on holiday.

'Inforoute'

If your car radio is equipped with RDS this will work in France, interrupting radio programmes with road news flashes (in French). You may also receive traffic news on 'Inforoute' on 107.7 MHz FM. These low-power transmitters cover the motorway routes and provide local up-to-date traffic reports, in French.

require a credit card and PIN number, are very unlikely to work with British issued cards due to incompatible computing systems. Keeping the fuel tank well-filled is good practice.

Information

You should take an up-to-date map with you. Changes in road numbers and motorway interchanges can booby-trap old editions. The Michelin 1:200 000 'yellow' maps are ideal. Free *Bison Futé* (Crafty Bison) maps showing alternative routes using secondary roads to avoid traffic problems, are available from the French Government Tourist Office or information offices in France. These routes are well signposted, make a pleasant change from main roads and are a great help in avoiding the predictable traffic problem zones. If you want to be a 'Crafty Bison' yourself, you could try taking an early or late lunch and stay on the road between 1200 and 1400. The French drop everything for lunch and the roads become much quieter.

Parking

Normally, parking is only a problem in large towns or cities. In the high season however, especially in the coastal resorts, demand for parking spaces exceeds supply.

There is some free parking in Disc Parking zones, where the bays are marked out in blue. Purchase a disc (*Disque de stationnement*) at petrol stations or supermarkets. Setting your arrival time on the disc automatically displays the expiry time in a cut-out window. Meter or ticket parking follows the usual pattern. Very often parking is free 1200–1400. These times are displayed on the ticket machine.

If parking in the street, you *must* park facing the direction of travel, i.e. on the right in two-way streets. It is, in any case, bad practice to park on the left, as you may drive off forgetting to move to the correct side of the road.

It is illegal to leave a vehicle parked in the same place for more than seven days, and a lesser time in some cities. Obstructive or illegal parking, especially in cities, often results in the offending vehicle being uplifted and taken to a pound. Foreign number plates will not save you.

Some parking zones work on the basis of parking on the odd-numbered side of the street for the first fortnight of a month (1st–15th) and on the even-numbered side for the second. A special sign indicates the entry to the zone. (*See page 29.*) Changeover time is between 2030 and 2100 on the last day of each fortnight.

Security

Sensible care should be taken, particularly where vehicles are left for long periods in vulnerable places such as tourist site car parks. Do not

Lights

All traffic must use headlights in rain or poor visibility. Right-hand-drive cars must have their headlight beam modified to prevent dazzle. This can take the form of masking off part of the headlamps (which unfortunately reduces the light output) or stick-on optical beam deflectors which cause the headlight to dip to the right. Some vehicles which have quartz-iodine headlamps cannot be modified in these ways and you should check with the car dealer. Driving with defective lights can result in a fine. The fine is less likely if you can remedy the defect right away. It is a legal requirement to carry a spare set of bulbs. Motorcycles must display headlights at all times.

Mobile phones

The use of a hand-held phone when driving is specifically forbidden. The use of hands-free phones is strongly discouraged. The only safe and legal way for the driver to use a mobile is to stop and switch off the engine beforehand.

Seat belts

Wearing of seat belts for front and rear passengers is compulsory when the vehicle engine is running. Children under 10 must occupy the rear seats but an infant up to 9 months may travel in the front seat if secured in an approved rear-facing seat, *but not if a passenger air bag is fitted.*

leave items on view inside the car, even if you know they are of little or no value, a potential thief does not.

In the large cities it is wise to keep car doors locked and windows up, if in slow-moving traffic or while stationary at traffic lights, as thieves on motorcycles occasionally reach inside to steal valuables. If hot weather means you must have the window open, be sure that handbags, wallets, cameras etc. are well out of sight and reach and, above all, never on a passenger's lap.

Should you have the misfortune to become a victim of crime, your insurers will require you to report the circumstances to the police and obtain a record that you have done so. In the country go to the *Gendarmerie* and in larger towns the *Commissariat de Police.*

Speed limits

Autoroutes – 130kph (110kph in rain). If windscreen wipers are needed it's 'raining'.
Dual carriageways – 110kph (100kph in rain)
Other roads – 90kph (80kph in rain)
All built up areas – 50kph on roads between the entrance sign to a town and departure sign (place name crossed with diagonal bar).
There's a 50kph limit on any road when visibility is less than 50m.
Drivers with less than two year's experience must not exceed the 'rain' speed limits even in fine weather.

Road signs

All major routes are clearly signed; even most minor roads have their destinations and route numbers marked. International European traffic signs are used throughout France

accôtement non-stabilisé – soft verge
aire – rest area
cédez le passage – give way
chaussée déformée – uneven surface
défense de stationner/stationnement interdit – no parking
dépassement interdit – no overtaking
déviation – diversion
gravillons – loose chippings
passage protégé – right of way
péage – toll
poste d'essence – petrol station
priorité à droite – priority to traffic from the right
priorité aux piétons – give way to pedestrians

ralentir – slow down
rappel – reminder of previous restriction
renseignements – information
rives dangereuses – dangerous roadsides
route barrée – road closed
sens interdit – no entry
sens unique – one way
seulement riverains – residents only
sortie de camions – HGV exit
stationnement gratuit – free parking
stationnement interdit – no parking
stationnement payant – paid parking
toutes directions – route for through traffic
un train peut en cacher un autre – one train may hide another
virage – bend
vous n'avez pas la priorité – you do not have priority

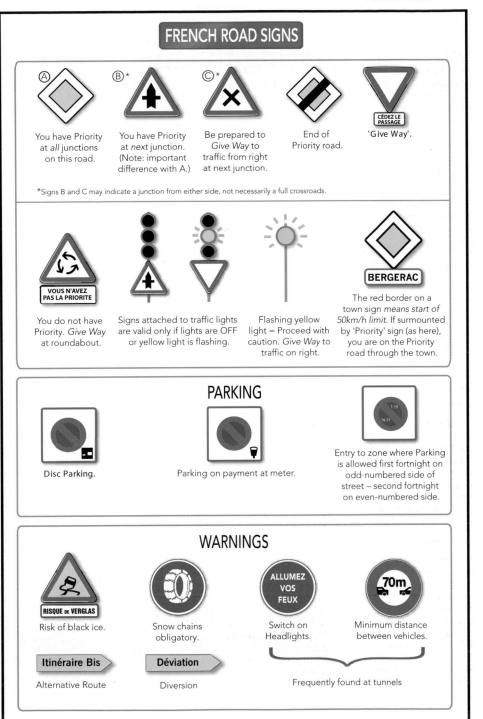

FRENCH ROAD SIGNS

Ⓐ You have Priority at *all* junctions on this road.

Ⓑ* You have Priority at *next* junction. (Note: important difference with A.)

Ⓒ* Be prepared to *Give Way* to traffic from right at next junction.

End of Priority road.

CÉDEZ LE PASSAGE 'Give Way'.

*Signs B and C may indicate a junction from either side, not necessarily a full crossroads.

VOUS N'AVEZ PAS LA PRIORITE You do not have Priority. *Give Way* at roundabout.

Signs attached to traffic lights are valid only if lights are OFF or yellow light is flashing.

Flashing yellow light = Proceed with caution. *Give Way* to traffic on right.

BERGERAC The red border on a town sign *means start of 50km/h limit.* If surmounted by 'Priority' sign (as here), you are on the Priority road through the town.

PARKING

Disc Parking.

Parking on payment at meter.

Entry to zone where Parking is allowed first fortnight on odd-numbered side of street – second fortnight on even-numbered side.

WARNINGS

RISQUE DE VERGLAS Risk of black ice.

Snow chains obligatory.

ALLUMEZ VOS FEUX Switch on Headlights.

70m Minimum distance between vehicles.

Itinéraire Bis Alternative Route

Déviation Diversion

Frequently found at tunnels

Getting to Languedoc and Southwest France

Rail Europe
tel: 08705 848 848;
www.raileurope.co.uk –
bookings for Eurostar and
TGV (high-speed) trains to
destinations throughout
France; also for Motorail
within France.

Eurotunnel *tel:* 08705 35
35 35; *www.eurotunnel.com*
– drive-on trains from
Folkestone to Calais
Coquelles through the
Channel Tunnel (35 mins),
direct access to the French
motorway system.

French Motorail
tel: 08702 415 415;
www.raileurope.co.uk – car-
carrying train services
operate in summer from
Calais to Avignon,
Narbonne and Toulouse.

Brittany Ferries *tel:*
08705 360 360, brochure
line: 08705 143 537;
www.brittanyferries.co.uk –
Portsmouth to St-Malo
(9 hrs) and Caen (6 hrs);
Poole to Cherbourg
(4 hrs); Cork to Roscoff
(13 hrs), summer only.

By car
If you are taking your own car, the autoroute system (mostly toll roads) is an excellent means of getting to your destination. Using the A16 from Calais and the A10, A71, A20 to Toulouse and beyond, or the A10, A71, A75 to the Mediterranean offer virtually uninterrupted motorway driving with high average speeds. France is bigger than it looks and this 1000km or so journey is best undertaken with an overnight break.

To reduce the driving distance in France, the longer sea crossings at the western end of the Channel, to St-Malo, Cherbourg, Caen or Le Havre are an option. They also have the advantage of avoiding both the London and Paris areas. The Brittany Ferries overnight crossing from Portsmouth to St-Malo, arriving at 0800, for example, enables the drive to Toulouse of about seven hours to be completed the same day, using motorways almost all the way.

You can avoid long-distance driving in France by using the French Motorail (*www.raileurope.co.uk*) which will transport your car and passengers to your destination overnight May to September in a purpose-built train. Services are from Calais to Avignon, Brive, Toulouse and Narbonne. Accommodation on the train, which is always exclusive to your party, is from two-berth sleepers to four- and six-berth couchettes. Light refreshments only are available on board and you are advised to bring your own food if you require something more substantial. The Calais terminal is a five-minute drive from the Channel Tunnel. Boarding begins two hours before the train departure and unloading takes a similar time.

Whilst transporting your car in this way saves on fuel, tolls and hotels, as well as wear and tear on the vehicle, it does come at a price and is really based on your desire to use your own vehicle on holiday. It is worth calculating the total cost of vehicle transportation against 'ordinary' rail travel and car hire upon arrival.

Car hire is expensive in France. It is normally cheaper to make arrangements before you leave, or consider an inclusive deal or fly-drive. You must be over 21 and have held a licence for at least one year, perhaps two.

All the usual main car hire firms have offices in France, and often at airports, main railway stations and ferry ports. It is wise to book ahead for peak holiday periods.

P&O Ferries *tel: 08705 202020; ww4.poferries.com* – Portsmouth to Cherbourg 2 hrs 45 mins (fast ferry) or 4 hrs 45 mins (ship), Portsmouth to Le Havre 5¼ hrs, Dover to Calais 1½ hrs, Rosslare to Cherbourg 19 hrs, Dublin to Cherbourg 16 hrs (summer only).

SeaFrance *tel: 08705 711 711; www.seafrance.com* – Dover to Calais 90 mins.

Hoverspeed *tel: 08702 408 070; www.hoverspeed.co.uk* – Dover to Calais services by SeaCat fast catamaran (60 mins), also Newhaven to Dieppe by SuperSeaCat (2 hrs).

Speedferries *tel: 01304 203000; www.speedferries.com* – Dover to Boulogne by large catamaran, 50 mins.

Condor Ferries *tel: 0845 345 2000; www.condorferries.co.uk* – Poole to St-Malo 5½ hrs (summer only).

Irish Ferries *tel: 08705 171717 (GB), 1890 313131* (Rep. of Ireland), *www.irishferries.com* – Rosslare to Cherbourg 19½ hrs, Rosslare to Roscoff 17 hrs (summer only).

Eurostar *tel: 08705 186 186; www.eurostar.com* – London Waterloo Intl to Paris (2 hrs 35 mins), also Lille Europe for connecting high-speed TGV trains to Bordeaux and Toulouse.

By air

The main international airports are Montpellier for the eastern end of the Languedoc and Toulouse for the western part of the area. Carcassonne, convenient for both, has a daily no-frills flight from Stansted in the UK. (See city chapters for full details of each airport.)

For touring, car hire can easily be arranged on arrival, but you are better off without a car in the area's six main cities. All airports have car-hire desks, though airlines also offer fly-drive arrangements. British Airways (*tel: 0870 850 9850; www.ba.com*) and Air France (*tel: 0845 0845 111; www.airfrance.com*) fly from Heathrow and Gatwick to Toulouse, Ryanair flies from Stansted to Carcassonne, Montpellier, Nîmes and Perpignan; *tel:* (UK) *0871 246 0000*, (Rep. of Ireland) *0818 30 30 50; www.ryanair.com*. Flybe (British European) has flights from Birmingham direct to Toulouse in summer; *tel: 0871 7000 123; www.flybe.com*, and there are also direct services to Toulouse from Shannon. For enquiries about internal flights in France with Air Liberté, *tel: 08 03 80 58 05*, or Air Littoral, *tel: 08 25 83 48 34*.

By rail

Eurostar trains take one hour forty minutes through the Channel Tunnel from London Waterloo to Lille, linking with SNCF's high-speed TGV trains to Montpellier and Toulouse. Some stop at Ashford in Kent. In July and August, Eurostar also runs a direct weekly service from London to Avignon (6 hours). Book through Rail Europe; *tel: 08705 848848; www.raileurope.co.uk*

From Paris, TGV services get you to the area in about five hours. TGV trains to Toulouse depart from the Gare Montparnasse and to Montpellier from the Gare de Lyon.

Inclusive holidays from the UK

To hire a pre-erected tent or mobile home, Eurocamp features a selection of sites along the Languedoc-Roussillon coast; *tel: 08703 338 338; www.eurocamp.co.uk*

A comprehensive selection of *Gîtes de France* and *Chambres d'hôte* is bookable through Brittany Ferries; *tel: 08705 360 360*. Operators featuring seaside villas, apartments and country houses include Interhome: *tel: 020 8891 1294; www.interhome.co.uk*; Vacances en Campagne: *tel: 08700 771771; www.indiv-travellers.com*. Holiday villages are available through Perfect Places: *tel: 08703 331771; www.perfectplaces online.co.uk*. For walking or riding holidays and also short breaks at small hotels (many in the Logis de France chain), try Inntravel: *tel: 01653 628811; www.inntravel.co.uk*

To get a full list of British tour operators to France contact ABTOF (Association of British Tour Operators to France): *tel: 01989 7691140; www.holidayfrance.org.uk*, or get the free *Traveller in France* available from the French Government Tourist Office, *178 Piccadilly, London W1J 9AL; tel: 09068 244 123 (premium rates apply); www.franceguide.com*

Setting the scene

Above
Festive decorations in Mirepoix

History

The North–South Divide Named after the ancient Langue d'Oc, the Languedoc was originally settled by people from various races who felt they had little in common with the French people who lived further north. This division came sharply into focus in the 12th century when the Counts of Toulouse were powerful and independent. Later, Protestantism was warmly embraced in the Languedoc, another cause of bitter division with the predominantly Catholic north which had subjugated them.

The Languedoc demonstrated a similar taste for independence during the French Revolution, but once again the forces of the north proved too strong.

Catharism Having first emerged as a branch of Christianity during the 10th century, Catharism lasted for about 400 years. It first acquired a name in 1163 when Canon Eckbert of Cologne mockingly called its supporters by the Greek word *katharos* (pure). The Cathars sought absolute purity. Believing the world had been corrupted, they did not worship the cross, regarding it simply as the instrument of Christ's crucifixion. They also denied Catholic teaching by rejecting the Eucharist as they felt bread and wine could not possibly represent Christ's flesh. For them the means to salvation was baptism, passed on by the laying on of hands from individual to individual in an unbroken line since Christ and the Apostles.

In many places this 'heresy' never emerged from the shadows but in the Languedoc it thrived. The powerful Counts of Toulouse were among many wealthy landowners who were sympathetic to its beliefs and willingly supported its followers, the *'Parfaits'*. But when it threatened to drive a wedge between political and religious power, both the King of France and the Catholic hierarchy got worried. At first the bishops and priests were content to attack the 'heresy' from the pulpit, but this failed to check its advance and they became increasingly concerned.

Early in the 13th century the Counts of Toulouse and other *seigneurs* who owned parts of the Languedoc seemed likely to unite with Catalonia to form a powerful rival to France. King Philippe Auguste, already infuriated by their support for the Cathars, decided to act against them. Making the most of the wholehearted support he got from Pope Innocent III, who was anxious to see an end to Catharism, he embarked in 1209 on a ruthless campaign designed to get rid of the heretics. The Pope declared it to be as worthy as a pilgrimage to the Holy Land.

Known as the Albigensian Crusade because Albi was the first place to offer refuge to Cathars, it led to the ravaging of many towns and villages. Hundreds of Cathars were martyred, mostly by being burned. The Crusade dragged on for over 20 years until the Languedoc was firmly under northern rule – but Catharism still retained its hold.

In 1233, Pope Gregory IX took even more drastic action, setting up the Inquisition. As a result everyone was forced to appear before tribunals made up of monks, usually Dominicans or Franciscans. Though run with ruthless efficiency and cruelty, their purge was severely handicapped by the fact that the Cathars had no fear of death as they believed hell was already on earth. Consequently nearly a hundred years passed before the 'heresy' was finally eradicated.

The Cathars' doctrine and influence have remained of absorbing interest to theologians and historians ever since. The prime source of information is the Centre d'Etudes Cathares research centre in Carcassonne (*tel: 04 68 47 24 66; www.cathares.org*).

Wars of Religion The divisions between France's Catholics and Protestants reached a new peak during the Wars of Religion in the second half of the 16th century. Assassinations and massacres were widespread until the Edict of Nantes in 1598 when King Henri IV, who had renounced his own Protestant faith to become a Catholic, granted Protestants freedom of worship. Sadly the Edict was revoked in 1685 as part of the north's determination to control the south where there were large numbers of them. During the following years many emigrated but others were tortured or killed by Catholics and their churches destroyed.

Camisards The peasants in the Cévennes mountains were among the most determined Protestants. They became known as the Camisards after *camiso*, the Languedoc word for shirt, because they sacked a shirt factory and wore the clothes they found in it. In July 1702 a group of them freed Protestant prisoners being held at Pont-de-Montvert and killed the Abbot while doing so. All hell broke loose. Though the Camisards never numbered more than a few thousand, they were able to put up strong resistance against the 25,000 royal troops ranged against them because they had three enormous advantages (which later proved equally useful to the Resistance during World War II): the rough countryside was ideal for guerrilla warfare, they knew it intimately, and they had strong local support. However, in 1704, when the troops deliberately destroyed 466 small towns and villages, most of the remaining Camisards surrendered. In 1787 the Edict of Tolerance officially ended their persecution.

Treaty of the Pyrenees Centuries of Franco-Spanish conflict ended in 1659 when the Treaty of the Pyrenees laid down that the border between the two countries should run along the crests of the Pyrenees.

Below
La Couvertoirade; the gatehouse to the fortified village.

This meant that Roussillon became part of France after years of being pulled to and fro. A less satisfactory outcome was that the Catalan people found themselves split in two. Nevertheless, their language has survived and many place names and streets are signed in both French and Catalan.

One quirk left behind by the Treaty is a small Spanish enclave just inside the French border. About 3km across, it is based in the small town of Llivia, whose occupants refused to join with the neighbouring places in becoming French. Today their descendants are more likely to tell you they are Catalan than Spanish.

Architecture

Bastides Many of the area's towns have developed from *bastides*, fortified medieval villages. The layout, still to be seen in places such as Carcassonne (Ville Basse), Mirepoix, Réalmont and Revel, was always similar – a grid of straight narrow streets and alleys with a square in the centre surrounded by covered arcades. Designed to enable the inhabitants to live safe from attack, they were surrounded by sturdy ramparts and gateways. Most date back to the height of the Franco-English wars in the 12th–14th centuries. At the time parts of the area were governed by France, others by England, and both sides built *bastides* to strengthen their positions. The seeds of the conflict had been set in 1152 when a large part of France passed to English rule following the marriage of Eleanor of Aquitaine (who had divorced King Louis VII two months earlier) and the 19-year-old Henry Plantagenet. Two years later he became King Henry II of England.

Southern Gothic Churches built in the style known as Southern Gothic in the west of the area have more in common with the austere Romanesque architecture of the 11th and 12th centuries than with the more flamboyant design and decorative stonework of traditional Gothic ones. Due to the lack of local stone, many were built in brick, whose lightness, compared with stone, enabled them to have vaulted roofs supported by interior buttresses with chapels between them.

Stepping inside these churches, however, you are struck most by the lack of light due to small windows. They are also notable for the considerable width of their naves which have no side aisles. After the Cathar movement had been stamped out, the Catholic clergy favoured this simple design, believing it helped unify their flocks and impressed on them who had the true and final word. The exterior of the churches is usually topped by a tower or wall of bells featuring tiers of arches.

Coastal development Until the 1960s the 200km-long coast between the Camargue and the Spanish border was a desolate stretch of lagoons, bogs and sand, interspersed by occasional harbours and a few small and rather faded resorts. Anxious to ease pressure on the Riviera and concerned that increasing numbers of French holiday-makers were heading for Spain each summer, the government decided to capitalise on the area's major asset – its succession of long sandy beaches.

Billions of francs were spent on creating new resorts grouped around smart marinas at places such as Agde, Leucate and Port-Barcarès. The architects were told the buildings must look modern and attractive, have pleasant landscaped settings and be affordable to ordinary people. Top-class campsites with pools and sports facilities were encouraged too. At the same time the hordes of mosquitoes that bred on the lagoons were eliminated, fast access roads constructed and sewage-treatment plants built to ensure that the beaches and sea remained unpolluted.

Just how successful the project has proved can be seen every summer when millions of holidaymakers descend on the area, not only from France but from all over the world.

Landscape

Geographically the region has a number of distinctly different features.

Mountains The Cévennes on the northeastern edge of the area rise in rugged ridges above wooded valleys; their highest peaks are Mont Lozère (1699m) and Mont Aigoual (1567m). The Pyrenees which border the south of the area are signicantly higher. The snowy peak of the Massif du Canigou (2784m) is visible from high points across the whole region on clear days. The Pyrenees are also more extensive, stretching away into Spain and from the Mediterranean to the Atlantic.

The Montagne Noire and Corbières which rise from the central Languedoc plain are hills rather than mountains. Nevertheless much of their scenery is just as spectacular, thanks to their rugged cliffs, thickly wooded valleys and crags topped by castle ruins.

Causses Four massive limestone plateaux, the Grands Causses – Méjean, Noir, Larzac and Sauveterre – lie to the west of the Cévennes. Topped by poor, dry soil because water drains easily away through the rock, they are impressively bleak and barren, though grazed by sheep in summer. Their coarse tufty grass is dotted with hardy plants such as thistles, lavender and juniper which manage to survive the summer heat and winter frosts and snow when cold winds whistle relentlessly across them.

Rivers such as the Dourbie, Jonte and Tarn have cut their way between the Causses. They now flow in deep wooded ravines which twist below cliffs that often tower 500m above them. The roads cut into the cliffsides enable visitors to enjoy some of the most dramatic scenery in France.

Etangs The saltwater lagoons which border much of the coast behind sandbars are a comparatively recent arrival. Places such as Narbonne, Agde and Marseillan were ports in Roman times, though they required constant dredging to prevent them silting up. During the Middle Ages this became uneconomic. In any case drifting sand was building up sandbars just off shore, creating a completely new coastline with sea water trapped in shallow lagoons behind it which were fed from the sea along *graus* (narrow channels). Salt used to be extracted from the lagoons, but now they are put to much more profitable use as oyster and mussel beds. They are also home to many species of sea birds including hundreds of pink flamingos.

Garrigues This is the name of the natural scrubland that covers the limestone hills, mainly to the southwest of the Cévennes. Despite the unrelenting summer heat, clumps of holm oak, broom and sweet-smelling plants such as lavender, thyme and rosemary manage to grow abundantly amongst the white rocks.

Caves Under the area's many limestone plateaux, particularly in the Ariège and Aveyron, caves have formed over the centuries. It is largely thanks to Edouard-Alfred Martel (1859–1938), originally a Paris lawyer, that this underground world has been so extensively explored. Always an enthusiastic traveller, he set out in 1883 to penetrate and map the many caves and tunnels under the Causses. Until then very little was known about what lay beyond the forbiddingly dark entrance holes, let alone how far the spaces stretched underground and whether any linked up. While exploring them, he also studied why the spaces had formed. By writing extensively about his discoveries, he inaugurated a new branch of science – speleology – based on the exploration and scientific study of caves. His work also had two other beneficial effects: it boosted both the area's water supplies and its tourist trade.

Wine

Languedoc-Roussillon is the largest wine-producing region in France, accounting for around two-thirds of the country's production. The majority of those produced in the Languedoc area are inexpensive but highly drinkable red 'unclassified' *vins de table*. However, over the last 25 years an increasing number of *viticulteurs* (producers) have been planting different varieties of grape in order to produce wines of a higher quality. Fifteen from the Languedoc plain have now reached France's top *appellation contrôlée* (AOC) grading (the first was in 1985), while others have achieved *vin de pays* status, either *Pays d'Oc* or *Pays de L'Hérault*.

Some of the wines from the Languedoc plain are produced co-operatively by the Coteaux du Languedoc areas and some by individual châteaux and *domaines*. Predominantly red, they are best drunk young and chilled.

Wines from the Languedoc's two other large wine areas, the Corbières and Minervois, are mainly strong dark reds, as are those from the highly regarded neighbouring Fitou vineyards, which reach their peak when aged for a few years.

In general, Roussillon produces better wines than Languedoc, having achieved its AOC status in 1977 for its Côtes du Roussillon, Côtes du Roussillon Villages (from 32 districts) and Collioure, which are mostly reds. In addition there are five *vins de pays*.

Roussillon is also well known for its *vins doux naturels*, sweet wines made from muscat grapes and fortified with wine alcohol. Served chilled mainly as an aperitif, they include Banyuls, Maury and Rivesaltes. The town of Gaillac is in the centre of the smaller Côtes du Tarn area which produces red, white and rosé wines. A Gaillac *appellation* denotes superior quality, yet prices are surprisingly low, even for Perlé, the top one.

The vineyards around Limoux have been producing sparkling white wine for 1000 years – the oldest in the world. Blanquette de Limoux, produced by the *méthode champenoise* (bubbles added chemically), is crisp and inexpensive compared with Champagne. Around 3 per cent is produced by the *méthode ancienne*, in which the bubbles occur naturally.

Armagnac, a brandy from the Gers *département* northwest of Toulouse, is thought to be the oldest distilled drink in France. It is made from white wine and matured in oak barrels.

Food

The area's gastronomy is influenced by Languedoc and Catalan traditions. It owes its flavours to the fruits and vegetables, both wild and cultivated, which flourish in the hot Mediterranean sunshine. Herbs, berries and garlic are used extensively.

Languedoc dishes tend to be robust and straightforward, using plenty of young lamb, particularly on the Causses where sheep's cheese is made in many places. Catalan dishes are prepared with generous quantities of olive oil and use many wild ingredients, from partridges to snails as well as local tomatoes, olives, peppers and mushrooms. The chestnuts which grow in abundance in the hills inland are used in sauces and stuffings or served as a vegetable.

Throughout the region, there is a strong tradition of preserved meats, sausages and pâtés. Duck appears in many forms, especially *confit* where the meat has been conserved in fat to be used in stews such as *cassoulet*.

Several kinds of fish stew are available on the coast as well as grilled and barbecued fish, though sea-water fish is suprisingly rare inland.

From spring to autumn, the wide variety of locally grown fruit and vegetables makes local markets a delight to visit. The triangle between Toulouse, Albi and Carcassonne, originally known as the 'land of milk and honey' because of the rich profits it made from growing woad, now produces all kinds of vegetables, particularly the white beans which are an indispensable component of both *cassoulet* and *fricassé de Limoux*.

Below
Narbonne: musicians in medieval costume

Language

In the Pyrénées-Roussillon *département*, once part of Catalonia, many people speak Catalan, though they also speak French (and probably Spanish) too. Catalan vaguely resembles Spanish and both have a common origin in Latin.

Some of the most common Catalan words you are likely to meet are *puig* (mountain peak), *riu* (river), *pla* (plateau) and *aplech* (festival). You will also notice that place and street names often appear in both Catalan and French.

The sing-song French accent which you hear throughout the Midi – and indeed the word Languedoc – is a hangover from the Oc language which was spoken locally in Roman times. Its name is derived from 'hoc ille', the Roman word for 'yes', which became 'oc' when spoken by the locals in the south. In northern France, people pronounced it 'oil' and the Langue d'Oil gradually developed into the French language.

However, the Langue d'Oc continued to thrive, a sign of the southern 'separatism' which troubadours helped to perpetuate between 1000 and 1200 by composing and singing romantic poems in it. These were performed in stately homes around the Midi, as well as further afield.

Although an edict in 1539 made French the official language in the Midi, people continued to speak in the *langue d'oc* until the beginning of the 19th century when children were forbidden to do so in school. It then declined sharply and is now no more than a local dialect, though some streets still have two names. Montpellier University offers courses in Occitan, which is the 19th-century name for the *langue d'oc*.

Some useful words

Causse – limestone plateau with dry rocky surface (a *can* is a small *causse*)

Corniche – escarpment (ledge)

Département – an administrative area; several make up a region such as Languedoc-Rousillon or Midi-Pyrénées

Dos-d'âne – hump in the road to slow down traffic (literally a donkey's back)

Draille – sheep track (often along a mountain ridge)

Étang – saltwater lagoon

Garrigue – poor terrain with scrub bushes, often rocky and hilly

Grau – narrow channel

Hôtel particulier – mansion

Lavogne – man-made pond on the *causses* for sheep

Lauze – flat slate or limestone slab used to cover roofs

Mas – prosperous 18th-century farm with lots of outbuildings

Parfait – Cathar

Serre – ridge

Vieille ville/centre médieval/ancien quartier – oldest part of a town or village

Vignoble – vineyard

Highlights

Best art galleries
- Hôtel d'Assézat, Toulouse (*see page 158*)
- Musée d'Art Moderne, Céret (*see page 65*)
- Musée Goya, Castres (*see page 184*)
- Musée Toulouse Lautrec, Albi (*see page 177*)

Best castles
- Brousse-le-Château (*see page 184*)
- Château de Montségur (*see page 97*)
- Château de Peyrepertuse (*see page 104*)
- Palais des Rois de Majorque, Perpignan (*see page 46*)
- Château de Quéribus (*see page 105*)
- Château de Salses (*see page 122*)

Best caves
- L'Aven Armand (*see page 250*)
- Grotte de Lombrives (*see page 96*)
- Grotte de Niaux (*see page 96*)

Best for children
- Cité de l'Espace, Toulouse (*see page 157*)
- Four Solaire (*see page 88*)
- Réserve Africaine de Sigean (*see page 121*)

Best churches
- Basilique St-Nazaire, Carcassonne (stained glass) (*see page 130*)
- Basilique St-Sernin, Toulouse (*see page 156*)
- Cathédrale Ste-Cécile, Albi (*see page 176*)
- Église St-Pierre, Prades (altarpiece) (*see page 73*)
- Ste-Eulalie et Ste-Julie, Elne (cloister) (*see page 55*)
- St-Martin-du-Canigou (*see page 75*)

Most unusual churches
- Cathédrale Ste-Cécile, Albi (*see page 176*)
- Église Ste-Marie, Rieux-Minervois (*see page 196*)
- Maguelone cathedral (*see page 273*)

Best events
- La Foire de la Cocagne, St Félix-Lauragais (*see page 170*)
- Les Feux de la St-Jean (*see page 18*)
- Procession de la Sanchí, Perpignan (*see page 47*)
- Limoux Carnival (*see page 141*)

Best gorges
- Gorges de Galamus (*see page 104*)
- Gorges de la Jonte (*see page 252*)
- Gorges du Tarn (*see page 252*)

Best coastal towns
- Cap d'Agde (*see page 273*)
- Collioure (*see page 53*)
- Sète (*see page 277*)

Best medieval towns/villages
- Carcassonne (Cité) (*see page 128*)
- La Couvertoirade (*see page 241*)
- St-Guilhem-le-Désert (*see page 226*)
- St-Jean d'Alcas (*see page 244*)
- Villefranche-de-Conflent (*see page 76*)

Most interesting towns/villages
- Cantobre (*see page 240*)
- Minerve (*see page 195*)
- Mirepoix (*see page 167*)
- Mont-Louis (*see page 90*)
- Rennes-le-Château (*see page 106*)
- Villeneuvette (*see page 227*)

Best museums
- Amphoralis (Musée des Potiers Gallo-Romains), Sallèles d'Aude (*see page 197*)
- L'Horreum, Narbonne (*see page 113*)
- Musée de Tautavel (*see page 123*)
- Musée de la Vigne et du Vin, Lézignan-Corbières (*see page 195*)
- Oppidum d'Ensérune (*see page 196*)
- Parc de l'Art Préhistorique, Tarascon-sur-Ariège (*see page 98*)

Perpignan

Ratings

Food and drink ●●●●●

Architecture ●●●●○

Shopping ●●●●○

Entertainment ●●●○○

History ●●●○○

Museums ●●●○○

Art ●●○○○

Children ●○○○○

asking almost continuously in Mediterranean sunshine, Perpignan has an attractive Franco-Spanish ambience – it used to be capital of French Catalonia – and always seems to buzz with activity. Its shops and pavement cafés are patronised as enthusiastically by its well-heeled citizens as by visitors taking time off from the beach. The Mediterranean is only 10km away at Canet-Plage. In the old town area, which is traffic-free and paved with glistening red marble, the narrow streets are crammed with shops and stalls. An aroma of spices wafts from the Arab quarter. By contrast, the avenues around the area are wide and lined with plane trees and palms, particularly beside the small River Basse which runs into the broader and less appealing Têt nearby. On high days and holidays, dancers take to the streets in traditional costumes to perform the *sardana*.

Getting there and getting around

Tourist Information *Palais des Congrès, place Armand Lanoux; tel: 04 68 66 30 30; e-mail: contact-office@little-france.com; www.perpignantourisme.com. Guided walking tours.*

Branch office in the Espace Palmarium, *place Arago. Open daily.*

By air: Aéroport Perpignan-Rivesaltes *avenue Maurice Bellonte; tel: 04 68 52 60 70*, is 7km northeast of the town centre. Facilities include car hire, restaurant and shop. A shuttle bus to the SNCF station, *avenue Général de Gaulle*, connects with flights.

By car: Leave A9 (La Catalane) autoroute at exit Perpignan Nord/ Airport. This leads across Pont Arago over the River Têt and to a convenient car park just beyond place de Catalogne.

By train: High-speed TGV trains run from Paris Gare de Lyon to Perpignan. A direct TGV service from Brussels calls at Lille Europe where it connects with Eurostar services from London at around noon each day.

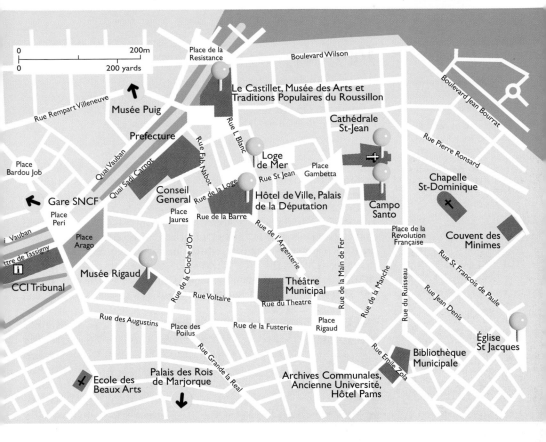

0   200m
0   200 yards

Place de la
Resistance

Boulevard Wilson

Rue Rempart Villeneuve

Musée Puig

Le Castillet, Musée des Arts et
Traditions Populaires du Roussillon

Boulevard Jean Bourrat

Prefecture

Quai Vauban

Rue L Blanc

Cathédrale
St-Jean

Rue Pierre Ronsard

Place
Bardou Job

Quai Sadi Carnot

Rue Fab Nabot

Loge
de Mer

Rue St Jean

Place
Gambetta

Chapelle
St-Dominique

Gare SNCF

Conseil
General

Rue de la Loge

Hôtel de Ville, Palais
de la Députation

Campo
Santo

Place
Peri

Place
Jaures

Rue de la Barre

Rue de l'Argenterie

Place de la
Revolution
Française

Couvent des
Minimes

i Vauban

Place
Arago

Rue de la Cloche d'Or

Rue de la Main de Fer

Rue St François de Paule

ttre de Tassigny

Musée Rigaud

Rue Voltaire

Théâtre
Municipal

Rue de la Manche

Rue du Ruisseau

Rue Jean Denis

CCI Tribunal

Rue du Theatre

Rue des Augustins

Place des
Poilus

Rue de la Fusterie

Place
Rigaud

Église
St Jacques

Rue Grande la Real

Bibliothèque
Municipale

Ecole des
Beaux Arts

Palais des Rois
de Marjorque

Rue Emile Zola

Archives Communales,
Ancienne Université,
Hôtel Pams

ℹ **Comité
Départemental
du Tourisme** *16 avenue
des Palmiers; tel: 04 68 51
52 53; e-mail:
tourisme.roussillon.france@
wanadoo.fr*

Gare SNCF *place de la
Gare. Train information,
tel: 36 35.*

Getting around: The main sights and main shopping area are easily
manageable on foot. At night the streets in the St Jacques quarter are
best avoided. The free P'tit Bus operates on a circle route around the
town; *Mon–Fri 0800–1200, 1345–1815, Sat from 0900.* Bus No 1 runs
every 30 minutes between place Péri and Canet-Plage, 30 minutes away
(until 2300 in summer). CTP bus information at the kiosk on place Péri;
tel: 04 68 61 01 13. Open Mon–Sat. **Taxis;** *tel: 04 68 34 59 49.*

Parking: Large parts of the old town area are pedestrian-only and
others one-way only, so park on the streets around it which are pay-
and-display, or head straight for an underground car park. Handiest
for the town centre are those in place du Pont d'En Vestit and place de
la République. You can also park free near the Palais des Rois de
Majorque and on Promenade des Platanes.

Sights

Campo Santo *rue Amiral Ribeil. Open daily, except Tue.*

Le Castillet *place de Verdun; tel: 04 68 35 42 05. Open Wed–Mon. Free.*

Cathédrale de St-Jean *place de Gambetta. Open 0800–1145 and 1500–1815.*

Campo Santo✦✦

This former cemetery next to the cathedral is completely surrounded by cloisters. One of only two of this kind in Europe (the other is in Pisa), it is now used for exhibitions and concerts.

Le Castillet✦✦

This 15th-century red-brick gatehouse with two towers, crenellations, windows with wrought-iron grilles and a pink dome is the only surviving part of the town's fortified walls, At one time used as a prison, it is now called Casa Païral and houses the **Musée des Arts et Traditions Populaires du Roussillon €**, which is devoted to local crafts, agriculture and festivals. One of the most striking exhibits is a life-size reconstruction of a typical home in the foothills of the Pyrenees. Climb the 142 spiral steps to the top for a splendid panorama stretching over the town's rooftops to the sea in one direction and the snowy Canigou mountain in the other.

Cathédrale St-Jean✦✦✦

The cathedral is a grand Gothic building, topped by a bell encased in an intricate wrought-iron cage. The attractive façade is made of river pebbles – frequently used in Roussillon because of the scarcity of stone – and thin red bricks. Inside, its most outstanding features, on either side of the large single nave which is typical of the Southern Gothic style, are sumptuously gilded baroque altarpieces dating from the 16th and 17th centuries. Whether they are to your taste or not, you cannot but marvel at the craftsmanship that went into sculpting the wood and then painting them, a process which occupied two artists for

Above
Local hero: memorial to François Arago

Eglise St-Jacques
place St-Jacques.

Hôtel de Ville *rue de la Loge.*

Loge de Mer *rue de la Loge.*

Musée Puig € *42 avenue de Grande-Bretagne; tel: 04 68 66 24 86. Open Tue–Sat.*

Musée Rigaud € *16 rue de l'Ange; tel: 04 68 35 43 40. Open Wed–Mon.*

An introduction, in English, to the museums and other cultural institutions of Perpignan is available on the Internet at *www.languedoc-tours.com/perpignan.htm*, and for a summary of the art displayed in Perpignan see *www.france-focus.com/perpignan.html*

three years. There is also a splendid organ whose unusual painted shutters are now displayed on the wall opposite. Outside, a doorway in the south transept leads to a chapel built specially to house the Dévôt Christ, a rather harrowing crucifix in gilded wood, thought to date from the early 14th century.

Eglise St-Jacques⁺

This 14th-century sanctuary is in the St-Jacques quarter which is now somewhat sleazy. Its large chapel was added in the 18th century for the Confrérie de la Sanch, the Brotherhood of the Holy Blood, formed in 1416 to comfort those condemned to death. The members are famous for the Procession de la Sanch on Good Friday when, hooded and dressed in macabre red or black robes with pointed hats, they parade a crucifix and huge '*misteris*' (scenes from the Stations of the Cross) through the streets to the cathedral.

Gare SNCF⁺

The town's railway station was immortalised as the 'Centre of the World' by Salvador Dalì. Arriving there in 1965, he claimed he suddenly felt free of the constraints of living in his native Spain.

Hôtel de Ville⁺⁺

The town hall is typical of the local Roussillon architecture, having wide wrought-iron gates and a façade of river pebbles. You have to be attending a wedding to visit its splendid Salle des Mariages but anyone can peep through the gates and see Maillol's famous bronze nude, *La Méditerranée*, on the patio.

Loge de Mer⁺

Built in 1397 as the headquarters of the town's maritime trade, the Loge de Mer is an impressive Gothic building with a decorative Renaissance extension added 200 years later. A wrought-iron weather vane on one side shaped like a galleon is a reminder of its connections with the sea, though the building has served many purposes and now, somewhat incongruously, a restaurant occupies the ground floor.

Musée Puig⁺

This museum in les Tilleuls, a turn-of-the-century villa, is devoted to a collection of coins donated by a local collector, Joseph-Puig, though less than half – about 1500 – are on show. Attractively displayed, they are mainly old Catalan and Mediterranean coins.

Musée Rigaud⁺⁺

Paintings by Hyacinthe Rigaud are displayed in this imposing 17th-century mansion. Born in the town in 1659, she became court painter to Louis XIV and Louis XV. The museum also has works by Picasso, Dufy and Maillol, a native of nearby Banyuls-sur-Mer (*see page 51*).

Palais des Rois de Majorque✦✦✦

The palace of the Kings of Majorca was built in 1276 when the town, part of the kingdom of Majorca, became the mainland capital but lacked a residence deemed fit for a king. More a fortress than a residence, it stands boldly on a hill, Puig del Rey, a few quiet streets away from the old quarter, reached by flights of steps which zigzag up to the ramparts and gardens surrounding it. The Kings of Aragon once kept lions in the moat while the mighty beasts' food – goats – grazed on the lawns. From the roof of the entrance tower, **Tour de l'Hommage**, there are splendid views over the town to the Massif du Canigou, ancient symbol of Catalan unity. Two stairways on either side of the palace courtyard lead to various grand rooms, including a reception hall and three chapels. The large courtyard in the centre is often used for concerts.

Shopping

The narrow streets in the old quarter are crowded with specialist shops. Look out particularly for traditional Catalan fabrics, and jewellery in the local red stone, *grenat*, at shops such as **Gilles et Jean**, rue Blanc. For gifts such as high-quality pottery, glass and household items, head for **Maison Quinta**, *3 rue Grande des Fabriques*, or **du Côté de l'Orangerie**, *2 rue de la Révolution Française*. Shops around Marché de la République specialise in dried fruits and spices. Rue de l'Ange is good for clothes. The main department store, **Galeries Lafayette**, is

Above
Perpignan's popular daily produce market

Eating outdoors on balmy evenings along the palm-lined avenues and narrow streets in the old quarter is one of the town's great pleasures, heightened by the wide choice of French and Catalan specialities. The most popular spot of all is place F Arago, a square with brasseries and cafés under magnolia trees. Small restaurants can also be found up what look like impossibly narrow alleys. Rue Fabriques-Nadal, for instance, is given over almost completely to small restaurants.

Al Très €€ *3 rue de la Poissonnerie; tel: 04 68 34 88 39*, is a small restaurant with ochre walls, which specialises in Catalan-style seafood. *Open Mon–Sat.*

L'Arago €€ *l place Arago; tel: 04 68 51 81 96*, is one of the lively brasseries with a shaded terrace around the relaxed place Arago.

Casa Sansa € *2 rue Fabriques-Nadal; tel: 04 68 34 21 84*, has gypsy musicians who serenade diners late into the night. *Open Mon–Sat.*

La Galinette €€ *23 rue Jean-Payra; tel: 04 68 35 00 90; regional dishes, some using chocolate as an ingredient. Open Tue–Sat.*

Le Jardin de l'Opéra €€ *impasse de la Division; tel: 04 68 51 46 72*, serves Catalan dishes; some tables outside in a very narrow and atmospheric alleyway. *Open daily.*

just across the River Basse in boulevard Clémenceau, with **Vergès**, a large store stuffed with household wares, opposite it. Two arcades of small shops, **Galerie Rive Gauche** and **Galerie Centre Ville**, lead off quai Vauban. The citizens love their markets, particularly the daily fruit and vegetable one on place de la République. A flea market is held every Sunday morning outside the Palais des Expositions and a bric-à-brac market on the second Saturday of each month at Promenade des Platanes.

Entertainment

Discos, piano and jazz bars, American theme bars, brasseries and pubs are scattered throughout the old quarter. Thursday is party night for the locals when you are bound to find live music in the old town at bars such as **Tio Pepe** (*15 rue de la Barre; tel: 04 68 51 32 98*) and **La Fabrique** (*1 rue Fabriques-Nadal; tel: 04 68 35 55 35*).

Events

Easter: **Festival of sacred music** during Holy Week and Spanish-style **Procession de la Sanch** on Good Friday when sacred relics and a crucifix are carried to the cathedral by the Brotherhood of the Holy Blood.
June: **Midsummer Festival of St-Jean** is celebrated in grand style with folk music, fireworks and dancing the *sardana*. Fires are lit on the 2784m Canigou mountain (40km inland) and torches from the surrounding villages are paraded into the town.
Sept: **International Festival of Photo Journalism** and **Medieval Market**.

Accommodation

Perpignan has a good choice of hotels of all prices, from modern to traditional. Avenue Général de Gaulle, leading to the railway station, is well endowed with one- and two-star hotels, though parking is a problem in the centre as only the larger hotels can offer garage facilities.

Hôtel de la Loge € *1 rue Fabriques-Nabot, place de la Loge; tel: 04 68 34 41 02; www.hoteldelaloge.fr*, is small and smart, occupying a 15th-century mansion in the old town centre. Twenty-two rooms. No garage.

Park Hotel €€ *18 boulevard Jean Bourrat; tel: 04 68 35 14 14; www.parkhotel-fr.com*, overlooks a leafy boulevard only steps from the old town.

La Villa Duflot €€€ *Rond-Point Albert Donnezan; tel: 04 68 56 67 67; www.villa-duflot.com*, is the top hotel, situated in large grounds on the southwest outskirts of town.

Suggested walk

Length: 3km.

Duration: 1½ hours, allowing time to go up to Palais des Rois de Majorque (though not inside).

The town is best explored on foot by wandering along the narrow streets and alleyways of the old quarter to admire its 14th- and 15th-century buildings and shady squares. Peep through the sturdy doorways of the old *hôtels particuliers* (mansions) whenever you get the chance as many have pretty courtyards, often featuring a well and balconies with carved stonework and wrought-iron balustrades. Even their drainpipes can be interesting as some of the old ones are made of glazed ceramic shaped with 'Dauphin' faces at the bottom. And note how the street names often appear both in Catalan and French.

Begin at **LE CASTILLET ❶** where narrow streets lead straight to the **LOGE DE MER ❷**. Take rue St-Jean to the **CATHEDRALE ❸**. On its left is St-Jean-le-Vieux, Perpignan's first church, consecrated in 1025. A century ago it was taken over by a M Bartissol to use as a store when he was in charge of installing electricity in the town. Though it is now being restored, it seems unlikely to reopen for some time yet. Nearby a wall plaque commemorates the visit of Frédéric Chopin and George Sand on their way to set sail from Port Vendres to Majorca in 1838.

Past the **CAMPO SANTO ❹** you arrive at the small **place de la Révolution Française** where rue de Ruisseau slopes up to the old St-Jacques quarter, now largely populated by Arab families and the scene of a lively market every morning on **place Cassanyes**. The **PALAIS DES ROIS DE MAJORQUE ❺** dominates this part of the town.

For a short cut, walk through place Rigaud and place des Poilus, window-shopping along the way, to **Maison Julia**, a 14th-century mansion in rue Fabriques-Nabot. With an attractive courtyard surrounded by two storeys of píllared galleries, it is one of the best preserved of Perpignan's *hôtels particuliers*. This is the old *parayres* area where drapers used to live.

The terrace brasseries and cafés around **place Arago** are ideal for lingering in the sunshine before strolling along the gardens bordering the **River Basse** back to **Le Castillet**. For a quieter retreat, the broad **Promenade des Platanes** is shaded by plane trees, palms and mimosas.

Also worth exploring

In the attractive Mediterranean-style **Jardin Sant Vincens**, on the southeast side of the town centre, an arts centre has been created in

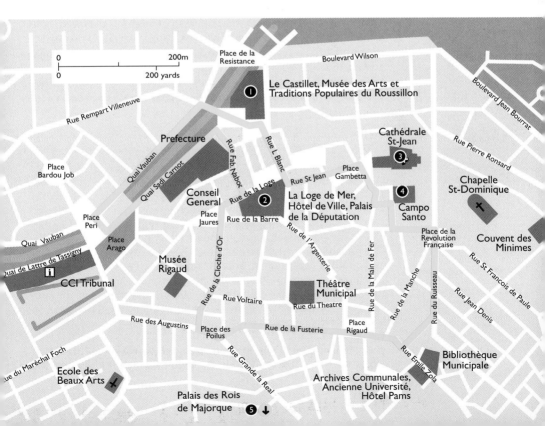

Jardin Sant Vincens
rue de Sant Vincens.
Open daily.

100-year-old wine cellars. Named **Centre d'Artisanat et d'Art Sant Vincens✦✦**, it displays striking ceramic pieces, tapestries and paintings by contemporary artists, including Jean Lurçat (1892–1966). Works by local artists are on sale.

The *sardana*

This traditional Catalan dance dates from the 16th century. Dressed in red and white, the dancers, young and old, move rhythmically and precisely in concentric circles, arms raised high, as they nimbly perform the intricate steps to the accompaniment of Catalan music. This is played on ancient woodwind instruments by bands called *cobles*. The *sardana* is performed frequently on summer evenings in Perpignan on place de la Loge and in front of le Castillet. You can also see it at summer festivals in other Catalan towns and villages throughout Roussillon.

The coast south from Perpignan

Ratings

Art	●●●●●
Beaches	●●●●●
Coastal villages/ towns	●●●●●
Wine	●●●●○
Children	●●●○○
History	●●●○○
Scenery	●●●○○
Walking	●○○○○

The Languedoc's flat coast is totally transformed when it reaches Les Albères, the foothills of the Pyrenees, shortly before the Spanish border. The long sandy beaches and sea-water lagoons suddenly give way to the rocky coves and steep hillsides of the Côte Vermeille, named after the silver-red glint of its rocky schist stone.

At the beginning of the 20th century, the painter Matisse discovered Collioure. Soon other Impressionist painters followed him. It's easy to see why as the harbour is one of the prettiest on the Mediterranean.

Like the railway line which first brought tourism to the area, the coast road south of Argelès is highly scenic, twisting around cliffsides and dipping through the small resorts. Sunset on the beach at Argelès (which boasts more campsites than anywhere else in France) is always a dreamy time as the Pyrenees become silhouetted above the sea.

ARGELES-PLAGE❖❖

ℹ️ **Argelès Tourist Information**
I place de l'Europe;
tel: 04 68 81 15 85;
www.argeles-sur-mer.com.
Open daily June–Sept.

🍴 **Casa de les Albères** € *Open Mon–Fri and Sat morning.*

🛒 There's a market on Wednesdays and Saturdays.

Argelès has the reputation of being the campsite capital of Europe! Over 60 sites are set in a 5km stretch of dunes and woods near the sea. Most have sophisticated facilities such as large swimming pools, tennis courts and restaurants. In summer many organise children's clubs and sports activities. Well-equipped pre-erected tents and mobile homes can be booked through tour operators in the UK (*see page 31*).

A promenade shaded by pines runs between the long sandy beach and a row of small hotels, holiday apartments, villas and shops. The beach offers children's clubs and watersports, as well as umbrellas for those who want to do nothing more strenuous than laze in the sun. However, the sand shelves quickly and is rather coarse for digging, so small children are best taken to the shallow lagoon beside a stream at the northern end.

Argelès-sur-Mer❖❖, slightly inland, is the oldest part of the town with narrow streets and alleys. In the centre, **Casa de les Albères❖❖** is a

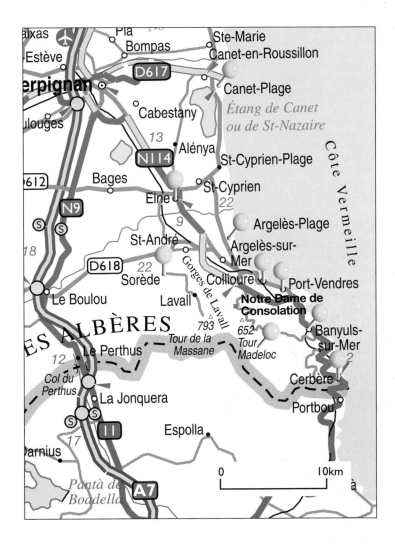

Catalan museum showing traditional arts and crafts including wooden toys, rope sandals and corks for bottles.

BANYULS-SUR-MER✦✦✦

With its pale pink and white buildings and shady squares, Banyuls feels distinctly Catalan. It spreads around two sheltered bays bordered by eucalyptus, palms and pavement cafés, with vineyards stretching over the hillsides around it.

Banyuls-sur-Mer Tourist Information avenue de la République; tel: 04 68 88 31 58; www.banyuls-sur-mer.com. Open daily June–Sept; Mon–Sat Oct–May.

Cellier des Templiers le Mas Reig, rue du Balcon de Madeloc. Open daily May–Sept. Guided visits (free) include sampling.

Musée Maillol €€ Vallée de la Roume; tel: 04 68 88 57 11. Open daily all year.

Les Elmes €€ plage des Elmes; tel: 04 68 88 03 12. Modern family-run hotel with 31 smart air-conditioned rooms and terraces beside the beach.

The sweet, dark brown aperitif, Banyuls, was first made here by the Knights Templar in the 13th century and there are plenty of opportunities for a free *dégustation* (tasting). On the edge of the town, you can see it being made at the **Cellier des Templiers**✦✦✦, the 600-year-old vaulted cellars of le Mas Reig, the castle where it was first produced. There is also a free exhibition and film about Banyuls in the **Grande Cave**✦✦ (*open daily*) opposite.

The **Aquarium**✦✦ **€€** (*tel: 04 68 88 73 39; open daily*) on the headland near the harbour is a centre for marine research as the sea on the Côte Vermeille is exceptionally clear, deep and well stocked with fish.

The sculptor Aristide Maillol (1861–1944) was born in Banyuls. One of his famous bronzes, *La Jeune Fille Alongée* (*Girl Lying Down*), stands on the seafront in Allée Maillol. He also sculpted the war memorial on the Île Grosse, a small island at the southern end of the bay. Although he lived mostly in Paris he returned every autumn to his aunt's country house, now the **Musée Maillol**✦✦✦, where he had a studio and is buried. His sculpture, *La Pensée* (*Thought*), can be found on his tomb (*see page 60*).

A lively festival, Fête Catalan, takes over the town every year from 3 to 11 July.

Canet-Plage❖❖

ⓘ Canet-Plage Tourist Information *éspace Méditerranée; tel: 04 68 86 72 00; www.ot-canet.fr*

ⓗ L'Aquarium €€ *beside the harbour; tel: 04 68 80 49 64. Open daily July–Aug, Tue–Sat Sept–June.*

Unlike many of its neighbours, Canet is a long-established seaside resort – with a casino – though it got a face-lift in the late 1960s when the coast was redeveloped. More recently it has transformed its long seafront, lined with bars, restaurants, shops and apartments, by restricting traffic and creating a large central piazza. At the north end, there is a busy harbour and boatyards.

The **Aquarium**❖❖ attracts visitors of all ages as it contains over 350 species of fish from all over the world; it is also an important research centre.

Accommodation and food in Canet-Plage

Hôtel le Galion €€ *20 avenue du Grand Large; tel: 04 68 80 28 23.* Comfortable 28-room hotel with restaurant, a mile from the sea.

Cerbere❖

ⓘ Cerbère Tourist Information *avenue Général de Gaulle; tel: 04 68 88 42 36; www.cerbere-village.com. Open daily in summer; Mon, Tue, Fri in winter.*

The coast road wriggles south to the French-Spanish border at Cap Cerbère, a magnificent viewpoint on both sides over sea and mountains. The little town itself huddles around a small pebbly bay surrounded by steep vineyards. Trains on the Paris-Barcelona line stop at its 'international' station. On the seafront a striking bronze statue of a woman holding a basket of oranges commemorates the workers who from 1878 to 1970 transferred freight, particularly oranges, between the French trains and the wider-gauge Spanish ones.

Collioure❖❖❖

ⓘ Collioure Tourist information *place du 18 Juin; tel: 04 68 82 15 47; www.collioure.com. Open daily all year.*

ⓗ Château Royal €€ *Tel: 04 68 82 06 43. Open daily.*

Left
Banyuls-sur-Mer

Nestling by the Mediterranean at the foot of the first hills after miles of flat coastline to the north, Collioure is the gem of the Roussillon coast. A charming little port, it has been a magnet for artists since Matisse settled there in 1905. His disciples, dubbed the 'Fauves' (deer), noted for their wild use of colour, soon followed. Narrow cobbled streets, now crowded with galleries and souvenir shops, lead back from its much-painted harbour and the small Eglise Notre-Dame-des-Anges whose tower, which has a small pink dome, was once a lighthouse. Inside the church, remarkable baroque wooden altarpieces, ornately carved and gilded, include a high altar by the Catalan artist Joseph Sunyer, sculpted in 1698.

Along the quay, colourful fishing boats tie up to deposit their catch, mainly the anchovies for which the town is renowned.

A succession of traditional fêtes from May to Sept includes **Fêtes de La St-Vincent** in mid-Aug, when you can rely on seeing the *sardana* danced. Don't forget to sample the local anchovies.

The **Château Royal***, which juts out into the centre of the harbour, was built by the Knights Templar in the 13th century and reinforced by the military architect Vauban in 1679, after Catalonia became part of France.

The town's four beaches are sandy but small so are usually crowded in summer. There are also diving and windsurfing schools.

Accommodation and food in Collioure

Hôtel Madeloc € *24 rue Romain Rolland; tel: 04 68 82 07 56; closed Nov–mid-Mar.* Small modern hotel with a pool in a quiet position on a hill behind the harbour (10-minute walk). No restaurant.

Les Templiers € *12 quai de l'Amirauté; tel: 04 68 98 31 10; www.hotel-templiers.com; closed Jan.* Restaurant overlooking the harbour and Château Royal, famous for its paintings which almost cover its walls. Many are by artist friends of the family who run it. Also notable for its fish.

Above
The harbour at Collioure

Elne❖

Elne Tourist Information *place St Jordi; tel: 04 68 22 05 07; www.ot-elne.fr. Open daily.* Follow the signs to the free parking place at the top of the town to join marked walking routes of different lengths around the old streets.

Ste-Eulalie et Ste-Julie (cloister €€) *Tel: 04 68 22 70 90. Open daily.* Admission includes entrance to the cathedral and archaeological and history exhibits in the cloister and *Musée Terrus* (paintings) opposite, *tel: 04 68 22 88 88.*

Hotel Week-end *€€ 29 avenue Paul Reig; tel: 04 68 22 06 68.* Small 8-room hotel handily-placed at end of main street with restaurant. Garden. Bicycles for hire. Private secure car park.

Below
Elne: cloister carving

Surrounded by apricot and peach orchards, Elne became the capital of the Roussillon area in Roman times so was superior to its now much bigger neighbour Perpignan. The Romans named it after Helena, mother of Emperor Constantine. Narrow streets wind up to the majestic Gothic cathedral, **Ste-Eulalie et Ste-Julie❖❖❖**. Its two towers, the original in stone and a 19th-century brick addition, are a landmark for miles around. Built between the 11th and 15th centuries (apart from the second tower), it has six chapels on its south side, all with fine vaulting showing how the Gothic style developed over the centuries. There is also a beautiful cloister, almost completely intact, with arches supported by superbly carved twin pillars telling the story of Adam and Eve. The view from the cathedral terrace high above the town stretches from the sea to the Pyrenees.

Hannibal

In 218 BC Hannibal arrived from Spain with 34 elephants on his way to attack Italy. Learning of his intentions, the Romans tried to persuade the local people to stop him, but they had no wish to get involved in battles to protect another country. Instead they signed a treaty with Hannibal at Elne, then one of the area's most important towns, and invited him to set up his headquarters there. Unusually, one clause stated that any dispute between his soldiers and the local men should be judged by a tribunal of Elne women.

PORT-VENDRES*

ⓘ **Port-Vendres Tourist Information** / quai François Joly; tel: 04 68 82 07 54; www.port-vendres.com. Open daily in summer; Mon–Fri in winter.

🛍 Daily fish auction at around 1600 at / Anse-Jerbal.

Port-Vendres – meaning the 'port of Venus' – has played many different maritime roles. Built around a deep cove which offered shelter for the Roman sailing galleys, it later developed into an important naval port when the military architect Vauban began strengthening the coast's defences in the late 17th century. Following bomb damage during World War II it was largely rebuilt. When Algeria was part of France, passenger ferries operated regularly to Algiers. Today the port is home to many fishing boats and has a well-equipped marina.

SOREDE*

ⓘ **Sorède Tourist Information** off rue de la Caserne; tel: 04 68 89 31 17; www.ot-sorede.com. Open daily July–Aug; Mon–Fri Sept–June.

ⓖ **Les Microcouliers** rue des Fabriques; tel: 04 68 89 04 50. Exhibition and shop open Mon–Fri.

Musée de l'Olivettes rue de la Coscolleda; tel: 04 68 89 12 47. Open daily July–Aug except Mon for conducted tours 1500–1800 in season; rest of year phone for an appointment.

In the days of horse transport, this small town used to make the whips and crops for which Perpignan was famous. Now production is confined to one factory, **Les Microcouliers***, a rehabilitation centre which is the only place where whips are still made by hand. **Musée de l'Olivettes*** displays railway and coal-mining memorabilia, with working models and a ride on a miniature railway.

TOUR MADELOC***

Above
Sorède door detail

Opposite
Elne cathedral cloister

This 14th-century signal tower, situated at a height of 652m, is ideally placed for keeping watch out to sea in this once sensitive border area. Very exposed, it is built in the local schist slate and topped with battlements. The road up to it off the D86 is narrow, steep and twisting and is often subject to strong winds, but offers superb views. From here you can see down across vineyards to Banyuls, Port-Vendres and Collioure, each tucked into its rocky cove, and to the flat sandy coast stretching away north.

Children's beach clubs operate on the long sandy beach at Cerbère during July and August. Watersports are available at several points and there is an Olympic-sized open-air heated pool.

Below
Elne cathedral

Suggested tour

Total distance: 125km. The detour to the Tour Madeloc adds 3km and the detour to Lavall adds 8km.

Time: 4 hours' driving. Allow 2 days to explore the little towns and enjoy the scenery and seaside. Those with limited time should concentrate on the coastal stretch from Collioure to Cerbère.

Link to another tour: From Sorède, the D2 and D618 lead west to Le Boulou (*see page 64*), 13km away.

Leave Perpignan on the straight D617 which runs through vineyards to the popular seaside resort of **CANET-PLAGE** ❶. The D81 enables you to skirt round it, but to see the sea – and get a better flavour of the

Restaurant de la Plage € *Cerbère; tel: 04 68 88 40 03. Open daily July–Aug, Thur–Tue Sept–June.* Large blue and white seafront restaurant with terrace in the centre of the bay at Cerbère, specialising in Catalan fare, especially fish.

coast – continue to the beachside road before turning right. Be warned, however, that this tends to be very busy at the height of summer.

On the way south to **St-Cyprien-Plage**, you have water on both sides – the sea on the left and the **Etang de Canet et de St-Nazaire** on the right. Continuing on the D81 you come next to **ARGELES-PLAGE ②**, the last of the beach resorts at the southern end of the French Mediterranean. Campsites can be found in the pine woods bordering the long straight road into the busy little town.

Afterwards the road begins to climb into the **Albères Hills** but drops down again into **COLLIOURE ③** and then up and down over the headland to **PORT-VENDRES ④**. Joining the N114 you hug the

hillsides, now covered by terraces of vineyards, on the scenic run down into **BANYULS-SUR-MER ❺**. Continue winding mid-way between sea and hilltop to **CERBERE ❻** where the Spanish border lies at the top of the high pass, 4km on the far side, though its customs' post is now invariably deserted.

Returning to Banyuls, follow the **TOUR MADELOC ❼** sign (just after the river bridge) by turning left to climb inland on the narrow D86. Several *tables d'orientation* beside the road identify the landmarks and explain the history of the vineyards.

Detour: The turn to the Tour Madeloc off the D86 takes you up a steep 1.5km climb around narrow hairpin bends. This is especially exciting on a windy day.

The D86 continues along the appropriately-named **Balcon de Madeloc** hillside past **Notre-Dame de la Consolation** chapel to rejoin the N114. Leave this at Junction 12, turn left through the centre of **ARGELES ❽** town and take the D2 to **SOREDE ❾**.

Detour: About 2km before Sorède, a left turn along a narrow road leads for 4km beside the River Massane into the **Gorges de Lavall** and the village of **Lavall**, with its tiny 12th-century chapel, **St-Martin**.
From Sorède the D11 takes you to **ELNE** and along the straight Roman road, now the N114, back into Perpignan.

Above
La Pensée

La Paella € *les Arcades centre, route de St-Cyprien, Latour bas Elne; tel: 04 68 22 23 72. Open daily July–Aug except Sun evening; otherwise lunchtime only. Small roadside restaurant where you eat inexpensively and well.*

Getting out of the car

The best reason to get out of the car along this route is to sit on the beach, but if you want to be a lot more energetic, try tackling the steep walk from the top of the village in Lavall to the **Tour de la Massane**, which takes you through a forest of ancient oaks and beeches. The tower at the top, 793m up and only 2km from the Spanish border, is a breathtaking viewpoint. Allow 2–3 hours. Alternatively, there's a gentler and shorter route up, starting from the Château de Valmy just outside Argelès, beside Junction 12 on the N114.

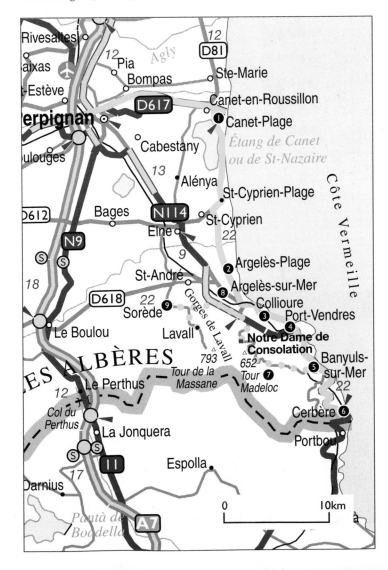

Into the foothills of the Pyrenees

Ratings

Mountains	●●●●●
Scenery	●●●●●
Food	●●●●○
History	●●●●○
Castles	●●●○○
Architecture	●●○○○
Art	●●○○○
Spas	●●○○○

This is a route of contrasts, starting in flat countryside covered in vineyards, orchards and cork woods which edges up to les Albères, the foothills of the Pyrenees. The further you go towards the Spanish border, the more alpine the scenery and architecture become. Prats de Mollo is very much a mountain town and in winter a cross-country skiing centre.

The area is also Catalan country. Many of the place names are distinctly un-French, you can often see the *sardana* danced and restaurants offer specialities such as spicy sausages and *anchoïade* (garlic and anchovy paste). The area did not become part of France until the border was finally settled in 1659 by the Treaty of the Pyrenees.

Though basically circular, the route has spurs up valley roads which lead to mountain passes on the border with Spain.

AMELIE-LES-BAINS✦✦

The particularly mild winters enjoyed by this spa town which spreads along the winding River Tech have given it an abundace of subtropical plants such as palms, oleanders and mimosa. It also has two spa centres, dating from 1902, using sulphurous springs, first discovered by the Romans, which are highly regarded for the treatment of rheumatism. General de Castellane, whose construction of a military hospital in the 1850s put the town's medicinal qualities on the map, was also responsible for the network of footpaths in the hilly woods all around. A short walk from the town centre in the direction of the Modony Gorge leads to the remains of Roman baths, the best preserved in France.

Across the Tech from the town centre, **Palalda**✦ is a medieval hillside village of steep narrow streets whose 400-year-old Chapelle du Rosaire has a fine carved wood altarpiece. The **Musée de la Poste en Roussillon**✦ is devoted to the local postal service, including the invention of stamps

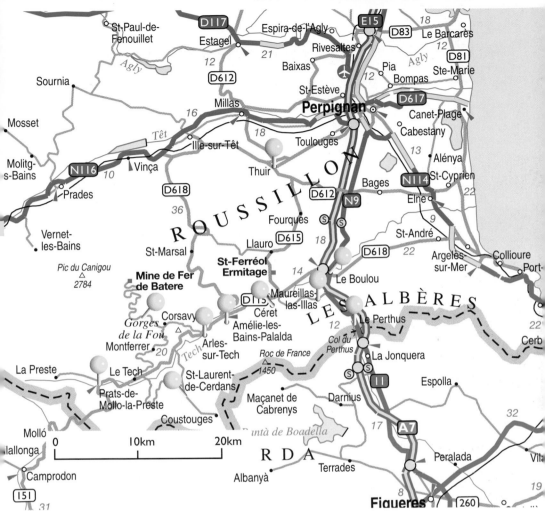

ⓘ **Amélie-les-Bains Tourist Information**

22 ave du Vallespir;
tel: 04 68 39 01 98;
www.amelie-les-bains.com.
Open Mon–Sat all year.

ⓜ **Musée de la Poste en Roussillon €**

Carrer de la Placette,
Palalda; tel: 04 68 39 34
90. Open Tue–Fri all year.
Shuttle bus services to
Palalda from Amélie or
2km on foot.

by a local man, Etienne Arago, and the code of smoke signals which could be sent from the nearby tower to alert the area in case of invasion from Spain.

Accommodation in Amélie-les-Bains

Hôtel Jeanne d'Arc € *place de la République; tel: 04 68 87 96 96; www.jeannedarc.fr.* Old-fashioned hotel overlooking the small market square. Own river terrace complete with palm trees. Ten en-suite rooms and 18 studio-apartments.

Le Palmarium €€ *44 avenue de Vallespir; tel: 04 68 39 19 38. Closed Dec–Jan.* Centrally positioned modern hotel with garden. Many of the 65 rooms have balconies.

Arles-sur-Tech❖❖

ⓘ Arles-sur-Tech Tourist Information *rue Jean-Baptiste Barjou; tel: 04 68 39 11 99; www.ville-arles-sur-tech.fr. Open daily July–Aug; Mon–Fri Sept–June.*

⬤ Tissages Catalans *rue des Usines; tel: 04 68 39 10 07. Open May–Oct Mon–Sat. Shop and museum.*

The tall 14th-century bell tower of the Eglise St-Sauveur welcomes you to this little town which grew up in the 10th century around a Benedictine abbey. The church has a soaring vaulted nave and peaceful 13th-century cloister. Don't miss the Sainte Tombe by the doorway as water, said to be holy, seeps into it for no explicable reason.

The small **Tissages Catalans❖** factory, which has produced traditional Catalan fabrics for over 100 years, has a museum beside it and a shop crammed full of colourful items from table napkins to dresses.

Le Boulou❖❖

ⓘ Le Boulou Tourist Information *I rue du Château; tel: 04 68 87 50 95; www.ot-leboulou.fr. Open Mon–Sat.*

ⓔ Espace des Arts *rue des Ecoles. Open daily, except Sun. Free.*

Les Thermes €€ *on the road to Le Perthus tel: 04 68 87 52 00. Open daily. Casino tel: 04 68 83 01 20.*

Situated beside the River Tech on the edge of cork woods which stretch up the Albères hillsides, le Boulou is a relaxed little spa town which benefits from its proximity to both sea and mountains. In the oldest quarter, the tiny 15th-century Chapelle de St-Antoine is a gem, particularly its gilded wooden altarpiece. Next door, the works of the local sculptor François Pous and other modern Catalan artists are on show in the **Espace des Arts❖❖**. The Eglise Ste-Marie, in the town centre, is remarkable for its splendidly carved 12th-century stone porch and a flamboyant baroque altarpiece in red and white Céret marble.

Le Boulou's most glorious moment in French history was in 1794 when it was the site of a battle which resulted in the French army pushing the Spanish back over the Pyrenees. The soldiers' success is commemorated by an imposing round monument and on the Arc de Triomphe in Paris.

Today the town's main industry is cork, which is stripped from the woods around to make corks for the local Roussillon wine producers. Its spa, **Les Thermes❖**, with a casino beside it, still offers treatments based on the thermal springs and gas.

Accommodation and food in le Boulou

Le Grillon d'Or €€ *40 rue de la République; tel: 04 68 83 03 60;*

www.grillon-dor.com. Family-run hotel on the edge of town with hillside views, and 35 good-sized rooms, outdoor pool and garage. The restaurant € offers a wide choice of menus in congenial surroundings.

CERET❖❖

❶ Céret Tourist Information
avenue Georges Clémenceau; tel: 04 68 87 00 53; www.ot-ceret.fr. Open Mon–Sat. Guided visits in English available.

❶ Musée d'Art Moderne €€ 8 *boulevard Maréchal Joffre; tel: 04 68 87 27 76. Open May–Sept daily; closed Tue rest of year.*

Maison de l'Archéologie € *Porte d'Espagne, place Picasso; tel: 04 68 87 31 59. Open Mon–Fri.*

◕ Saturday morning is a good opportunity to buy *tielles*, the local tartlets of cuttlefish and tomato, in the market.

◔ Sardana festival Mid-July.

This lively little town is known throughout France for the delicious plump red cherries which grow in the local orchards, providing a mass of beautiful white blossom in spring. On sale in markets and shops from April, they are one of France's earliest varieties.

Being strong in Catalan traditions, Céret is a good place to watch the *sardana* being danced and, if to your taste, attend a bullfight. Avenues of plane trees, plenty of smart shops and the remains of ancient fortifications around its web of narrow streets and small squares make it a pleasant place to stroll round. Picasso was a frequent visitor and many of his ceramics are on show in the small but excellent **Musée d'Art Moderne❖❖❖**, together with works by contemporary artists, particularly from the local area. A small Picasso memorial based on one of his drawings stands opposite the Arènes bullring. The **Maison de l'Archéologie❖**, an archaeological museum, occupies one of the town's old towers.

Accommodation and food in Céret

La Terrasse au Soleil €€€ *route de Fontfrède; tel: 04 68 87 01 94; www.la-terrasse-au-soleil.fr.* You pay for the hillside setting of this comfortable, 44-room hotel on the edge of the town with beautiful views to the Canigou mountain and the Roussillon plain. Outdoor pool. Congenial surroundings.

Restaurant les Feuillants €€€ *1 boulevard la Fayette; tel: 04 68 87 37 88. Closed Sun Oct–Feb.* Top-class town-centre gourmet restaurant in a belle-epoque villa whose specialities include lobster with chestnuts (*Oct–Mar only*). Or you can eat in its simpler Brasserie Le Carré.

GORGES DE LA FOU❖❖❖

❶ Gorges de la Fou €€ *off the D115, 2km west of Arles-sur-Tech; tel: 04 68 39 16 21. Open Apr–Nov, except in bad weather. Visits last 1½ hours, including a 15-minute walk from the car park.*

Reputed to be the narrowest canyon in the world, this 250m-deep slit has been cut through rock by a stream (*fou* in Catalan means precipice). The canyon is 2km long and often less than a metre wide; you walk between its often slimy sides on a metal 'bridge'. Though so much smaller than America's mighty Grand Canyon, it is no less impressive.

MAUREILLAS-LAS-ILLAS✧

ⓘ **Maureillas-las-Illas
Tourist Information**
*at the Musée du Liège,
avenue Maréchal-Joffre;
tel: 04 68 83 15 41.*

Ⓜ **Musée du Liège €**
*avenue Maréchal-Joffre,
tel: 04 68 83 15 41. Open
daily except Tue, all year.*

The main reason for pausing in this large village is its cork museum, the **Musée du Liège✧✧**, which shows the full process of cork-making from tree to wine bottle. Cork sculptures by local craftsmen are also on show alongside a collection of oak casks.

The ancient church, Chapelle St-Martin-de-Fenollar (*open daily except Tue all year*), has frescoes dating back to the 12th century which provided inspiration for Picasso and Braque.

LE PERTHUS✧

Ⓜ **Fort de
Bellegarde €** *Tel:
04 68 83 60 15. Open
June–Sept daily.*

This little town has an almost South American feel as its long main street, avenue de la France, is crowded with shops and stores catering for day-trippers from Spain. Earlier travellers were more likely to have been nomads, armies and refugees as it was a major border crossing point until 1976 when the A9 *autoroute* (la Catalane) opened, sweeping most of the traffic straight past it.

Fort de Bellegarde✧✧✧, an impressive fortress, stands guard over the town on a rock (420m). You reach it over a drawbridge beyond a smaller fort. Originally Spanish, it was strengthened by the military architect Vauban in the 1680s and most of his improvements are still intact. There is a large central courtyard and terrace with extensive views. Permanent exhibitions are devoted to its history and the Romans' *Via Domitia* highway.

Vauban

Sébastien le Preste de Vauban (1633–1707), Louis XIV's military architect, was the principal exponent of the new design of fortress required to meet the challenge presented by the introduction of the cannon. Until then, attacks involved digging tunnels to undermine fortresses, weakening the walls with battering rams or building towers so the marauders could climb over the top. The only alternative was to wait until the defenders ran out of food or water which, if they had livestock and a well, might not happen for months.

The cannon changed the situation completely, necessitating a major re-think in military architecture. Huge curtain walls, sometimes 6m thick, became essential and towers lost their importance.

Although Vauban built or strengthened a large number of the area's fortresses and castles, he claimed to be much more proud of his work on the Canal du Midi where he oversaw the construction of 49 aqueducts.

Opposite
Le Perthus: the Fort de
Bellegarde

Prats-de-Mollo***

Prats-de-Mollo Tourist Information / *le Foiral; tel: 04 68 39 70 83; www. pratsdemollolapreste.com. Open daily July–Aug, Mon–Fri Sept–June.*

Fort Lagarde €€ *Tel: 04 68 39 70 83. Open daily Apr–Oct; live shows Sun–Fri,* including cavalry displays, fencing, shooting and actors re-enacting life there in the 18th century.

Hôtel le Bellevue €€ *place El Firal; tel: 04 68 39 72 48.* Small hotel situated just outside the old quarter. Some rooms have balconies overlooking the lively town square. *Open mid-Feb–Nov. 17 en-suite rooms.*

Above
Prats-de-Mollo

Left
Prats-de-Mollo church

This lively mountain town is overlooked by **Fort Lagarde***, a formidable citadel which Vauban constructed in 1692 around the remains of an older castle. Below it beside the River Tech, the original medieval part of the town, Ville d'Amoun, has straight narrow streets and thick ramparts. Among its interesting old buildings are the Maison des Rois d'Aragon, once the hunting lodge of the Kings of Aragon, and the Eglise Ste-Juste et Ruffine which has several splendid altarpieces. The town's large square, outside the old walls, is the scene of festivities throughout the year which often include *sardana* dancing; it is also popular for the game of *pétanque* (boules). In winter, cross-country ski routes lead around the base of the Costabonne peak (2465 m) from the little spa of La Preste (1130 m), 8km up the valley.

St-Laurent-de-Cerdans*

St-Laurent-de-Cerdans Tourist Information 7 *rue Joseph Nivet; tel: 04 68 39 50 06; www.ville-saint-laurent-de-cerdans.fr. Open daily July–Aug; Sat–Sun Sept–June.*

Traditional Catalan fabrics and espadrilles are made in this unexpectedly busy little town surrounded by mountains. The **Musée d'Arts et Traditions Populaires** €** (*rue Joseph Nivet; open daily July–Aug; Sat–Sun Sept–June*), housed in a redundant textile factory, shows traditional crafts including the production of shoes.

Thuir*

The Cusenier wine cellars have made a name for this otherwise unremarkable town. On a visit to the **Caves-Byrrh***, you can see its

Caves-Byrrh € 6
*blvd Violet; tel: 04 68
53 05 42; www.byrrh.com.
Guided tours daily July–Sept;
Mon–Fri Oct and Apr–June;
Mon, Tue and Thur
Nov–Mar.*

800 vats, including the world's largest oak one which holds more than a million litres, and can watch aperitifs such as Byrrh, Cinzano and Dubonnet being made.

Suggested tour

Total distance: 150km. The detour to Le Perthus adds 18km, the detour to St-Laurent-de-Cerdans adds 20km, the detour to La Preste adds 16km and the detour to Batère adds 26km.

Time: 4 hours' driving. Allow a day for the main route, but more with detours. Those with limited time should concentrate on the stretch from Céret to Prats-de-Mollo.

Link to another tour: From le Boulou, the D618 and D2 lead east to Sorède (*see page 56*), 13km away.

From Perpignan (*see page 42*), take the N9 south to **LE BOULOU ❶** – a quieter and more peaceful road than the A9 autoroute which runs parallel with it.

Detour: To visit **LE PERTHUS ❷** on the Spanish border, leave le Boulou on the N9, once a busy cross-border road but now superseded by the autoroute which soars over lofty viaducts beside it. At the start of the detour (9km each way), the tiny **Chapelle St-Martin-de-Fenollar** on the left is noteworthy for its 12th-century murals in bold ochres, reds and greens; they provided inspiration for both Picasso and Braque.

From Le Boulou take the D618 through **MAUREILLAS-LAS-ILLAS ❸** and **CERET ❹** to join the D115. Follow it beside the Tech through **AMELIE-LES-BAINS ❺** and **ARLES-SUR-TECH ❻**. Just after Arles-sur-Tech, the **GORGES DE LA FOU ❼** are prominently signed on the right.

Detour: Shortly after the Gorges de la Fou sign, turn left off the D115 on to the D3 to **ST-LAURENT-DE-CERDANS ❽** (10km each way).

Continuing on the D115 through a wide wooded gorge, you come to **PRATS-DE-MOLLO ❾**.

Detour: About 8km beyond Prats-de-Mollo on the D115a, **la Preste** is a small spa town offering thermal treatments.

Below
Céret

From Prats-de-Mollo you can return towards Arles-sur-Tech along an even more scenic route by turning left off the D115 at **le Tech** on to the narrow D44. This goes through the village of **Montferrer** where you can pause to admire the mountain views from the terrace of its tiny museum.

Detour: Just before **Corsavy** on the D44, take the D43 left for a detour (13km each way) on the lonely road up to the abandoned mine workings and remote inn at **Batère**.

From Corsavy, return to the D115 at Arles-sur-Tech and head back towards Céret but skirt it by turning left on to the D615 to go through **Llauro** to THUIR **❿**. As the road climbs through cork woods, it passes the **Hermitage de St-Ferréol** with views over the coast and to the snowy Canigou mountain inland. The hills give way to flat countryside covered in the neat vineyards which produce the famous aperitifs of Thuir.

Return to Perpignan on the D612, going through **Toulouges**, which was put on the map in 1027 when the Synod held there tried to promote peace throughout Western Europe by proclaiming the Truce of God which restricted warfare to certain days of the year.

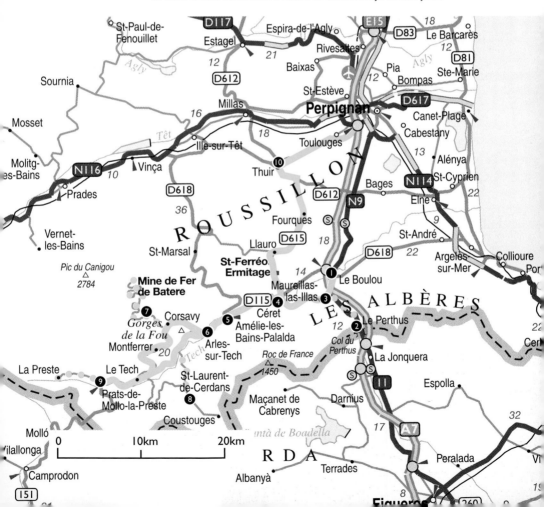

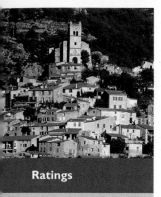

In the shadow of the Canigou

Ratings

Architecture	●●●●●
Mountains	●●●●●
Scenery	●●●●●
Churches	●●●●○
Outdoor activities	●●●●○
Walking	●●●●○
Villages	●●●○○
Spas	●●○○○

Y ou can't escape the spell of the Pic du Canigou, the dramatic snow-topped mountain, when you are in the Perpignan area. Rarely out of sight, it has been loved and revered for centuries by the local Catalans. They light the first midsummer bonfire on it and enjoy walking, riding, cycling and climbing on the wooded slopes that stretch for miles below it. For those who prefer less energetic pursuits, the castles, monasteries and picturesque little towns ranged around offer plenty to explore.

An opportunity not to be missed in summer is to look in the village churches, which are usually closed out of season, to see the surprising wealth of treasures inside. Many have beautiful carved and gilded wooden altarpieces inspired by the work of the 17th-century Catalan sculptor Joseph Sunyer. His own most famous pieces are to be seen in Perpignan and Prades.

ILLE-SUR-TET✢

ℹ **Ille-sur-Têt Tourist Information** *place de la Poste; tel: 04 68 84 02 62; www.ille-sur-tet.com. Open daily July–Aug; Mon–Fri Sept–June.*

🏛 **Centre d'Art Sacré** *€€ Tel: 04 68 84 83 96. Open daily July–Aug; Wed–Mon Sept–Nov and Feb–June; closed Dec–Jan.*

This little town nestles between two rivers, the Têt and Boules. Its main tourist attraction is the **Centre d'Art Sacré✢**, housed in Hospici d'Illa, a 16th-century pilgrims' hospice which highlights the treasures of the area's churches by staging different exhibitions each summer as well as having permanent displays of processional crosses and gold and silver plate.

PRADES✢✢

Surrounded by peach orchards, Prades nestles below the Canigou mountain. The town, which has many street names in Catalan, is

Prades Tourist Information *4 rue des Marchands; tel: 04 68 05 41 02; www.prades-tourisme.com. Open daily July–Aug; Mon–Fri Sept–June.*

P Pay-and-display parking on market square, free on streets further away.

Eglise St-Pierre *Tel: 04 68 05 23 58. Open Mon–Fri July–Sept. Church silver on show in the Treasury €.*

strung out along narrow straight streets, some with kerbstones and doorsteps made of the local pink marble quarried at Villefranche-de-Conflent (*see page 76*). Dominating the central square, the 17th-century **Eglise St-Pierre✣✣✣** has a tall, square bell tower, 500 years older, with three tiers of open paired arches, typical of the area's Lombardy style. Inside, the church has a single nave lined with side chapels. Its rather austere design sets off the lavish altarpiece which takes up the entire wall behind the high altar. Elaborately carved, painted and gilded, it is the largest in France and depicts scenes from the life of St Peter. The artist was Joseph Sunyer, the famous Catalan sculptor who came to Prades with his brother around 1690 and worked in churches throughout the area.

The distinguished Spanish cellist Pablo Casals made Prades his home in 1939 when he could no longer stomach life in Spain under Franco. An exhibition about his life and work can be seen in the Mediathèque (*33 rue de l'Hospice. Free. Open Tue–Sat*). In 1950 he inaugurated a Bach Festival which, with several other musical events, continues today, staged mainly in the Abbaye de St-Michel-de-Cuxa (*see page 75*) in the countryside 3km south of the town.

Musée de la Soie is devoted to the area's silk production from worm to fabric (*€ boulevard de la Gare; tel: 04 68 05 33 75. Open daily Apr–Oct*).

⬛ **Market** Tue.

🅰 **Music Festival** *Late July–early Aug.* Tickets bookable by credit card through the tourist office; booking opens May.

Accommodation and food in Prades

Les Glycines €€ *129 avenue du Général de Gaulle; tel: 04 68 96 51 65. Closed Oct–mid-Nov.* Simple but comfortable town-centre hotel noted for its floral displays. Nineteen rooms. Bright, cheerful restaurant.

L'Hôtel Hexagone €€ *La Plaine St-Martin; tel: 04 68 05 31 31.* Plain but comfortable modern hotel (definitely the town's best) with garden and sun terrace on the edge of the town, handy for the N116. No restaurant. Thirty rooms.

PRIEURE DE SERRABONE***

🅸 **Prieuré de Serrabone €** *Boule d'Amront; tel: 04 68 84 09 30. Open daily.*

This 12th-century priory is regarded as one of the area's best examples of the Romanesque style. Although the outside is rather austere, the interior is richly decorated, including flowers and animals on the capitals and an elaborate pink marble tribune (bishop's throne) with carving so delicate it looks like embroidery. Take a stroll, too, in its small botanical garden.

ST-MARTIN-DU-CANIGOU***

🅸 **St-Martin-du-Canigou €** *Tel: 04 68 05 50 03. Open daily.* Walk up to it from the village of Casteil (45 minutes) or book to go by 4×4 vehicle with a guide from Vernet or Villefranche-de-Conflent.

Perched on a rocky outcrop (1055m), 3km south of Vernet-les-Bains, this monastery's red rooftops and square bell tower provide a landmark for miles around. When founded in the 11th century, its church was one of the first to have a vaulted nave and aisles supported by massive pillars. Since then it has had a chequered history. It was severely damaged by an earthquake in 1428 and the monks had to abandon it during the French Revolution. In 1902 the ruins were bought by the Bishop of Perpignan and gradually restored until the monks were finally able to move back in 1972.

ABBAYE DE ST-MICHEL-DE-CUXA****

🅸 **Abbaye de St-Michel-de-Cuxa €** *Codalet. Open daily except Sun morning.*

🅰 **Music festival** *Late July–early Aug.*

Left
Prades church

After being abandoned during the French Revolution, this ancient monastery at Codalet, where Benedictine monks first settled in 878, was eventually restored, becoming a monastery again in 1919. Parts of the building are original, dating back to the 10th to 12th centuries, including the attractive four-tier square bell tower and delicately sculpted cloisters. However many of the columns from it were bought in 1907 by an American sculptor, George Grey Bernard, and are now on show in New York. In the west wing, a model and photographs tell the story of the abbey.

St-Paul-de-Fenouillet*

ℹ️ **St-Paul-de-Fenouillet Tourist Information** 26 boulevard de l'Agly; tel: 04 68 59 07 57; www.st-paul66.com. Open Mon–Sat July–Aug; Tue–Sat Sept–June.

🎫 **Le Chapitre €** Next to tourist office. Open Mon–Sat July–Aug; Tue–Sat Sept–June.

Situated between the Fenouillèdes and Corbières hills, this little town promotes itself as a base for a wide variety of outdoor activities, from mountain biking to canyoning. You can see layers of its long history in what remains of its ancient church which was part of a chapter house, **Chapitre de St-Paul-de-Fenouillet***.

Accommodation in St-Paul-de-Fenouillet

Le Chatelet €€ *Route de Caudiès; tel: 04 68 59 01 20. Closed mid-Nov–mid-Mar.* Small, pink, countryside hotel on the D117 towards Quillan. Fifteen rooms, swimming pool May–Sept.

Vernet-les-Bains**

ℹ️ **Vernet-les-Bains Tourist Information** 6 place de l'Ancienne Mairie; tel: 04 68 05 55 35; www.ot-vernet-les-bains.fr. Open daily July–Aug; Mon–Fri Sept–June.

🎽 **Championnat du Canigou** is a 30km race, first held in 1905, on footpaths on the Canigou mountain. More challenging than a marathon! To take part, just turn up on the day (first Sun in Aug).

🌀 **Fête de la Belle Epoque** takes place on Ascension weekend in May when everyone dresses up and old vehicles parade through the streets.

Vernet-les-Bains is a relaxed hillside town with lush gardens, thermal springs and shaded boulevards. In its heyday as a fashionable spa around the turn of the century, it attracted many British visitors, including Rudyard Kipling. Today some people still come to drink its waters (reputed to help the treatment of rheumatism and ear, nose and throat diseases) but most visitors are more interested in walking, riding or mountain biking in its glorious mountain surroundings. The square bell tower of the Eglise St-Saturnin beside the restored castle crowns the old quarter at the top of narrow streets whose old houses are bedecked with flowers. The castle's terraces have good views of the wooded mountains.

Accommodation in Vernet-les-Bains

Le Mas Fleuri €€ *25 boulevard Clémenceau; tel: 04 68 05 51 94; www.hotellemasfleuri.fr. Open mid-May–mid-Oct.* Comfortable family-run hotel in sunny position with large pool and gardens. Thirty rooms.

Villefranche-de-Conflent***

ℹ️ **Tourist Information** in the ramparts at the entrance to Bastion de la Montagne; tel: 04 68 96 22 96; e-mail: otsi-villefranchedeconflent@voila.fr. Open daily.

Walking round the **ramparts*** of this strongly fortified medieval town, you can easily feel transported back in time. Twenty-two of the buildings within its thick two-storey-high walls are classed as historic monuments. Often built in pink marble from the nearby quarry, they date from the 13th and 14th centuries. Though most are now occupied by souvenir shops or restaurants, Villefranche is definitely a

 Ramparts € *Open daily, except Jan.*

Fort-Libéria €€ *Tel: 04 68 96 34 01. Open daily. Shuttle bus (navette) from Le Canigou café, place du Génie.*

Above
Vernet-les-Bains

place to linger and absorb the unique atmosphere. It is also the starting point of le Petit Train Jaune (Little Yellow Train), one of Europe's most scenic railway lines. **Fort-Libéria****, which stands guard on a hillside above the town, was built by the military architect Vauban in 1679 as a deterrent to any snipers who might have been tempted to take pot shots down into the town. It has three tiers and high stone walls topped by bricks and wrought-iron rails. L'Escalier de Mille Marches ('staircase of 1000 steps' though there are actually 734) leads up to it from the town across Pont St-Pierre, an attractive

Grotte des Grandes Canalettes €€ *2 rue Saint-Jacques, Villefranche-de-Conflent; tel: 04 68 96 23 11; www.grotte-grandes-canalettes.com. Open daily Apr–Oct; Sun afternoons Nov–Mar.*

fortified bridge. The climb is rewarded by a magnificent panorama over the valley and the Canigou mountain.

Grotte des Grandes Canalettes, one of several large caves in the area, is in the hills on the southwest edge of the town.

VINÇA

Vinça Tourist Information *9 place Bernard Alart; tel: 04 68 05 84 47. Open Mon–Sat July–Aug only. Visits to the local church in the mornings during summer. July–Aug organ recitals.*

Big old houses with decorative stone doorways are gathered along a network of narrow streets and tiny squares, all clustered around the village's fine Southern Gothic church, Eglise St-Julien, which has several beautiful altarpieces and an organ built by the famous Cavaillé family.

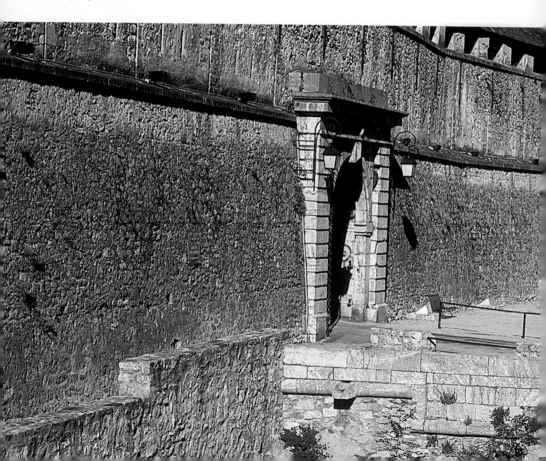

Suggested tour

Total distance: 140km, plus 25km each way between Perpignan and Ille-sur-Têt. The detour to Prieuré de Serrabone adds 24km, the detour to St-Martin-du-Canigou adds 6km and the detour to Eus adds 8km.

Time: 5 hours' driving. Allow at least a day for the main route, more with detours. Those with limited time should concentrate on the circuit from Prades through Vernet-les-Bains and Villefranche-de-Conflent. A trip on the Little Yellow Train can take almost a full day.

Links to other tours: From St-Paul-de-Fenouillet, the D117 leads east to Maury (*see page 108*), 8km away, and the D10 leads north to Cubières-sur-Cinoble (*see page 108*), 10km away. From Villefranche-de-Conflent the N116 leads west to Mont-Louis (*see page 90*), 30km away.

Below
Villefranche-de-Conflent

Take the N116 west out of Perpignan to **ILLE-SUR-TET** ❶ where the route proper begins, then continue on it as it climbs from the

Le Petit Train Jaune stops at seven stations – and 13 more by request. Daily services. Timetable and information: *tel: 04 68 96 63 62.* A leaflet about walks and places to visit from various stations is available from stations and TICs. *www.ter-sncf.com/yellow-train*

Roussillon plain along the valley into the mountains, getting nearer to the snow-capped Canigou (on the left) all the way. In early spring the peach orchards which thrive in the shelter of the valley are a mass of pink blossom.

Detour: To visit the **PRIEURE DE SERRABONE ❷**, turn left off the N116 3km beyond Ille-sur-Têt on to the D618 and then follow the River Boulés on the D84 (12 km).

As the N116 bypasses **VINÇA ❸** and **PRADES ❹**, leave it each time and follow their *centre ville* signs to visit them.

On the edge of Prades, turn south on the D27 (signed Codolet). This leads up through cherry orchards to the **ABBAYE DE ST-MICHEL-DE-CUXA ❺** and has a glorious view of the Canigou ahead. Continuing to climb through open countryside, you pass the village of **Taurinya** and its attractive 11th-century bell tower, enjoying superb views back down over Prades and ahead of **VERNET-LES-BAINS ❻** spreading down from its ancient church.

Detour: To visit **ST-MARTIN-DU-CANIGOU ❼**, follow the D116 south from Vernet-les-Bains for 3km.

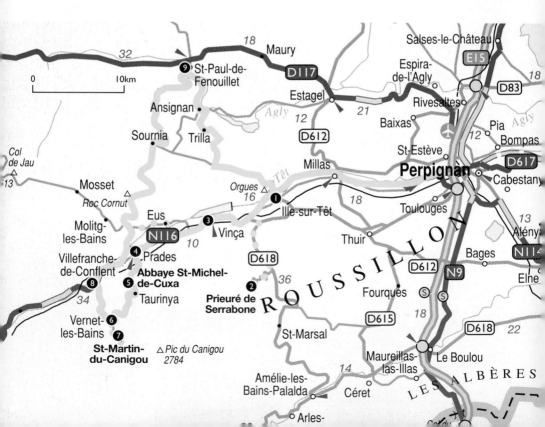

Le Petit Train Jaune

Constructed between 1910 and 1927 to connect the remote villages in the foothills of the Pyrenees, the line is now mainly used by tourists. Its bright yellow metre-gauge electric trains (with open-top carriages in summer) climb to the 1200m-high Cerdagne plateau near the Spanish border on their way to Latour-de-Carol where they connect with the Toulouse-Barcelona line on the main SNCF network. On the 63km journey, they rattle around hillsides, through deep gorges, over lofty viaducts, in and out of 19 tunnels and past terraced vineyards and tiny red-tiled villages that cling to the hillsides. Several run each day and the full journey takes 2½–3 hours.

After following the wooded Têt valley in the shadow of the Canigou, the line crosses wide mountain pastures below Font-Romeu and passes the huge solar oven at Odeillo. The scenery becomes positively alpine at the highest point (1593m) where it crosses the Col de la Perche at Bolquère-Eyne, the highest SNCF station in France.

Below
Le Petit Train Jaune

From Vernet-les-Bains the D116 leads north down a wide gorge to **VILLEFRANCHE-DE-CONFLENT** ❽ , with Fort-Liberia brooding over it on the hillside beyond. A ride on **le Petit Train Jaune**, which starts from Villefranche-de-Conflent, is a memorable experience. The 63km line to Latour-de-Carol is one of the most scenic in Europe.

From Villefranche-de-Conflent, take the N116 towards Prades, turning left on to the D619 to **Sournia**.

Detour: A short detour (4km each way) off D619 on D24 leads to **Eus**, a picturesque hillside hamlet whose old houses cluster around a fortified church in typical Catalan style. It spreads down the sunny side of the valley among boulders of granite and patches of broom.

Then as the D619 twists and climbs towards Sournia in the Fenouillèdes hills, you get splendid views south across the valley not only to the Canigou but also the mountains across the border in Spain. Trees give way to scrubby bushes as the road winds up and up through wild rocky moorland past huge boulders and strangely-shaped rocks, such as the **Roc Cournut**. You'll certainly want to stop

Below
Les Orgues, at Ille-sur-Têt

and get your binoculars out at the highest point, the Col de Roque-Jalère (976m), where the white ridge of the Corbières hills comes into view to the north and the Mediterranean to the west. The Compoussey plateau beyond it is a very quiet stretch of countryside with just a few red-roofed villages clustered around their square bell towers. The final descent into **ST-PAUL-DE-FENOUILLET** ❾ is dramatic as the road drops down to go through the Clue de la Fou, a narrow gap between two cliffs gouged out by the River Algy. From St-Paul-de-Fenouillet, the D619 and D77 return you south via **Ansignan** where the road passes close to an aqueduct built by the Romans. Bear right on the D9b via **Trilla** for the scenic run down to the Têt valley and the N116 back to Perpignan. Just before Ille-sur-Têt the road passes **les Orgues**, curious pillars of rock which look remarkably like organ pipes. There are two groups of these *cheminées de fées*. The one on the eastern side, in the middle of an 'amphitheatre' of craggy white walls, is easily accessible. Enjoy this spectacular site while you can as geologists reckon it will disappear within about 50 years due to erosion by wind and rain.

Up into the Pyrenees

Ratings

Mountains	●●●●●
Outdoor activities	●●●●●
Scenery	●●●●●
Spas	●●●●○
Architecture	●●●○○
Food	●●●○○
History	●●○○○
Wildlife	●●○○○

This route takes you south through the Pyrenees to the wide Cerdagne plateau on the border with Spain. Although the tops of the mountains do not match the height of the Alps, this part of Catalan-speaking Roussillon – fought over with Spain for centuries – is all high. Its meadows, where sheep, cattle and horses graze, blaze with wild flowers in summer when wild crocuses, gentians and lupins mingle with the buttercups and daisies. And a huge variety of mushrooms sprout up in the woods.

Criss-crossed by footpaths, the area rewards those who get out of their car to enjoy the fresh mountain air and scenery on foot – or, in winter, on skis. Indeed snow makes many of the minor roads impassable until spring and the narrow mountain road which twists between Ax and Mijanès often remains blocked until even later.

Ax-les-Thermes ❖❖

This elegant town is typical of the 19th-century spas which became fashionable with the arrival of the railway. Today most summer visitors prefer to go walking and winter ones to go skiing, but it still has two pump rooms – the Teich and Grand Tétras – and 80 thermal springs. These range in temperature from 18–78°C (64–172°F) and are used to treat rheumatism, skin problems and breathing disorders. Anyone can use the Bassin des Ladres (lepers), the public pool on place du Breilh which was built in 1260 for soldiers suffering from leprosy. You could take a very public dip in it but most people are content simply to soak their feet; wonderful after a long walk or day's skiing! The town also has a large selection of hotels. The Eglise St-Vincent, built in 1811 on the site of an earlier church, is remarkable for its 4-ton granite altar and modern stained glass.

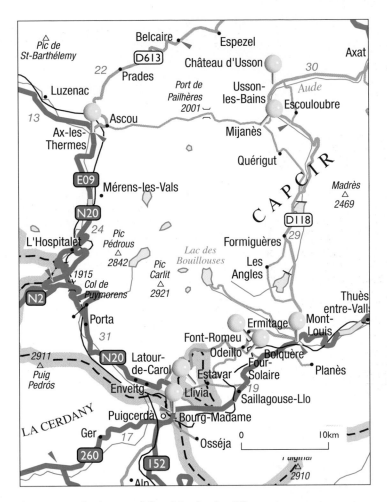

Accommodation and food in Ax-les-Thermes

Auberge l'Orry le Saquet € *route de l'Espagne; tel: 05 61 64 31 30. Closed Jan.* Fifteen-room hotel with pretty garden on southern edge of town. Parking.

Hôtel l'Auzeraie €€ *avenue Delcassé; tel: 05 61 64 20 70. Closed mid-Nov–mid-Dec.* Noted for its regional cuisine. Fitness room, garden and car park. Thirty-three rooms.

Hotel de France € *10 avenue Delcassé; tel: 05 61 64 20 30. Closed Mar–mid-Apr and mid-Nov–Jan; restaurant closed mid-Nov–mid-Apr.* Traditional French hotel with modern block behind. Many of the 38 rooms have balconies. Garage.

BOURG-MADAME❖

ⓘ Bourg-Madame Tourist Information *place de la Catalogne; tel: 04 68 04 55 35. Open Mon–Sat July–Aug; Mon–Fri Sept–June.*

ⓗ Eglise St-Martin *Guided visits to Hix.*

ⓐ Two-week **Hix festival** in August.

As befits a border village, Bourg-Madame once thrived on smuggling. It was originally called Guingettes d'Hix because people from Hix, a hamlet 1km away, liked to go to its *guingettes* (cafés with dancing) for a night out; the first opened in 1693. Its present name was given after the Duc d'Angoulême and his wife, known as Madame Royale, passed through on their return from exile in Spain after the downfall of Napoleon. He gave permission for it to be renamed in honour of the event.

Hard as it is to believe, Hix was the capital of the region until the 12th century, mainly because of the country fairs which were held there. Today it consists only of a few few stone buildings beside a small Romanesque church, **Eglise St-Martin❖**.

FONT-ROMEU❖❖❖

ⓘ Font-Romeu Tourist Information *avenue E Brousse; tel: 04 68 30 68 30; www.font-romeu.fr. Open daily.*

ⓗ Chapel *300m before the Col du Calvaire de Fort-Romeu on the D618, 1km east of Font-Romeu. At the Col itself, on the other side of the D618, a footpath leads past Stations of the Cross to a panoramic view over the Cerdagne and surrounding mountains.*

ⓒ Hotel Carlit €€ *rue Dr Capelle; tel: 04 68 30 80 30. Modern family-run 58-room hotel in town centre enjoying good views over the plain. Swimming pool.*

This large year-round holiday resort, the highest town in France (1800m), was purpose-built in the 1920s on the edge of pine forests. Occupying a sheltered sunny position on a south-facing hillside, it enjoys a panoramic view aross the Cerdagne plateau to the ridges of the Pyrenees.

In winter it is a busy ski resort, equipped with 460 snow cannons to ensure the season remains in full swing until April. Throughout the year leading sportsmen and women arrive from all over the world for altitude training, as well as holiday-makers who go walking or climbing. The Grand Hotel, which occupies a commanding position on the skyline, was built as a prestigous railway hotel but is now divided into holiday apartments.

The town got its name from the nearby pilgrim's spring (*foun roumeu* in Catalan) which has been the site of pilgrimages since – the story goes – the Vierge de l'Invention, a statue of the Virgin Mary, was discovered in a crack in the rock by a bull as it scraped earth from the spring. The small 17th-century **chapel❖❖** beside it has a lavish altarpiece by the Catalan sculptor Joseph Sunyer. The statue spends each summer in the chapel until 8 September when it is carried downhill with much pomp and ceremony to the church in Odeillo. It is brought back with similar ceremony on Trinity Sunday. The large hermitage building beside the chapel is now used as university accommodation.

Left
A rural community

FOUR SOLAIRE✧✧✧

Four Solaire €€
*Odeillo; tel: 04 68 30
77 86; www.imp.cnrs.fr.
Open daily. Exhibition with
video on how the solar
oven works.*

The Four Solaire, a vast 40m-high curving screen of tiny mirrors near the village of Odeillo dominates the countryside. Built in 1969, it is the world's largest solar oven and is used to research the effects of very high temperatures on materials. The sun's rays are reflected onto the screen from 63 large mirrors set up on the hillside facing it and then reflected again into a single spot where the temperature can reach over 3000°C (5400°F).

LLIVIA✧✧✧

**Llívia Tourist
Information** *Musée
municipal de Llívia, Spain;
tel: (Spain) (+34) 972 89 63
13; www.llivia.com. Open
Mon–Sat all year.*

You are now entering Spain. This small enclave, only 3km across, remained Spanish when everywhere around it became part of France following the Treaty of the Pyrenees in 1659. On the road which crosses it you slip over the 'border' without realising until you stop and find everyone speaking Catalan (though they also understand Spanish). A large number of holiday villas enjoying views over the Cerdagne are springing up around the road, but if you turn off it into the old part of Llívia you are immediately plunged into narrow streets clustered beneath an imposing 15th-century church with a spired bell tower. The stone buildings house a handful of shops and restaurants. The old pharmacy is now a small museum.

Spain's Llívia

Llívia has remained 'temporarily' part of Spain since 1659 when the Treaty of the Pyrenees ceded 33 villages on the northern slopes of the Cerdagne to France. At the time, the exact course of the border was not precisely specified but was basically understood to be the north/south watershed where rivers flowed either into France or Spain.

The population of Llívia strongly objected to being moved into France, arguing that it could not possibly be classed as a 'village' as it had been capital of the Cerdagne since the 10th century. They also pointed out that the River Sègre which passes it flows into Spain even though its source is a spring on the northern side of the Pic de Sègre.

No-one has yet got round to settling the matter, but meanwhile Llívia determinedly retains Spanish signs, Spanish menus and – until the euro – used Spanish currency. The tiny village of Eyne, 7km east of Llívia, has tried to become a second Spanish enclave, but so far the French government has loftily ignored its petitions.

Accommodation and food in Llívia

l'Esquirol € *Avinguda Catalunya, 17527 Llívia; tel: (Spain) (+34) 972 89 63 03.* For a taste of genuine Catalan food, including specialities such as duck with peas and *crème Catalan.*

A music festival takes place in the church in August. For information *tel: (Spain) (+34) 972 89 60 49; www.llívia.com/festival/index.htm*

Hotel Llívia €€ *avenue Catalunya 111; tel: (+34) 972 14 60 00.* Big modern hotel with pool, large garden, children's playground and tennis. Expect the staff to speak Catalonian or Spanish – and to understand English better than French. Seventy-six rooms. Disabled access.

Right
The Solar Oven (Four Solaire) on Mont-Louis

MIJANES*

Mijanès Tourist Information *at le Pla (2km south on the D16); tel: 04 68 20 41 37; www.donezan.com. Open daily July–Aug, Mon–Fri Sept–June.*

This quaint little terraced village, whose stone houses spread along narrow cobbled streets down the sunny side of a hillside, has been occupied since prehistoric times. Once home to Gauls and Romans, it was at its busiest durng the 18th century when iron was mined in the area. Now in winter it turns into a mini ski resort for slopes about a 10-minute drive away.

MONT-LOUIS***

Mont-Louis Tourist Information *3 rue Lieutenant Pruneta; tel: 04 68 04 21 97. Open daily July–Aug; Mon–Sat Sept–June.*

Puits de Forçats € *in the military fort. Guided visits July and Aug. Tickets available at Office de Tourisme.*

Four Solaire €€ *Résidence Vauban; tel: 04 68 04 14 89; www.four-solaire.com. Open daily.*

Still completely surrounded by ramparts which have never had to withstand an attack, Mont-Louis is a perfect example of an old fortified town. Its watchtowers and bastions have remained intact since Louis XIV instructed his military architect, Vauban, to build it in 1679 to guard the border between France and Spain following the Treaty of the Pyrenees when Rouissillon was ceded to France. Today the citadel is used as a commando training centre – so don't be surprised to see soldiers out and about. Inside it the original well, the **Puits des Forçats***, built in case of siege, still has its wooden winding gear in working order.

Four Solaire**, the world's first solar oven, an amazing combination of mirrors and panels, was installed in the Résidence Vauban in a corner of the ramparts in 1949. Guided tours show how solar energy is produced, reaching temperatures of over 3000°C (5400°F). Pottery baked in the oven is on display.

Accommodation in Mont-Louis

La Taverne-Bernagie €€ *10 rue Victor Hugo; tel: 04 68 04 23 67.* Eight-room hotel with an intimate restaurant in the extraordinary surroundings of this small fortress town.

CHATEAU D'USSON*

Château d'Usson € *Tel: 04 68 20 43 92. Open daily July–Sept, Sat–Sun May–June. Other days by appointment through Mijanes tourist office; tel: 04 68 20 41 37.*

This ruined castle stands on a rocky outcrop above the village of Usson-les-Bains. Originally constructed in wood in the 10th century, it was a Cathar refuge when the 'heretics' were in retreat. Later it became redundant and fell into ruin during the French Revolution when much of its stone was removed for other buildings. The village below has also seen better days as its former spa buildings beside the River Bruyère are fast falling into disrepair.

Above
Magnificent autumn colours in the Pyrenees

Suggested tour

Total distance: 135km. The detour to Lac des Bouillouses adds 28km and the detour to Château d'Usson adds 6km.

Time: 4 hours' driving. Allow at least a day for the main route, two with detours. Those with limited time should concentrate on the Cerdagne area, particularly Font-Romeu and Mont-Louis.

Links to other tours: At Ax-les-Thermes, the route meets the 'Castles and caves from Foix' route (*see pages 98–101*). From Mont-Louis the N116 leads east to Villefranche-de-Conflent (*see page 76*), 30km away.

Leave **AX-LES-THERMES ❶** along the N20 which climbs beside the railway up the River Ariège valley in a wide wooded gorge. It's easy to sweep through **Mérens-les-Vals** without noticing its ruined chapel, one of the oldest in the region. Thought to date back to the 10th century, it has a three-tier bell tower in typical Catalan style.

Further south you can shorten the journey over the Col de Puymoren (1915m) by paying the toll to go through the 6km-long tunnel under it from **l'Hospitalet**, but the ride over the top on the twisting road through the mountains is much more scenic. Dropping down along the wide valley of the River Carol, still beside the railway, you pass the twin towers of a ruined castle, Tours Carol, and reach the villages of **Latour-de-Carol** and **Enveitg**, where trains on the Toulouse-Barcelona line meet up with the Petit Train Jaune (*see page 81*).

Continuing south the N20 goes through **Ur** on the way to **BOURG-MADAME** ❷ and its tiny suburb **Hix**, framed by a ridge of the Pyrenees across the border in Spain. Take the N116 east (towards the charcuterie-producing town of **Saillagouse**), but turn left after 4km on to the D30 and then right onto the N154. This whisks you imperceptibly into the Spanish enclave and its small town of **LLIVIA** ❸. Leaving Llívia is trickier as you need to spot the sign to **Estavar** in the town centre. Beyond Estavar the D33e runs scenically up to **FONT-ROMEU** ❹ past **Odeillo** and its extraordinary-looking solar oven, **FOUR SOLAIRE** ❺. Leaving Font-Romeu on the D618 you soon come to the hermitage on the left with the chapel behind it and then go over the Col du Calvaire de Font-Romeu (1836m) on the way to **MONT-LOUIS** ❻.

Detour: The D60 (left off the D198 just north of Mont-Louis) leads up a wooded road through the Fôret de Barrés to the **Lac des Bouillouses**, 14km north. This big mountain reservoir, over 2000m high, feeds irrigation channels and hydroelectric plants in the Têt valley. Altogether there are over 20 lakes on the bleak Bouillouses plateau between the Carlit, Péric and Aude peaks.

From Mont-Louis the D118 runs north past **Formiguères**, a village notable for its distinctly alpine feel and 14th-century church, Ste-Marie. Six kilometres beyond it turn left on to the D32 and then the D16 for Quérigut and **MIJANES** ❼. In Napoleonic times, this was an important stretch of highway. Named the Chemin des Canons, it was built in 1659 following the Treaty of the Pyrenees so munitions could be transported to the Mont-Louis fort. Indeed the village of **Quérigut**, watched over by the ruins of a castle abandoned after the Treaty, boasted a population of 600 inhabitants at the end of the 19th century.

Detour: From Mijanès the D16 leads to **CHATEAU D'USSON** ❽ (3km).

From the car park in Mijanès, a 25-minute woodland walk leads to one of the few remaining Catalan forges, a relic from the 18th-century iron industry. Oxen were used to operate the presses which enabled a team of eight men to do work which previously required 100 – clearly a significant step towards industrialisation.

Along the D25 which takes this route back to Ax-les-Thermes from Mijanès, the mountain tops are crowned by cairns, thought to have been placed there by Napoleon's officers to mark the summits. It is one of the remotest mountain roads in the area, often steep and narrow with hairpin bends over the Col de Pailhères (2001m). It is invariably blocked by snow in winter and can remain closed until May; the alternative route back to Ax-les-Thermes is via Usson-les-Bains, Aunat, Espezel and Belacaire, but this adds 20km to the journey.

Various trips are possible on the Petit Train Jaune as it makes frequent stops on its scenic 63km journey between Villefranche-de-Conflent and Latour-de-Carol. Timetable and information: *tel: 04 68 96 63 62.*

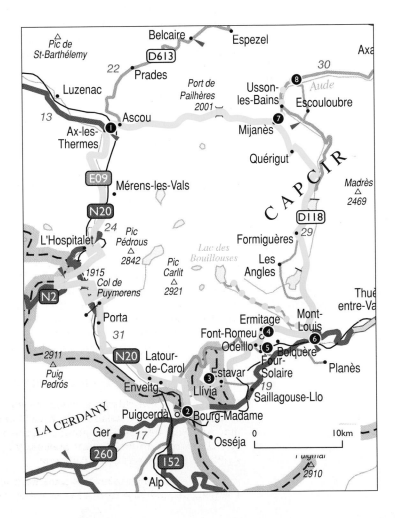

Castles and caves from Foix

Ratings

Castles	●●●●●
Caves	●●●●●
Historical sights	●●●●○
Children	●●●○○
Mountains	●●●○○
Outdoor activities	●●●○○
Scenery	●●●○○
Museums	●●○○○

Two of the region's most characteristic features are included in this route – castles and caves. Foix Castle was a major political stronghold in the 13th century and Monségur, one of the most historic sites in France, was the scene of the terrible slaughter that ended the Albigensian Crusade.

In the limestone hills crossed by the River Ariège and its tributaries, hundreds of caves have formed. The prehistoric paintings in the Grotte de Niaux are among the finest in Europe – and are being carefully cherished. The Grotte de Lombrives is the largest cave open to the public in Western Europe.

Although several towns along the route have an industrial side, this scarcely impinges on their attraction. The busy main roads which link them take you through peaceful countryside and hills where it is easy to head off along less beaten tracks and find places to explore on foot.

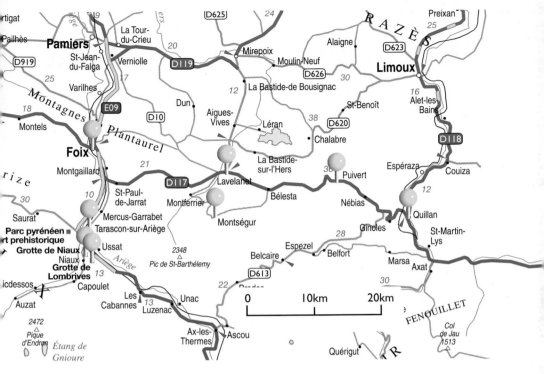

FOIX✦✦

The most important town between Toulouse and Carcassonne benefits from its commanding position on the edge of the Plantaurel hills where two rivers meet, the Arget and Ariège. Though comparatively small, its castle, **Château des Comtes de Foix✦✦**, occupies an impressive position on a rock in the centre, with its three towers silhouetted against the mountains. One of the lower rooms houses the **Musée Départemental de l'Ariège✦**, a collection of weapons and prehistoric finds from over 60 caves around the Ariège area (250 more caves have been identified but not yet explored). The castle's finest hour was early in the 13th century when the Count of Foix was a force to be reckoned with. Indeed Simon de Montfort never dared attack it during the Albigensian Crusade though the town was a Cathar stronghold (*see page 33*). There are good views from the top of the 15th-century round tower (the two 13th-century ones are square) and the terrace.

The town has two distinct areas. In the old part, narrow streets and alleys with half-timbered buildings radiate from small squares including place de Labistour which has a charming bronze fountain in the shape of a swan. The newer area has broad boulevards and two 19th-century covered markets. Traditional Catalan fabrics are made in the town but nobody now pans for gold in the river. Iron was mined

Left
Foix château

P Pay-and-display parking.

nearby until 1931. The composer Gabriel Fauré (1845–1924) grew up in the town, attending school at the Ecole Normale d'Instituteurs in Montgauzy, just above the castle on the north side of town, which has a good view over the town. The Chapelle Notre Dame, next to the Ecole, was formerly part of a convent.

Accommodation in Foix

Hôtel Pyrène €€ *rue Serge Denis; tel: 05 61 65 48 66. Closed mid-Dec–Jan.* Well-placed at southern entrance to the town with good view of the castle. Garden and pool. No restaurant. Twenty rooms.

GROTTE DE LOMBRIVES✦✦✦

Grotte de Lombrives €€€
Ussat-les-Bains, beside the N20, 4km southeast of Tarascon-sur-Ariège; tel: 05 61 05 98 40; www.cathares.org. Open daily Apr–Oct for 90-min tours of the caves on a little train.

This extensive network of caves near Tarascon-sur-Ariège has featured in the *Guinness Book of Records* as the biggest open to the public in Western Europe. The galleries extend for over 3km and the main cathedral-like chamber (100m high) has an almost vaulted roof. Stories abound about activities in the caves over the centuries. Hercules is said to have buried Pyrène, his beautiful young mistress, there. Religious and political refugees sought refuge in them. And did the Cathars hide their treasure somewhere inside?

GROTTE DE NIAUX✦✦✦

Grotte de Niaux €€€ *Above Niaux village, 5km south of Tarascon-sur-Ariège, off the D8. Open daily but reservations essential as only 20 people allowed in at a time for the 90-minute guided tours; tel: 05 61 05 88 37; www.sesta.fr*

Extensive galleries have been excavated in this network of caves halfway up a steep rocky hillside south of Tarascon-sur-Ariège. The remarkably well-preserved prehistoric paintings in them are the best of all those discovered so far in 23 caves in the area. Dating from palaeolithic times around 12,000 BC, they depict mainly animals – bison, ibex, deer and horses – all neatly outlined in black and red. The colours were created by using animal fat and charcoal made from burnt twigs. Visitors are restricted to 200 a day to prevent the sort of deterioration that has necessitated closing the caves at Lascaux in the Dordogne.

LAVELANET✦

i **Lavelanet Tourist Information** *place Henri du Nant; tel: 05 61 01 22 20; www.paydolmes.org. Open daily July–Aug; Mon–Sat Sept–June.*

This is a busy industrial town with several fabric factories, plenty of shops and a museum, The **Musée du Textil et du Peigne en Come✦ €€** (*65 rue Jaurès; tel: 05 61 03 01 34. Open afternoons July–Aug, except Sun*), devoted to local cloth-making, has looms from the 18th century to the 1980s and a reconstruction of a typical mountain mill. During the summer, the town holds festivals with fireworks.

MONTSEGUR✦✦✦

ⓘ Montségur Tourist Information Tel: 05 61 03 03 03; www.montsegur.org. Open daily July–Aug; Tue–Sat Sept–Nov and Apr–June.

ⓗ Château de Montségur €€ Open daily. Access from the car park above the village on the D9.

Village museum Tel: 05 61 01 10 27; www.montsegur.org/museum. Open Feb–Dec.

The small village of Montségur, with its craft studios and souvenir shops, nestles at the bottom of a 300m-high crag where a ruined castle, the **Château de Montségur✦✦✦**, the third to occupy the site, perches (1216m), silhouetted above a white cliff. The second castle once provided refuge for over 200 Cathars in 1244 during the Albigensian Crusade until they were martyred on a burning pyre after they descended. The Crusade was over but the Inquisition continued for 80 more years. Speculation has continued ever since about whether Cathar treasure is hidden on the site though excavations, on show in the village's small **archaeological museum✦**, have not revealed it – yet!

Accommodation and food in Montségur

Hôtel Costes € Tel: 05 61 01 10 24. Open Apr–mid-Nov. Small nine-room hotel with modern comforts in well-converted stone farm buildings in the centre of the village. Lots of atmosphere, sun terrace and good selection of books and souvenirs. Tasty home-cooked meals.

PUIVERT✦

ⓜ Musée du Quercorb €€ 16 rue Barry du Lion; tel: 04 68 20 80 98; www.quercorb.com/musee. Open daily Apr–Oct.

Château de Puivert €€ Tel: 04 68 20 81 52; www.chateau-de-puivert.com. Open daily.

Right
Puivert

All that remains of **Château de Puivert✦**, this sleepy village's medieval castle, once a Cathar stronghold, is its 32m-high keep, now a dominant landmark as you approach. The **Musée du Quercorb✦** in the village has a model showing how the castle would have looked in its heyday in the 14th century. The most interesting section of the museum (which covers local history) is devoted to medieval musical instruments displayed in a reconstruction of the castle's music room – a reminder of the time when troubadours were frequent visitors.

QUILLAN✦

Set in a bowl of wooded hills beside the River Aude, the town (once a famous shoe-making centre offers visitors a variety of activities from

i **Quillan Tourist**
Information *square*
André Tricoire, Quillan;
tel: 04 68 20 07 78;
www.ville-quillan.fr.
Open daily July–Aug;
Mon–Sat Sept–June.

◆ Folklore Festival
Throughout July and
Aug.

The Pyrenees

The mountain range that stretches for 430km from the Atlantic to the Mediterranean, separating France from Spain, is said to be named after Pyrène, a beautiful young girl who fell in love with Hercules, the Greek hero famed for his strength. She was the daughter of King Berbryx who lived in the huge Lombrives cave and ruled the mountain folk, the Bekrydes.

When Hercules was called away to continue his labours she found she was expecting his child. Too frightened to tell her father, she fled into the mountains but was mauled by a bear. Hearing her agonised cries echoing around the peaks, Hercules rushed to her aid, leaping over mountains and raging rivers. But he arrived too late to save her. As he buried her in the Lombrives cave, he said 'Gentle Pyrène, so that your name will always be remembered by those who people this land, these mountains where you now sleep for eternity will henceforth be named the Pyrenees'.

potholing to horse riding and is a good base for exploring both the foothills of the Pyrenees and the Corbières hills. Its ruined 12th-century castle, high above the river, is shaped in a perfect square.

Accommodation and food in Quillan

Opposite
Tarascon-sur-Ariège

Hôtel Cartier €€ *31 boulevard Charles de Gaulle; tel: 04 68 20 05 14. Closed mid-Dec–mid-Mar.* Comfortable 28-room hotel facing the station with renowned restaurant, les 3 Quilles.

TARASCON-SUR-ARIEGE❖❖

i **Tarascon-sur-
Ariège Tourist
Office** *espace François
Mitterrand; tel: 05 61
05 94 94;*
www.pays-du-montalm.com.
Open daily July–Aug;
Mon–Fri Sept–June.

The round 14th-century St-Michel clock tower watches over this small town from a hilltop near the remains of its medieval quarter. The large square, Place Garrigou, has several 16th-century buildings around it including L'Eglise de la Duarade. The area's many caves have made the town an important base for speleologists. At the **Parc de l'Art Préhistorique**❖❖❖ (just off the N20 1km north of the town), full-size replicas of paintings from the nearby Grotte de Niaux are on show.

Suggested tour

Total distance: 190km. The detour to Grotte de Niaux adds 10km.

Time: 4 hours' driving. Allow at least a day for the main route. Those with limited time should concentrate on Montségur and the Grotte de Niaux.

 **Parc de l'Art Préhistorique €€€**
route du col de Port; tel: 05 61 05 10 10. Open daily Apr–Oct.

 **P Francerie Pâtisserie** *3 avenue St-Roch (on the N20 just south of the town) is very handy for picnic items, cakes and ice cream.*

Links to other tours: At Ax-les-Thermes, the route meets the 'Up into the Pyrenees' route (*see pages 91–93*). From Foix the N20 leads north to Pamiers (*see page 168*), 20km away. From Quillan the D118 leads northeast to Couiza (*see page 102*), 12km away.

From **FOIX** ❶ (87km south of Toulouse on the N20), follow the scenic N20 south beside the River Ariège to **TARASCON-SUR-ARIEGE** ❷. Just north of the town, the Parc de l'Art Préhistorique is signposted 1km off the N20.

Detour: GROTTE DE NIAUX ❸ is 5km south of Tarascon-sur-Ariège. To visit it, turn right onto the D8 off the N20.

☾ **Hôte Bayle** € 38
avenue d'Ax-les-
Thermes, Belcaire; tel: 04 68
20 31 05. Closed first half
of November. Twelve-room
hotel with garden and
exhilarating mountain
views. Restaurant.

Caves

The reason why the area has so many caves is that the limestone ground readily absorbs rainwater. This causes a chemical reaction which can slowly dissolve some of the limestone, creating shafts or tunnels inside it. When these widen out they can become underground rivers and caves, often linked in a complex network. Rushing water and roof falls help enlarge the spaces, sometimes creating enormous cathedral-like caverns.

Leaving Tarascon-sur-Ariège, stay beside the Ariège on the N20 which passes **GROTTE DE LOMBRIVES ❹**. Go through **Les Cabanannes** and **Unac** to **AX-LES-THERMES ❺** (see page 84) and then take the long climb out of it on the D613 up to the Col de Chioula (1431m), a popular base for cross-country skiing in winter. After passing wooded hillsides and terraces and crossing plains, you come to **Belcaire** and the wide flat Plateau de Sault. Four kilometres beyond Belcaire, turn right onto the D29 to **Espezel** and drop sharply down to the D107. This goes along a valley to **Belfort**, the Défilé de Joucou gorge and Marsa (whose church has a distinctive flat bell tower), before dropping gently to **Axat**, a pretty village beside the River Aude, with a medieval quarter clustering around the church, where the D117 leads beside the River Aude through **St-Martin-Lys** to **QUILLAN ❻**. The 8km stretch between St-Martin-Lys and Quillan is named the Défilé du Pierre-Lys. In 1814 Félix Armand, the priest of St-Martin-Lys, got his parishioners to build it by hacking through solid rock; he is commemorated by a small monument in front of Quillan's railway station. From Quillan take the D117 which climbs west onto a plateau of farmland towards **PUIVERT ❼**, whose castle is silhouetted on the skyline as you approach, and then **Belesta**. Turn left there on to the D5 and head for **MONTSEGUR ❽**, past the roadside cave where water often gushes from the Fontaine des Fontestorbes spring.

From Montségur take the D107, through the cloth-making town of **Montferrier** with its distinctive bell tower, to **LAVELANET ❾**. From there the quiet D10 (signed Raissac) is a much more pleasant way to return to Foix than the faster D117 as it crosses hillsides and farmland.

Getting out of the car

From the car park beside the D9 above Montségur village, a short track leads to the foot of the steep path which leads up through trees and bushes to the ruins of its bleak fortress. Part steps, part rocks, it takes

Grotte du Mas d'Azil €€ *Tel: 05 61 69 97 71. Open for guided tours (1 hour) of caves and museum daily July–Aug; Tue–Sun Sept and Apr–June; Sun Mar and Oct–Nov; closed Dec–Feb.*

about 20 minutes to climb. Sensible shoes are essential. Seeing the small area at the top, it's hard to believe that over 1000 Cathars once lived there under siege. The last 205 were surrounded by an army of 10,000 Catholics. When they eventually descended on 16 March 1244, refusing to recant, they were burned alive. A memorial stone at the bottom in the 'Prat dels crematz' (field of the burned) commemorates them – 'Martyred in the name of pure Christian love'. How ironic that the name Montségur means 'safe mountain'.

Also worth exploring

To visit the **Grotte du Mas d'Azil**, take the D117 from Foix, turning right just beyond La Bastide de Sérou on to the D49 (34km). This cave is of great importance to archaeologists because in 1887, Edouard Piette found evidence of human habitation there between 30,000 and 9500 BC. The cave, 420m long and about 50m wide, has winding galleries beside a river. Painted stones were found there but no-one has come up with an explanation for what they depict.

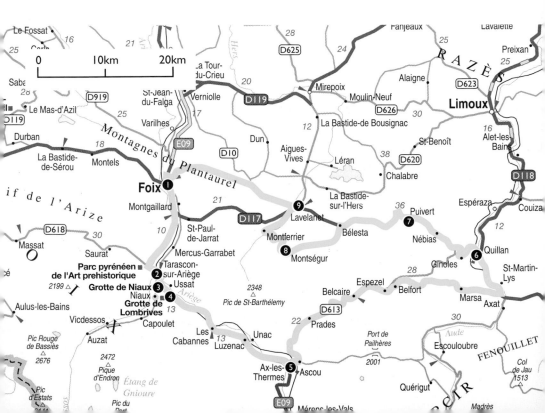

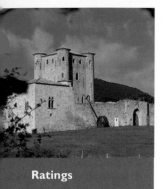

A taste of Cathar country

Ratings

Castles	●●●●●
Scenery	●●●●●
History	●●●●○
Children	●●●○○
Nature	●●●○○
Villages	●●●○○
Architecture	●●○○○
Walking	●●○○○

History was made in the Corbières hills during the Middle Ages. If you let your imagination roam, this route will take you back to the noble, ferocious and mysterious events which took place there in the days of the Cathars, the troubadours and the Knights Templar.

Although the Corbières themselves are hills rather than mountains, the scenery is often dramatic with rocky limestone ridges and crags peeping above the *garrigue* and small vineyards. The roads can twist and turn but are never difficult.

Two famous castles, Peyrepertuse and Quéribus, which both played a crucial part in the Cathar movement, stand on rocky pinnacles that look startlingly inaccessible even today. It would be a pity not to allow time to walk up to at least one of them. The reward is not only superb views but a better understanding of former lifetimes and struggles.

ARQUES✦✦✦

Château d'Arques
€€ *Tel: 04 68 69 84 77; www.perso.wanadoo.fr/ chateau.arques.* Combined admission with Maison Déodat Roché; *tel: 04 68 69 82 87. Open daily Apr–Oct.*

Only the sturdy four-storey orange sandstone keep survives from **Château d'Arques✦**. Built in 1284, it was severely damaged during the Wars of Religion. It overlooks the flat countryside around the village which was the birthplace of Déodat Roché, a leading historian on the Cathars. After he died in 1978, his home, **La Maison Déodat Roché✦✦** €€ (*tel: 04 68 69 82 87; open daily*), became a small museum devoted to Catharism.

COUIZA✦

Tourist Information
route des Pyrénées; tel: 04 68 74 02 51; e-mail: pays.couiza@wanadoo.fr. Open Mon–Fri.

On the River Aude, Couiza's fortunes grew from the hat-making industry but declined when uncovered heads became fashionable. It boasts a totally restored 16th-century castle, the Château des Ducs de Joyeuse, whose four round towers, typical of the Languedoc, are a

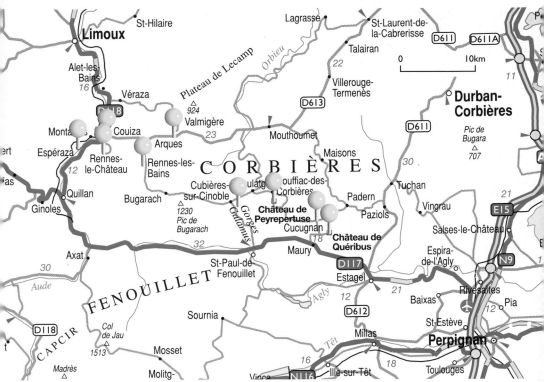

landmark on the edge of the town. Used as a military hospital and then as a prison, it is now a hotel.

Accommodation in Couiza

Château des Ducs de Joyeuse €€ *Tel: 04 68 74 23 50; www.chateau-des-ducs.com*. A 35-room hotel in the 16th-century castle, completely restored in 1996. Top-class restaurant, swimming pool and four-poster beds in ten of the rooms. For a real treat, book the Gothic suite.

CUCUGNAN✧✧

Théâtre Achille Mir
€€
Tel: 04 68 45 03 69.
Open daily Feb–Dec.
Combined ticket with the
Château de Queribus
(see page 105).

This smart little village was surrounded by olive groves until 1956 when they were destroyed by frost. Few people have heard of Cucugnan unless they are fans of the French writer, Alphonse Daudet. An audio-visual version of *Le Sermon du Curé de Cucugnan*, his short story based on verses by Achille Mir, a local teacher who died in 1901, is presented in the **Théâtre Achille Mir✧**, the village's 49-seat theatre.

Accommodation in Cucugnan

Auberge du Vigneron €€ *Tel: 04 68 45 03 00.* Small six-room hotel with terrace looking down on vineyards and up to Château de Quéribus. Closed mid-Nov–Feb.

ESPERAZA*

ⓘ Espéraza See Tourist information in Couiza; *tel: 04 68 74 02 51 (see page 102).*

🏛 Musée de la Chapellerie €€ *avenue Gare; tel: 04 68 74 00 75. Open daily Feb–Dec.*

Musée des Dinosaures €€ *avenue Gare; tel: 04 68 74 26 88. Open daily Feb–Dec.*

The **Musée de la Chapellerie**** occupies an old warehouse in this small town. Laid out like a factory, it shows the different stages in the making of hats. Over 150 wigs, ancient and modern, are also on display, and hats are for sale. Next to it, **Musée des Dinosaures*** displays the enormous skeleton of a dinosaur which was found locally, together with fossils and a life-size tableau of an archaeological dig. **Campagne-sur-Aude**** € (*open July–Aug daily*), 2km south of Espéraza, has an archaeological trail where some of Europe's most important dinosaur remains have been excavated.

GORGES DE GALAMUS***

🏛 Ermitage St-Antoine-de-Galamus is a 15-minute walk from the car park on the D7; *www.nature.fr.fm*

The drive along this rugged 3km-long gorge high above the River Agly is one of the most dramatic in the region. The road, built in 1892, twists tightly along a shelf carved out of the white rock which frequently overhangs it as the gorge becomes narrower and narrower. At the southern end, from a car park/viewing platform you look down on the small **Ermitage St-Antoine-de-Galamus****, now a café, clinging to the hillside halfway down the gorge. Its tiny chapel is behind it in a cave.

CHATEAU DE PEYREPERTUSE***

Seen at its best from the village of Rouffiac-des-Corbières, this medieval fortress is the least ruined of the area's castles. Built on top of a rocky crest, a site first used by the Romans, it is one of the marvels of the Corbières. As you discover when you climb up, the ruins of two castles are spread along a 300m-long ridge. The upper one (796m) has never been accessible except on foot, as the steps cut in the rock to it are too steep even for mules. As you wander round the remains of the courtyards, towers and arches, the most amazing thing to reflect on – apart from the view – is the feat of building them with the simple tools of the 12th century.

Château de Peyrepertuse €€
Duilhac-sous-Peyrepertuse; tel: 06 71 58 63 36; www. chateau-peyrepertuse.com. Open daily Feb–Dec. Access to the winding 3.5km road up to the car park is from Duilhac, just below it at the foot of the ridge; then allow at least 15 minutes to walk up – and wear walking shoes. On a windy day the experience can be particularly exhilarating!

Accommodation near Château de Peyrepertuse

Auberge de Peyrepertuse € *Rouffiac-des-Corbières; tel: 04 68 45 40 40. Closed mid-Dec–mid-Jan and Wed.* Six-room guesthouse in the small village that has the best view up to the Château de Peyrepertuse.

Auberge du Vieux Moulin € *9 rue de la Fontaine, Duilhac-sous-Peyrepertuse; tel: 04 68 45 02 17. Closed Dec–Feb.* Old mill converted into a 14-room inn.

CHATEAU DE QUERIBUS✧✧✧

Château de Québirus € *Cucugan; tel: 04 68 45 03 69. Open daily Feb–Dec. Combined ticket with Théâtre Achille Mir (see page 103).* Access from the D123 south of Cucugnan, signposted left up a steep narrow road to the car park and ticket office.

The ruined Château de Quéribus is one of the Languedoc's most dramatic sights, perched perilously on the Grau de Maury, a narrow rocky crag 728m high above the village of Cucugnan. From a distance,

Right
Château de Peyrepertuse

Opposite
Château de Quéribus

it's hard to believe there is any way up, but a steep rocky path leads to this 'eagle's nest' from the car park. The walk up, always exhilarating, is distinctly perilous in wind so it's definitely not suitable for anyone without a good head for heights.

The ruin itself is a maze of passages, staircases and doorways with a high vaulted wall supported by a sturdy pillar in the centre. First recorded in 1020, it was a Cathar stronghold in the 13th century and was the last refuge, sheltering the Bishop of Razès until 1254. Subsequently it was a royal fortress guarding the Spanish border until Roussillon became part of France in 1659. Arrow slits provide hair-raising views down, though you get a 360-degree panorama from the terrace – across the Roussillon plain to the Mediterranean in the east and south to the Canigou mountain with the Pyrenees beyond.

RENNES-LES-BAINS*

ⓘ Rennes-les-Bains Tourist Information *Grande Rue des Thermes; tel: 04 68 69 88 04. Open daily July–Aug; Mon–Fri Sept–June.*

You can do your body a favour by bathing in mineral and thermal water in this village nestling beside the crystal-clear River Sals. Its spa, **Thermes de Rennes-les-Bains***, offers various medicinal programmes and also has a large outdoor pool overlooking a pretty riverside walk.

Accommodation in Rennes-les-Bains

ⓗ Thermes de Rennes-les-Bains *Grand rue des Thermes; tel: 04 68 74 71 00; www.thermes.org/rennes*

Hostellerie de Rennes-les-Bains €€ *rue de Montferrand; tel: 04 68 69 88 49. Closed mid-Jan–Mar.* Riverside hotel with seven rooms, pool and sun terrace.

RENNES-LE-CHATEAU***

ⓗ Espace de l'Abbé Saunière €€ *Villa Bethania; tel: 04 68 74 72 68. Open daily.*

ⓑ The village bookshop (*tel: 04 68 74 26 71*) has a good selection of books about L'Abbé Saunière, Catharism and the local area.

From its hilltop position above the Aude valley, this intriguing little village has a good view of the red rooftops of Espéraza and Campagne-sur-Aude nestling in the valley below. How could the parish priest, Béranger Saunière (1852–1917), afford to build himself the grand Villa Bethania and the curious neo-Gothic Tour Magdala on the cliff edge as his library? And where did the money come from in 1891 to restore and lavishly decorate the almost derelict village church, Ste-Marie-Madeleine?

A visit to the **Espace de l'Abbé Saunière**, the priest's former home and now a museum, sheds a little light on the mystery of his unexplained wealth. Maybe he discovered the treasure of the Knights Templar who, in the 12th century, had one of their headquarters nearby. He had been arrested for digging up graves at night, and he refused to allow the use of his water tower when the villagers were fighting a fire – so was it really full of water?

Blanquette de Limoux

Vines have been cultivated in the Limoux region since ancient times but in 1531 the Benedictine monks at St-Hilaire abbey made a historic discovery. They found that wine produced in glass flasks with a cork top – rare at the time – acquired a natural fizz. This was the origination of Blanquette de Limoux, the world's first sparkling wine, now enjoyed all over the world. The production process begins with crushing grapes in whole bunches as soon as they are picked and then involves a careful timetable of fermentation and ageing lasting almost a year or, for special vintages, up to three years. Most is produced by the *méthode champenoise* where the bubbles are added chemically, but about 3 per cent is the sweeter organic *méthode ancestrale* version which has no additions and is always bottled on the third day after a full moon.

Above
Arques

Suggested tour

Total distance: 185km. The detour through the Gorges de Galamus adds 8km, the detour to Espéraza and Campagne-sur-Aude adds 12km and the detour to Rennes-le-Château adds 10km.

Time: 5 hours' driving. Allow at least a day for the main route or two to include walking up to the Château de Peyrepertuse and Château de Quéribus. Those with limited time should concentrate on the stretch between the Château de Quéribus and Rennes-le-Château.

Links to other tours: From Maury, the D117 leads west to St-Paul-de-Fenouillet (*see page 76*), 8km away. From Cubières-sur-Cinoble, the D10 leads south to St-Paul-de-Fenouillet (*see page 76*), 10km away. From Couiza the D118 leads southwest to Quillan (*see page 97*), 12km away, or north to Limoux (*see page 138*), 15km away. From Mouthoumet, the D613 leads northeast to Villerouge-Termenès (*see page 141*), 7km away. From Padern, the D14 leads east to Tuchan (*see page 125*), 8km away.

From Perpignan take the D117 past the airport beside the River Agly to **Estagel** and then **Maury**. Turn right here into the Corbières hills on the steeply climbing D19 which takes you over the Grau de Maury, a 432m-high pass, remarkable both for its views and vegetation. The Maury valley below, made up of fossils having originally been covered by the sea, is famed for its scented bushes such as thyme as well as boasting several varieties of wild orchids. Just beyond the pass, the **CHATEAU DE QUERIBUS** ❶ is on the right; then 2km beyond it, turn left at **CUCUGNAN** ❷ on to the D14. This takes you over the Col du Tribi (344m), through **Duilhac-sous-Peyrepertuse** (below the **CHATEAU DE PEYREPERTUSE**) ❸, and over the Col de Grès (406m) to the quaint little village of **Rouffiac-des-Corbières** from where the Château de Peyrepertuse looks like a piece of the rocky ridge. Continue through **Soulatgé** to **Cubières-sur-Cinoble**.

Detour: At Cubières-sur-Cinoble, turn left off the D14 to drive through the narrow **GORGES DE GALAMUS** ❹; the distance to the viewpoint at the end is 4km.

After Cubières-sur-Cinoble the D14 goes through tiny **Bugarach**, a thriving hat-making centre in the 19th century, which is overlooked by a rugged massif. It then continues through wooded valleys to join, 3km beyond **RENNES-LES-BAINS** ❺, the D613. Turn left onto it to **COUIZA** ❻.

Detour: From Couiza the detour (4km) to **ESPERAZA** ❼ crosses over the River Aude to **Montazels** and then south along the D12. The Campagne-sur-Aude trail is 2km further beyond Espéraza. While in

Montazels, watch for the signs to Domaine St-Jacques, 1km north of the town, as it is one of the few vineyards which produce sparkling white wine, Blanquette de Limoux, by the *méthode ancestrale*. This means the bubbles form naturally rather than by chemical injection.

Detour: Also from Couiza, the detour to **RENNES-LE-CHATEAU** ❽ (5km) climbs southeast up an unnumbered road off the D118 in the town.

Next drive north on the busy D118 beside the River Aude, turning right after 5km onto the D70 to go east through **Véraza** and across peaceful wooded countryside. Turn right again onto the D54. From the viewpoint just past **Valmigère**, you can see south on a clear day over the Corbières to the snowy top of the Canigou mountain with the Pyrenees beyond. As the road twists prettily down into **ARQUES** ❾ , the castle (to the right of the village) is a notable landmark overlooking the dark green Rialsesse forest and cliffs with red gulleys behind it. The D613 then leads east through **Mouthoumet**. Two kilometres beyond it, turn right on to the D139 to join the D410 and go over the bleak Col du Prat (444m) to **Maisons**. The D123 follows the gentle gorge of the River Torgan past small vineyards to **Padern** which is overlooked by its 17th-century ruined castle – and boasts a handy *cave coopérative* where you can sample and buy local wine. Return to Perpignan through Cucugnan and Maury.

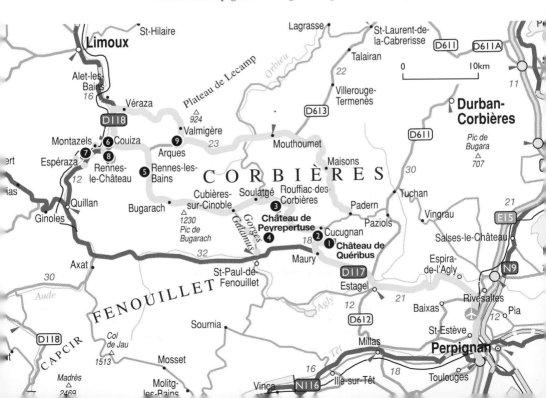

Narbonne

Ratings

History	●●●●●
Food and drink	●●●●○
Museums	●●●●○
Architecture	●●●○○
Entertainment	●●●○○
Shopping	●●●○○
Art	●●○○○
Children	●●○○○

This small but vibrant city is bound to fire a sense of history in every visitor. In the centre you can even walk on the flat grey stones of a Roman road, the Via Domitia. Founded by the Romans as Narbo Martius in 118 BC, the city became capital of Gaul, their largest province. Its next great era came in the 12th century when it was a thriving port. The cathedral, founded then by its rich and powerful archbishops, was intended to be the biggest in Christendom. Though never completed, it remains a remarkable symbol of that time. The wars and plagues which followed brought the city to its knees for two centuries until the construction of the Canal de la Robine and later the railway helped revive its fortunes. Today, surrounded by vineyards and only a few kilometres from the Mediterranean, it is certainly a place to savour.

Getting there and getting around

From the south, leave the A9 autoroute at Narbonne Sud, where the roundabout has an eye-catching centrepiece – a giant amphora (Roman vase). From the north, the N113 and N9 join straightforward routes along main roads into the city centre.

Public transport: The town centre is compact and all the sights are within a short walking distance. There are regular bus services to the beach at Narbonne Plage in July and August. The railway station is in Route de Montpellier, a 10-minute walk from the centre.

The Motorail terminal is on the north side of the tracks, linked by a minibus service to the main station. Overnight Motorail services run to and from Calais in summer.

ⓘ **Tourist Information** *place Salengro; tel: 04 68 65 15 60; www.mairie-narbonne.fr. Open all year.* Information also available at the **Town Hall** *place de l'Hôtel de Ville.*

Narbonne-Plage Office du Tourisme *avenue du Théâtre, tel: 04 68 49 84 86.*

Museum information *Tel: 04 68 90 30 65.*

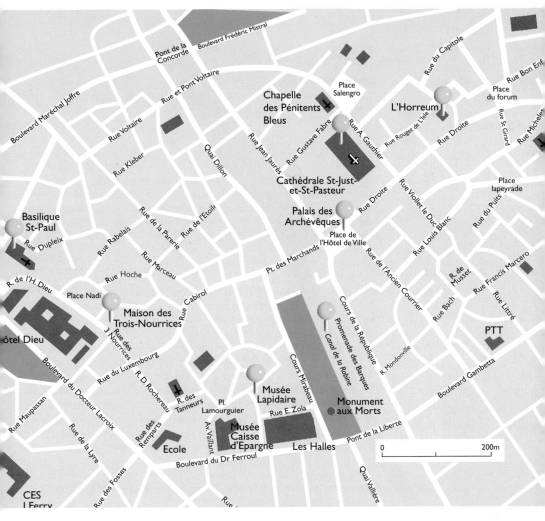

For boat trips on the canal, cruisers can be hired through Connoisseur Cruisers, *7 quai d'Alsace; tel: 04 68 65 14 55; www.connoisseur.fr*

Cycle hire at Cycles Cancel, *50 boulevard Frédéric Mistral; tel: 04 68 65 12 26; www.bouticycle.com*

Parking: Car parks are well signposted and there are pay-and-display meters on the central streets; free on Sundays. South of the centre, parking is free on both sides of the Canal de la Robine, which is particularly convenient when driving in from Narbonne Plage, 10km away, and other beaches. In summer, traffic can be heavy along this route.

Sights

Basilique St-Paul
rue Dupleix.

Cathédrale St-Just-et-St-Pasteur *rue A Gauthier.*

Basilique St-Paul⁺⁺

This lofty Romanesque building is notable for its soaring arches and elegant vaulting, on the Bourg side of the canal. Don't miss the small stone frog which sits on the font.

Canal de la Robine⁺

The canal cuts through the centre of the city, dividing the old Bourg district, where the lower classes lived, from the Cité, which was the home of the ecclesiastical authorities and the ruling *vicomtes* on the other. It was built in the 1680s along the bed of the River Aude (which had changed course 200 years earlier following massive floods) and joins the Canal du Midi, 15km and ten locks to the north.

Cathédrale St-Just-et-St-Pasteur⁺⁺⁺

This massive building in the heart of the city was destined to be one of the biggest churches in Christendom, designed to chase away once and for all any thoughts of heresy which the local population might have been harbouring. However, only the chancel was completed before work stopped in 1340, 60 years after the first stone had been laid, because the municipal authorities refused to allow their clerical opposite numbers to pull down part of the city wall to make way for the nave. While the tussle was still dragging on, their resolve to keep the wall intact was strengthened when England's Black Prince stormed the city in 1355, overrunning the working-class Bourg district across the River Aude. (At that time the river divided the city in two, though later after it changed course this section was turned into the canal.) By the time the walls were no longer needed for defence, the city could no longer afford to extend the cathedral.

The cathedral has superb stained-glass windows and Aubusson and Gobelins tapestries on its walls. The elaborately carved choir stalls date

Via Domitia

In 118 BC the Romans built a highway stretching over 250km from Beaucaire (75km east of Montpellier) to le Perthus in the Pyrenees. They named it after Domitius Ahenobarbus, the proconsul of their Gallia Narbonensis province which was governed from Narbonne and extended from Toulouse to Lake Geneva. Though originally intended to help their legions march between Rome and Spain, it quickly became an important commercial artery, facilitating trade within the Roman Empire and further afield by sea. Earlier Hannibal had used the same route on his way from Spain to Italy with his elephants in 218 BC. In Narbonne, the road joined up with another Roman highway, the Via Aquitania, which led northwest through Toulouse to Bordeaux. Some of the standing stones which once marked each mile are on show in local museums.

L'Horreum €€ 7
rue Rouget-de-l'Isle; tel:
04 68 90 30 54. Open daily
Apr–Sept; Tue–Thur
Oct–Mar.

Musée Lapidaire €€
Eglise de Lamourgier, place
Lamourgier; tel: 04 68 90
30 66. Open daily Apr–Sept;
Tue–Sun Oct–Mar.

Palais des Archévèques
€€ place de l'Hôtel de Ville;
tel: 04 68 90 30 30. Open
daily Apr–Sept; Tue–Sun
Oct–Mar. Entrance to the
Gilles Aycelin keep is
through the town hall.

The entrance ticket for
any of the above is valid
for three days and includes
entrance to the other
museums.

from the 16th century and the fine organ, also richly carved, from the 18th. The altar, designed by Jules Mansart, is made of local pink marble from Caune. What should have been the transept is now a courtyard with delicately vaulted 14th-century cloisters leading into the Archbishop's Palace.

L'Horreum***

This extraordinarily well-preserved underground Roman storehouse has a warren of vaulted stone cellars with grain chutes where perishable goods would have been kept. As Narbonne was an important port and also on the Via Domitia, it traded extensively with other parts of the Roman Empire, exporting meat and cheese from the Cévennes as well as oil, woad, wood and hemp. Stone containers and fragments of engraved stonework from Roman buildings are dotted along the galleries and in the small cubicles which open off them. An exhibition in the entrance area includes Roman objects and drawings showing what other buildings in Narbo Martius must have been like.

Maison des Trois-Nourrices*

The 'House of the Three Wet Nurses' in rue des Trois Nourrices gets its unusual name from the stone pillars shaped like curvaceous maidens which support the lintel of its magnificent Renaissance façade. Actually, there are five of them, not three! The interior is not open to the public.

Musée Lapidaire**

This unusual museum in a deconsecrated church displays an extensive collection of stone fragments from sculptures and bas-reliefs dating back to Gallo-Roman times and the Middle Ages. The church, which in typical Southern Gothic style has a single nave, is all that remains of a Benedictine convent.

Palais des Archévèques***

The opulent Archbishops' Palace, built between the 12th and 14th centuries, is a grand and complicated complex of halls, passages, towers and courtyards. This is now attached to the neo-Gothic town hall which was added under the auspices of Eugène Viollet-le-Duc, the famous military architect, in 1846. Within the complex, the **Palais Neuf** houses the **Musée d'Archéologie et de Préhistoire**** which has a fascinating collection of Roman objects and fragments of buildings. The Chapelle de la Madeleine houses amphorae (vases) and mosaics. **Musée d'Art et d'Histoire**** in the former archbishops' apartments has paintings by Canaletto and Brueghel. Steps lead to the top of the formidable Gilles Aycelin keep, which the archbishops had built to remind the town's *vicomtes* who had a residence opposite that they held the reins of power in the city. It also kept watch over the river port which then existed directly below.

Shopping

Les Halles, the turn-of-the-century market hall, at cours Mirabeau, merits a visit whether or not you want to buy anything. Recently restored, it's an iron-framed glass building with elaborate stuccoed columns and a grand stone doorway crowned by a huge clock. Inside, the 80 stalls selling local produce and wine will certainly tempt you to stock up.

The most interesting small shops are to be found off place de l'Hôtel de Ville in rue Droite and rue de l'Ancien Courrier. **Monoprix**, on the place itself, is the only large store in the centre. A **Géant Casino** supermarket can be found on route de Perpignan and Carrefour on the way to Narbonne-Plages.

Entertainment

Théâtre Narbonne
Scene Nationale de Narbonne 2 avenue Domitius; tel: 04 68 90 90 00; www. letheatre-narbonne.com

Narbonne is justifiably proud of its **Théâtre** complex inaugurated in 1994, where concerts, conferences and exhibitions are staged as well as plays. **L'Espace de Liberté** (*route de Perpignan; tel: 04 68 42 17 89*) includes an Olympic-size pool, skating rink, bowling alley and a range of outdoor sports facilities. International sporting events take place at **Parc des Sports** (*tel: 04 68 90 90 68*).

Narbonne Médiévale in mid-Aug includes re-enactments of medieval times with shows, costumed parades, music and street performances. A **Wine Festival** is staged mid-Oct. Events information, *tel: 04 68 90 30 68*.

Accommodation and food

La Dorade €€ *44 rue Jean-Jaurès; tel: 04 68 32 65 95*. Narbonne's oldest hotel, founded in 1648, has seen better days and this is reflected in its modest price. However, it is very central, overlooking the canal near place de l'Hôtel de Ville, has a garage and exudes a traditionally French atmosphere.

Hotel d'Occitanie €€ *23 avenue de la Mer; tel: 04 68 65 47 60*, is a modern hotel on the outskirts in the direction of the sea. Its excellent leisure facilities include a pool, fitness centre and tennis.

Le Régent € *13–15 rue Suffren, tel: 04 68 32 02 41*, is a small family-run hotel in a quiet area, about a 10-minute walk from the centre. Free on-street parking. Fifteen rooms.

La Résidence €€ *6 rue du 1er Mai; tel: 04 68 32 19 41*, became a hotel in the 1960s when the Aiguille family converted their splendid 19th-century mansion. It's situated in a quiet central street with garage parking. Twenty-six rooms.

L'Alsace €€€ *2 avenue Pierre Semard; tel: 04 68 65 10 24*, opposite the railway station, is one of the best restaurants in town for seafood.

Brasserie Co €€ *1 boulevard Docteur Ferroul: tel: 04 68 32 55 25*. Trendy brasserie where the food matches the contemporary decor. Noted for its weekend brunches.

Le Coq Hardi €€ *75 rue Droite; tel: 04 68 65 27 38. Closed Wed and Sun.* Fresh fish and grills are always on the menu, but it is best known for its crème brûlée.

Le Gaulois €€ *4 rue B Crémieux; tel: 04 68 65 86 61. Closed Sun.* Duck dishes are a speciality at this small restaurant in old vaulted cellars.

Le Petit Comptoir €€ *4 boulevard M Joffre; tel: 04 68 42 30 35.* An attractive little restaurant serving local specialities, particularly fish and duck.

Suggested walk

Length: 2.5km.

Duration: Under an hour just to walk round, but allow a full day to see all the sights.

Start in the steps of the Romans by treading the flat grey slabs of the **Via Domitia** in the centre of **place de l'Hôtel de Ville**. There was a huge outcry from the shopkeepers around the square when plans to re-tile and pedestrianise it were announced, but the discovery of the Roman road during the works changed all that. Now the square's well-presented centrepiece, it attracts more people to the area.

To get your bearings, particularly as the layout of the **Palais des Archévêques** (Archbishops' Palace) ❶ and the adjacent CATHEDRALE ❷ is complicated, climb the 162 steps to the upper terrace of the keep whose entrance is through the **town hall**. The views from the 43m-high tower stretch past pinnacles and flying buttresses over the city rooftops and far beyond. Another high spot is the cathedral's north tower.

Fontfroide Abbey
€€ *Fontfroide; tel: 04 68 45 11 08; www.fontfroide.com.* Take the N113 and D613 from Narbonne. *Open daily for guided tours.*

The narrow rue Droite follows the straight route of the original Via Domitia past **L'HORREUM** ❸ whose entrance is now in the parallel rue Rouget de l'Isle. A little further up it, the pillars of a **Roman temple** stand in place Bistan as a reminder that it is the site where the Roman forum is thought to have been. On the way to place Lapeyrade, the 15th-century **Eglise St-Sébastian** is said to stand on the spot where the saint was born.

Narrow streets lead across rue Viollet le Duc and rue de l'Ancien Courrier to the busy **cours de la République** which runs alongside a broad promenade shaded by plane trees beside the **CANAL DE LA ROBINE** ❹. Cruisers tie up along the quay below it.

Crossing the water by the wrought-iron footbridge you will see the remains of the arched **Roman bridge** which once spanned the **River Aude** here. In summer the **waterside gardens** with their fountains beside Cours Mirabeau make a pleasant spot to sit and watch the comings and goings on the canal, but you might want to bear in mind that the nearby **market hall** closes at 1300. Behind it is the **MUSEE LAPIDAIRE** ❺ in the **Eglise Notre-Dame-de-la-Mourguié**.

Many of the old buildings in this area, particularly along rue Belfort, have attractive façades, particularly **LA MAISON DES TROIS-NOURRICES** ❻ in the road of the same name. Just beyond it in rue Arago is the **BASILIQUE ST-PAUL** ❼.

The most interesting way to return to **place de l'Hôtel de Ville** is along rue Hoche and across the intimate old **place des 4 Fontaines** which has a pretty fountain. The **Pont des Marchands** footbridge, a continuation of the Via Domitia, seems more like an arcade as there are shops on both sides. As an alternative you can stroll along quai Dillon and take the footbridge next to a lock across to an old mill building now occupied by a library.

Also worth exploring

Narbonne is divided from the sea and the busy resort of Narbonne-Plage by **Montagne de la Clape**, a rugged area of hills and ridges with rocky grey cliffs. Beneath them, narrow roads twist through pine woods and *garrigue* – moors of sweet-smelling thyme, rosemary and lavender. A poignant cemetery, **Cimetière des Marins**, occupies one of the two highest hilltops; its memorial stones are dedicated to sailors lost at sea. Small vineyards cover the lower slopes of the hills, producing good quality la Clape Coteaux du Languedoc wines. There are few buildings around as it is a conservation area. The best way to explore is on foot or by bike.

A 14km drive southwest from the city takes you into the Corbières hills where a huge 12th-century Cistercian abbey, **Abbaye de**

Fontfroide***, built in the local ochre and pink sandstone, nestles peacefully amongst cypress trees and terraced gardens in a small secluded valley. At its peak in the 15th century over 200 monks lived there but it gradually declined until being abandoned altogether in 1791. The buildings, privately owned since 1908, have now been restored at vast expense. They include a perfectly-proportioned Cistercian church with modern stained-glass windows, a pretty cloister, chapterhouse and monks' dormitory. A rose garden planted with over 3000 bushes in 1990 has won awards for its design.

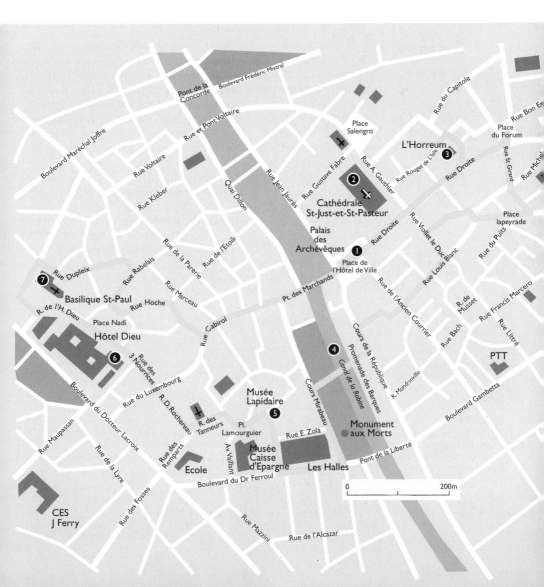

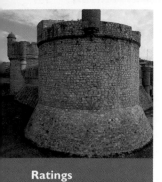

The coast and lagoons

Ratings

Beaches	●●●●●
Children	●●●●○
Outdoor activities	●●●●○
Wildlife	●●●●○
Castles	●●●○○
Coastal villages/ towns	●●●○○
Vineyards	●●●○○
Historical sights	●●●○○

W hen this route moves away from the sea along the Golfe du Lion and heads into the Corbières hills, the atmosphere changes markedly – a happy combination. Within a few easy kilometres, the remote and often desolate countryside inland offers an interesting alternative to sun-worshipping resorts such as Leucate and Bacarès. Summer brings thousands of holidaymakers to them in search of a tan or to sail either on the shallow sea-water lagoons or the Mediterranean itself.

The highlights inland include the mighty castle at Salses, which once guarded the border between France and the Kingdom of Aragon, and the cave at Tautavel, where the earliest remains of human existence in Europe have been found.

This is also the land of the famous Rivesaltes and Fitou vineyards, while children – and adults – will find plenty to interest them at the African safari park at Sigean.

Etang de Bages et de Sigean❖❖

ⓘ Peyriac Tourist Information
promenade de la Saline; tel: 04 68 41 38 22. Open daily July–Aug.

** Musée Archaéologique €**
rue de l'Etang, Peyriac-de-Me. Open daily July–Aug by appointment through the tourist office.

In Roman times, when Narbonne was a busy port, the shores of this lagoon were well populated. Ancient finds from that time are on show in the **Musée Archaéologique❖** in the village of Peyriac-de-Mer. Subsequently the area around the lagoon lay deserted for centuries because of the mosquitoes which infested it until coastal development started in the 1960s. Today the mosquitoes have gone from the lagoon but there are plenty of midges about in summer.

Fitou❖❖

This delightful wine-making village, overlooked by the ruins of a hilltop

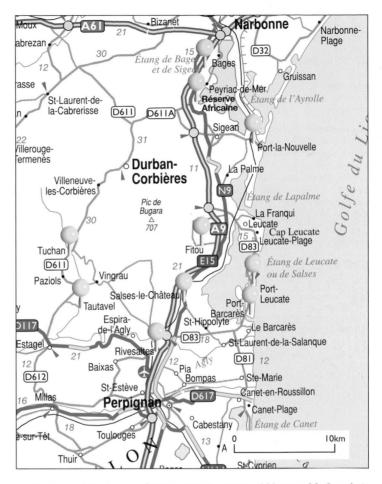

ℹ Fitou Tourist Information 6 rue de la Mairie; tel: 04 68 45 71 65; www.fitou.fr. Open Mon–Fri.

castle, has a distinct air of prosperity. Its quaint 800-year-old church is named – unusually – after a married couple, St-Julien and Ste-Basilisse.

PORT-BARCARES ✧✧

ℹ Port-Barcarès Tourist Information place de la République; tel: 04 68 86 16 56; www.portbarcares.com. Open daily all year.

Le Lydia✧, a large white liner, was deliberately grounded in 1967 to become the centrepiece of the beach of this purpose-built resort and its near neighbour, Port-Leucate. All along the coast, pastel apartment and villa complexes with neat gardens and hotels have risen up on the flat sandbar between sea and lagoon, aiming to cater for every need of the 21st-century holidaymaker. A thalassotherapy centre offers to

Le Lydia *Open July–Sept daily; then weekends only; tel: 04 68 86 07 13.* The 'Paquebot des Sables' has a wide selection of entertainments, including a casino, bars and restaurants.

Atlantide Marina *avenue du Roussillon; tel: 04 68 86 32 65; open July–mid-Sept.* Has a swimming pool, discos and laser show. There are also children's beach clubs July–Aug.

soothe away aches and stress, while watersports provide activity for those who want to do more than just lie in the sun. Bars and discos ensure that no-one needs to retire to bed early. Sardines have been fished locally for centuries and throughout the summer you can feast on them at stalls and restaurants, barbecued over vine twigs.

Accommodation in Port-Barcarès

Hôtel de la Mer € *43 avenue Annibal; tel: 04 68 86 08 07.* Cheerful summer holiday hotel with 17 rooms, 100m from beach.

PORT-LEUCATE❖❖

Port-Leucate Tourist Information *espace Culturel; tel: 04 68 40 91 31; www.leucate.net. Open daily Apr–Nov; Mon–Sat Dec–Mar.*

Like its neighbour, Port-Bacarès, this lively resort was purpose-built in the 1960s to cater for sun-loving holidaymakers. Together the two resorts now have the biggest marina complex on the French Mediterranean, fed by channels from the 10km-long Etang de Leucate lagoon which stretches behind the sandbar on which they have been built. The winds which frequently blow from either sea or land provide plenty of days when conditions are ideal for windsurfers. Sunset over the Etang de Leucate can be magical as the Corbière hills behind it become tinged with purple. The north end of the beach has a naturist village.

Below
Port-Leucate

THE COAST AND LAGOONS

PORT-LA-NOUVELLE❖

ⓘ Port-la-Nouvelle Tourist Information *place Paul Valéry; tel: 04 68 48 00 51; www.portlanouvelle.com. Open daily June–Sept; Mon–Sat Oct–May.*

Unlike other towns along the Languedoc-Roussillon coast, Port-la-Nouvelle is not primarily geared to tourism. Instead it is an industrial port handling oil supplies for the whole of Southwest France, and as such it has some rather unsightly refinery buildings, though the giant tankers which constantly come and go can be interesting to watch. The town also has a long beach, marina and canal basin where the Canal de la Robine reaches the sea. The nature reserve on Ile Ste-Lucie in the salt flats is a pleasant spot for walks.

RESERVE AFRICAINE DE SIGEAN❖

ⓘ Tourist Information *place de la Libération, Sigean; tel: 04 68 48 14 81. Open daily July–Aug; Mon–Sat Sept–June.*

Ⓗ Réserve Africaine de Sigean €€€ *off the N9; tel: 04 68 48 20 20; www.reserveafricainesigean.fr. Open daily. Allow 30 minutes for the safari drive and 2 hours on foot for the nature trail.*

This large safari park (7km north of Sigean), is one of the few 'formal' attractions in this part of France. Ideal for families to visit, it has 3000 animals including lions, bears and white rhinos. They roam freely in brushland that looks almost like their natural habitat. In addition, various exotic birds such as flamingos have joined the indigenous ones on the nearby lagoons. Cars drive round on a 5km route. Pedestrians can follow a nature discovery trail with observation posts for watching antelopes, zebras and cheetahs. Alligators bask in the warmth of a solar-heated house.

Accommodation and food in Sigean

Le Sainte Anne €€ *3 avenue de l'Hospital; tel: 04 68 48 24 38. Open all year.* Picturesque hotel with restaurant, quietly situated on the edge of the town. Colourful garden with children's playground.

RIVESALTES✦✦✦

🛈 **Rivesaltes Tourist Information** *avenue Ledru-Rollin; tel: 04 68 64 04 04. Open Mon–Sat July–Aug; Mon–Fri Sept–June.*

🏛 **Musée Maréchal Joffre** € *rue de la Republique;. tel: 04 68 64 24 98. Open daily June–Sept; Mon–Fri Oct–May.*

From the north you enter this little town, the centre of the area that produces the sweet Muscat de Rivesaltes aperitif wine, across a suspension bridge over the River Agly. A large plane tree, over a hundred years old, stands in the centre of the old quarter beside an elegant bell tower which – typical of the area – is built in brick and pebble. One of the narrow streets off it leads to the **Eglise St André**✦✦ which has a gilded altarpiece. On the church's exterior, notice how its olive-green glazed ceramic drainpipes each have a face at the bottom. The crenellations on the red brick Portail Nef, one of the ancient fortified gateways into the old quarter, make it look like a small castle. An equestrian statue of Maréchal Joffre, one of France's famous World War I commanders, who was born in the town, stands in the modern part looking down a broad avenue of plane trees. His birthplace houses the **Musée Maréchal Joffre**✦, a museum dedicated to him. Don't miss a *dégustation* of the local muscat wine at one of the *caves*.

Accommodation and food in Rivesaltes

La Tour de L'Horloge € *11 rue Armand Barbès; tel: 04 68 64 05 88. Closed Jan–Feb.* Small 17-room traditional hotel in centre of old quarter with restaurant serving Catalan dishes. Garage.

SALSES-LE-CHATEAU✦

🏛 **Château de Salses** €€ *Tel: 04 68 38 60 13; www.monum.fr. Open daily.*

When the narrow neck of land between the Corbières hills and the coastal lagoons formed the border between France and Spain, Salses-le-Chateau was an obvious place to have a castle. The King of Aragon built one in the 1300s. Today's **Château de Salses**✦✦✦, a vast building in yellow stone and pink brick, dates from 1497. Standing incongruously amongst vineyards, its 10m-thick walls – designed to withstand attack from the newly invented gunpowder – certainly look impregnable, though the moat around them has long since dried up. Constructed in just six years, the castle could house 1500 men and 300 horses in vaulted stables. Its central courtyard was defended by an underground corridor with traps from which the word 'ha-ha' (meaning sunken fence) may have been derived. The five-storey keep beyond the interior moat is where the governor and officers lived.

When the border was moved to the Pyrenees, the castle was handed over to France. Louis XIV's military architect Vauban improved its defences, but it was never attacked and subsequently became a prison.

Opposite
The Château de Salses

TAUTAVEL*

Musée de Tautavel
€€ *avenue Jean Leon Gregories; tel: 04 68 29 07 76; www.tautavel.com. Open daily. Special events, lectures and exhibitions throughout the year; also 'prehistoric' banquets in July and Aug.*

Human bones estimated to be 450,000 years old, the oldest found in Europe, were discovered in 1971 in the **Caune de l'Arago***, a cave near the village which is situated in a vine-growing plain on the edge of the Corbières hills. The 40m-long cave, which opens out onto the plain from one of the surrounding cliffs, was excavated by Professor Henry de Lumley who organised digs in the area and set up the Centre of European Prehistory in the village (visits by special arrangement).

In the excellent **Musée de Tautavel***, part of the Centre, ancient objects found in the area bring prehistory to life. The highlight is a vivid life-size reconstruction of the cave made from castings. Videos depict the various stages of the cave's occupation, including prehistoric men returning from a hunt and hacking up game they have caught.

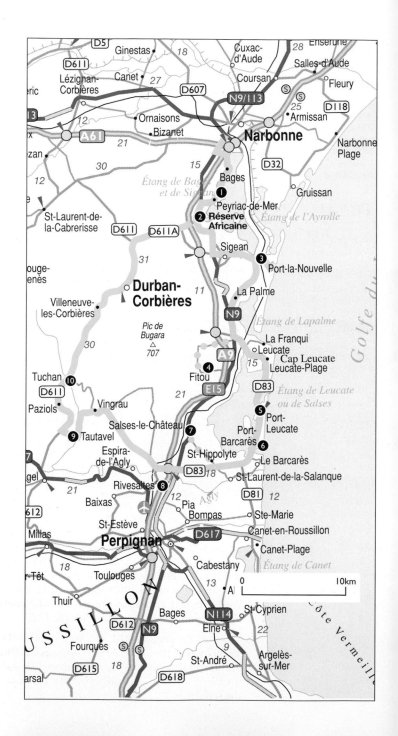

Ha-has

The word 'ha-ha', meaning a sunken fence which forms a boundary without interrupting a view, is said to have originated at Salses castle – as they proudly tell you on a visit there. To aid its defenders an underground corridor was built around the courtyard with water traps along it to catch spies. When they fell in, they would exclaim in surprise 'ah ah'. Those who did not drown were likely to knock themselves out on stone lintels which were deliberately set at different heights.

TUCHAN*

The village of Tuchan is brooded over by the Montagne de Tauch, an austere ridge of hills which makes this part of the Corbières feel wild and remote, especially if you happen to be driving through it at dusk. Surrounded by vineyards, it is the centre for the production of Fitou wine.

Suggested tour

Total distance: 160km. The detour to Fitou adds 14km and the detour to Salses adds 6km.

Time: 4 hours' driving. Allow about a day for the main route, or at least a full day with detours and time on the beach. Those with limited time should concentrate on Sigean and Tautavel.

Links to other tours: From Tuchan, the D611 and D14 lead southwest to Padern (*see page 109*), 7km away. From Port-Bacarès, the D81 leads south to Canet-Plage (*see page 53*), 15km away.

Leaving Narbonne south on the N9 (towards Perpignan), turn left after 5km on to the D105. This hugs the shore of the **ETANG DE BAGES ET DE SIGEAN** ❶ through **Bages** and then rejoins the N9 just beyond **Peyriac-de-Mer**. After 5km on the N9 (past the **RESERVE AFRICAINE** ❷ safari park on the left), leave it again by turning left onto the N139 to go through **Sigean** to the sea at **PORT-LA-NOUVELLE** ❸. Then take the D709 back to the N9 again, through **Lapalme** where the cliffs northwest of the village have a glorious view over the lagoon to the sea. Two kilometres after rejoining the N9, you come to its junction with the D627.

Detour: To visit **FITOU** ❹, stay on the N9 for 5km beyond its junction with the D627. At **Les Cabanes-de-Fitou**, turn right on to the unnumbered road which goes over the A9 autoroute to Fitou (2km), then return north along the N9 to rejoin the route at its junction with the D627.

The 20km train journey (30km by car) from Narbonne to Port-la-Nouvelle (on the line to Perpignan) takes 15 minutes. Frequent services. Boat trips on the Canal de la Robine also cross the lagoon.

At the N9/D627 junction, take the D627 east towards the sea. It runs spectacularly along the narrow strip of land between the sea and the **Etang de Leucate** lagoon. The old village of **Leucate** overlooks the lagoon while **Leucate-Plage**, the original resort, is on the Mediterranean.

The new resorts of **PORT-LEUCATE** ❺ and **PORT-BARCARES** ❻ are unusual in having no seafront road. Instead access to the beach is down cul-de-sacs, so unless you leave the D627 you will quickly sweep past them. Beyond Port-Barcarès, turn inland on the D83.

Detour: Turn right off the D83 on to the D11 through **St-Hippolyte** to visit **SALSES-LE-CHATEAU** ❼ (7km), and then pick up the route again by returning to the D83 along the N9 (5km).

From the D83 continue inland over the A9 autoroute, turning left to go over a small suspension bridge into **RIVESALTES** ❽. From there the D12 twists dramatically up beneath a ridge of white limestone cliffs into the Corbières hills and the village of **Vingrau** from where the D9 leads to **TAUTAVEL** ❾. Next take the D59 to join the D611 which goes through **TUCHAN** ❿ and past the **Château de Aguilar**, built on an isolated rocky outcrop. It was strongly fortified in the 13th century to guard the gorge below from Spanish attack. Now the hilly countryside covered in *garrigue* – sweet-smelling scrubby bushes – is wild and austere. The Montagne de Tauch broods over the lonely road as it makes its way through vineyards to the villages of **Villeneuve-les-Corbières** and **Durban-Corbières**. The latter is very much a southern wine village, with wineries along its plane-lined main street and the ruins of a castle on a hillock in the centre. The Fitou vineyards are all around and the countryside becomes much softer with cherry trees and pink outcrops as the D611 continues northeast to join the N9 back to **Narbonne**.

Getting out of the car I

The **Cap Leucate** cliffs, just north of Leucate-Plage offer glorious views over the Golfe du Lion coastline. A scenic path leads from them down to **La Franqui**.

Getting out of the car II

Although it is easy to drive to Port-la-Nouvelle from Narbonne, why not go by train? The line is one of the most scenic in France, running between two large lagoons, the **Etang de Bages et de Sigean** and the **Etang de l'Ayrolle**, on a narrow sandbar which it shares with the **Canal de la Robine**. Look out of the window and you seem to be almost floating as there is scarcely any 'land' on either side, just patches of dune – home to hundreds of sea birds – lapped by rippling water. Sunset, when the pink sky is reflected in it, is the most beautiful time of all.

Opposite
Leucate-Plage on the Golfe du Lion coast

Ratings

History   ●●●●●

Architecture   ●●●●○

Food and drink
               ●●●○○

Children   ●●○○○

Entertainment
               ●●○○○

Museums   ●●○○○

Shopping   ●●○○○

Art   ●○○○○

Carcassonne

The town has two distinct faces – la Cité and the Ville Basse – separated by the River Aude. Most visitors are attracted by la Cité, a formidable medieval citadel built on a high crag which looks particularly spectacular when floodlit at night. Across the river is the lower town, Bastide St-Louis, where the main offices and shops are to be found. Originally the town thrived on cloth-making but now it is mainly an administrative centre.

It's easy to see why la Cité has become a museum piece. At the end of the last century it was saved from falling into complete decay by Viollet-le-Duc, the architect who specialised in military renovation. He restored it to its 12th-century form. In contrast the Ville Basse, the 'new town' which King Louis IX had built in 1260, has the grid layout typical of a *bastide* (fortified town).

Getting there and getting around

Carcassonne's small **Salvaza Airport** (*tel: 04 68 71 96 46*) is 3km northwest of the town. It has flights to Stansted in the UK by Ryanair. There is a restaurant and car-hire desks, but no shops. A shuttle bus to the Ville Basse and la Cité operates daily. A coach service to and from Toulouse connects with the Ryanair flights.

The **railway station** is on the northern edge of the Ville Basse, with parking opposite it across the Canal du Midi.

ⓘ **Carcassonne Tourist Information** *Office Municipal de Tourisme in the Ville Basse, 15 boulevard Camille-Pelletan; tel: 04 68 10 24 30; e-mail: accueil@ carcassonne-tourisme.com; www.carcassonne.org. Open Mon–Sat (Sat morning only). Guided tours. In la Cité, Porte Narbonnaise; tel: 04 68 10 24 36. Open daily. Guided visits in English June–Sept. Small charge.*

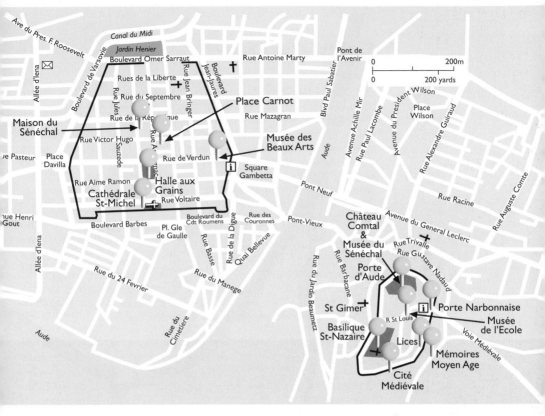

To reach la Cité by car, take exit Est from the A61 autoroute and follow signs to car parks. For the Ville Basse, exit Ouest is also convenient.

Parking: Access to la Cité by car is severely restricted. Cars are normally banned from mid-Apr–Sept. Instead they have to be left in the well-signposted car park outside the walls with moderately priced day-long parking rates. Pedestrians walk in through the Porte Narbonnaise. Hotel guests should check parking arrangements with their hotel. There is also free on-street parking in the suburbs to the north of la Cité for those prepared to face the hilly walk up. Pay-and-display car parks are situated beside the boulevards surrounding the Ville Basse. The grid of narrow streets in the centre is all one-way. The Vieux-Pont, one of two bridges over the river, is also one-way in the direction of la Cité.

Public transport: A shuttle bus operates every 15 minutes in high season from 0930 to 1230 and 1400 to 1930 between la Cité and square Gambetta on the edge of the Ville Basse; *tel: 04 68 47 82 22*, and also, more frequently and year-round, the No 2 bus. To walk between la Cité and the Ville Basse takes about 15 minutes. Go via the Pont-Vieux.

Sights – La Cité✧✧✧

La Cité✧✧✧

The citadel is a very convincing 19th-century restoration of the original medieval fortified town. Indeed some say it is too perfect. Standing on a strategically sited hilltop first settled by the Romans, it was more or less abandoned when its position was no longer militarily useful and fell into serious disrepair until being restored, at enormous cost to the state, by Viollet-le-Duc. Now it is much as it was originally, with high double walls stretching for over 1km, 52 towers, a castle and basilica. Only 130 people actually live there, but its narrow streets are lined with small shops, mostly selling souvenirs. All summer it is a tourist honey pot.

Basilique St-Nazaire✧✧✧

The outstanding feature is its 14th- to 15th-century stained glass, including two beautiful rose windows. The sun shining through them dapples the interior with colour. Only the barrel-vaulted nave is original from the 11th century. Viollet-le-Duc took it upon himself to put crenellations around the belfry wall outside.

Below
La Cité

Château Comtal
€€ 1 rue Violet Leduc;
tel: 04 68 11 70 77. Open
daily.

**Musée Mémoires
Moyen Age** €€ Espace
Pont Levis, Chemin des
Anglais, La Cité; tel: 04 68
71 05 65. Open daily.

Musée de l'Ecole € 3
place St Jean, La Cité,
Carcassonne; tel: 04 68 25
95 14. Open Tue–Sun.

Im@ginarium € 3–5 rue
Saint Jean – La Cité; tel: 04
68 47 78 78. Open daily.
Interactive museum using
technology to present the
history of Carcassonne.

Château Comtal*

Château Comtal, the inner bastion, was built in the 12th century by the Viscounts of Carcassonne, the Trencavels. It has been knocked around extensively – though never by military attack – over the years, ending up with five towers, two courtyards and wooden galleries, part of its defences, along the outer walls. One of the towers contains the **Musée Lapidaire*** which has a collection of Roman pottery and stone fragments; also old prints showing what la Cité looked like before it was restored.

Lices**

A 3km-long broad grassy bailey or ditch – les lices – runs round la Cité between the high inner wall and lower outside one. It was used for jousting tournaments and archery practice as well as storage.

Musée de l'École*

This nostalgic 1900 classroom is complete with old-fashioned desks, blackboards and ink pens.

Musée Mémoires Moyen Age*

Mémoires Moyen Age is a 30-minute video presentation with music and sound effects about the history of la Cité and its military construction. The museum is situated just outside the walls.

Porte Narbonnaise*

The pedestrian gateway, which sports two huge towers, formerly guarded the entrance to la Cité with a heavy chain backed up by trapdoors and two portcullises. Today over a quarter of a million visitors pass through it each year.

Sights – Ville Basse**

Bastide St-Louis (Ville Basse)**

The 'new town' was built following the wholesale destruction of the area during the Albigensian Crusade which ended in 1240. Wide boulevards shaded by plane trees have replaced the ramparts which originally encircled its grid of straight narrow streets.

Cathédrale St-Michel**

The cathedral, in rue Voltaire, is typically Southern Gothic in style with a single large nave. The altar is built in the local warm red/cream marble from Caunes. The stained-glass windows are 19th century.

Halle aux Grains*

The town's open-sided corn market dates from the 17th century and has a lofty wooden roof. A circle (now often covered by parked

Halle aux Grains
rue du Dr Albert Tomey.

Musée des Beaux-Arts
1 rue de Verdun; tel: 04 68 77 73 70. Open Wed–Sun mid-June–mid-Sept; Tue–Sat mid-Sept–mid-June.

cars) marked on the square beside it is where traders found guilty of cheating had to stand for an hour wearing a placard proclaiming their misdemeanour.

Musée des Beaux-Arts⁕

The museum's collection ranges from 17th- to 19th-century French, Flemish and Dutch masters to local pottery and memorabilia from the Chéniers, a well-known local family who had strong Greek connections.

Place Carnot⁕

This big square, the centre of the town, was originally surrounded by arcades, part of the traditional architecture of a *bastide*, but they disappeared long ago and the buildings are now a mixture of styles. Now traffic-free, it has a decorative Italian fountain in the centre depicting Neptune.

Shopping

The Ville Basse is dotted with small shops, particularly in the pedestrianised streets across from the station, such as rue Georges Clemenceau and Courte Jaire. For pâtisserie and chocolate, such as the famous Pavés de la Cité, head for place Carnot. There's also an open-air market there on Tue, Thur and Sat mornings. There's a daily market (fresh and cooked meat and fish) in the **Halle aux Grains**. **Monoprix** is the only department store, though several hypermarkets are situated on the outskirts near the autoroute. Most of the shops in la Cité are very touristy though the **Cellier des Vignerons** in rue du Grand Puit has an excellent selection of local wines.

Entertainment

La Cité stages a summer festival during July and August when open-air concerts, plays and medieval re-enactments take place near the castle. On Bastille Day, 14 July, the town puts on one of the best firework displays in France, making the whole of La Cité look as if it is going up in flames. The best place to watch is on the Vieux Pont or the banks

of the River Aude. This is not an evening to try driving through the town as both its bridges are closed to traffic.

Accommodation and food

The three hotels in la Cité are handy if you enjoy being in the centre of the action but they charge for the privilege. There are many more just outside the walls and others lower down in the Basse Ville. The tourist offices can book accommodation but you have to go there in person. The streets of la Cité abound in eateries of varying quality, but you are much more likely to rub shoulders with local people in the Basse Ville.

La Cité

Le Donjon €€ *2 rue du Comte Roger; tel: 04 68 11 23 00*. Medieval setting with modern comforts; transformed from an orphanage into a mid-priced hotel. Thirty-six rooms.

Hotel de la Cité €€€ *place de l'Eglise; tel: 04 68 71 98 71*. Everyone from Queen Elizabeth II to Walt Disney and Michael Jackson has checked into this exclusive wood-panelled, near-château which boasts a swimming pool and one of the few gardens in la Cité.

Auberge Dame Carcas €€ *3 place du Château; tel: 04 68 71 23 23*. Reasonably priced menus in traditional surroundings.

Brasserie le Donjon €€ *2 rue du Comte Roger; tel: 04 68 25 95 72*, serves local classics in bright surroundings.

Ville Basse

Le Cathare € *53 rue Jean Bringer; tel: 04 68 25 65 92*. Inexpensive small hotel in the centre of town. Its restaurant which occupies part of a 13th-century former monastery specialises in grills on an open fire.

Des Trois Couronnes €€ *2 rue des Trois Couronnes; tel: 04 68 25 36 10*. A modern hotel boasting one of the best views of la Cité from its riverside position, particularly for diners in quai Bellevue, its terrace restaurant. Sixty-eight rooms.

Grand Hôtel Terminus €€ *2 avenue du Maréchal Joffre; tel: 04 68 25 25 00; open Mar–Nov*. This hotel opposite the railway station is indeed grand. It has an imposing mirrored and marbled lobby in true *fin-de-siècle* style, yet surprisingly affordable rooms. One hundred rooms.

Hôtel du Pont Vieux € *32 rue Trivalle; tel: 04 68 25 24 99; closed mid–late Jan*. A quiet family-run hotel nestling in a small street in the oldest quarter of the town just below la Cité. Nineteen rooms.

La Rotonde € *13 boulevard Omer Sarraut; tel: 04 68 25 02 37*. A lively brasserie near the station which is popular with students, not least because its inexpensive menu includes a cinema ticket.

Suggested walk

Length: 3km.

Duration: At least an hour, including 15 minutes from la Cité down to Ville Basse.

Before heading into **LA CITE** ❶ through the **PORTE NARBONNAISE** ❷, stroll around the broad ditch – **LES LICES** ❸ – between the high inner wall and lower outside one, then walk along the walls and enjoy the view down over the **River Aude** and **VILLE BASSE** ❹ with hills in the distance.

Inside **la Cité** the narrow streets, jam-packed in summer, are lined with small shops and cafés occupying quaint old stone buildings. The most notable sights are the **CHATEAU COMTAL** ❺ and **BASILIQUE ST-NAZAIRE** ❻.

Two routes lead down to the Ville Basse. Through the **Porte d'Aude**, a steep cobbled path named **Montée d'Aude** zigzags down to the **Eglise St-Pimer**; or the easier **Montée G Combéléran** leads down from the Porte Narbonnaise. Cross the 600-year-old **Pont-Vieux**, which has pointed recesses where pedestrians can stand to avoid vehicles, and turn left to walk down Boulevard du Cdt Roumens past the grand 18th-century entrance gate, **Portail des Jacobins**, and on to the **cathedral**.

Dotted around the narrow grid of streets within the Ville Basse, particularly rue de Verdun and rue Aimé Ramond, are a number of fine mansions dating from the 18th century when the town grew rich from cloth-making. Although they are closed to the public, you may pass open doorways where you can peep into their secluded courtyards. These invariably have attractive balconies and staircases and often a well with a palm tree beside it. To have such an exotic feature was regarded as a status symbol. The oldest is the **MAISON DU SENECHAL** ❼ in rue du Dr Albert Tomey. Nearby is the covered market place, **HALLE AUX GRAINS** ❽.

The traffic-free **PLACE CARNOT** ❾ is the town's centre. Its new red marble paving and cobbles provide a smart setting for a market on Tuesday, Thursday and Saturday mornings and pavement cafés at other times.

Eglise St-Vincent in rue du 4 Septembre has the second widest nave in France (after the one at Mirepoix) and is topped by a flamboyant 54m-high tower with 47 bells. Nearby the **Préfecture de Police** in rue Jean-Bringer occupies the former bishop's palace.

Also worth exploring

The **Canal du Midi✦✦✦** passes through the Ville Basse in front of the railway station. Its wide basin and lock are a hive of industry in summer. Leafy Jardin Chenier beside it is an attractive spot for sitting or strolling and has a playground for children. You can walk along the tow-path as far as you like in either direction.

The town's citizens made a serious mistake when they declined to contribute towards the cost of bringing the canal through the town centre as Pierre-Paul Riquet suggested when he was building it in 1669 (*see page 199*). Instead it followed the valley of the Fresquel, 2kms north, which meant they missed out on the valuable trade it might have brought, unlike Castelnaudary – 32km west – which prospered from it. The canal was re-routed between 1786 and 1810, including a superb aqueduct over the Fresquel, but this was far too late for the town to benefit fully from water-borne business.

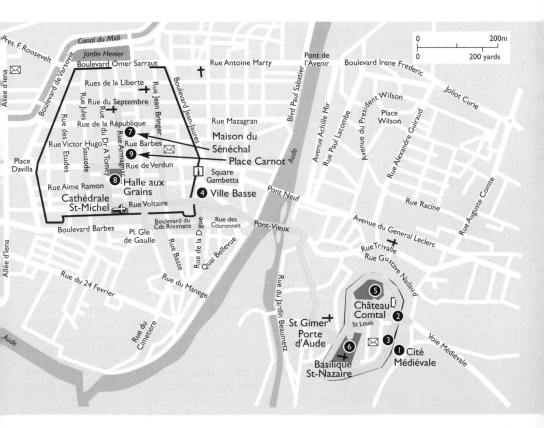

The Corbières hills

Ratings

Scenery	●●●●●
Food and drink	●●●●○
Villages	●●●●○
Castles	●●●○○
Churches	●●●○○
Vineyards	●●●○○
Walking	●●●○○
Spas	●●○○○

The lively little town of Limoux is one of the highlights of this otherwise rural route around the Corbières hills, particularly during its entertaining carnival weekends.

To the west this is Blanquette country where, nearly 500 years ago, the world's first sparkling white wine came to fruition in the monastery at St-Hilaire. To the east, around Lagrasse, the vineyards which produce Corbières wines stretch up the hillsides, dotted with *domaines* (estates) where you can sample and buy.

Everywhere the scenery is stunning for this is hill country even though it lacks the drama of high mountain peaks. Limestone crags peep through wooded hillsides and there are long views to the distant Pyrenees. Ruined castles and the remains of ancient monasteries are forlorn reminders of its turbulent past.

Petrol stations – as well as shops and restaurants – are in short supply on this route so stock up before starting out.

ALET-LES-BAINS❖❖

ⓘ **Alet-les-Bains Tourist Information** *avenue Nicolas Pavillon; tel: 04 68 69 93 56. Open daily.*

ⓗ **Benedictine abbey** *€ Open daily.*

True to the tradition of France's spa towns, Alet has a casino to complement its range of mineral waters, said to be helpful for gastric problems. Nostradamus, the French visionary, recommended them anyway. Situated in a sheltered spot beside the River Aude, the old quarter is a charming area with half-timbered and pink stone buildings surrounded by ramparts. Its **Benedictine abbey**❖, burnt out during the Wars of Religion, is a forlorn ruin.

LAGRASSE❖❖❖

The capital of the Corbières is one of the most beautiful little towns in France – and that's official! It is classified as such. Certainly its setting, beside the River Orbieu surrounded by hills, could scarcely be

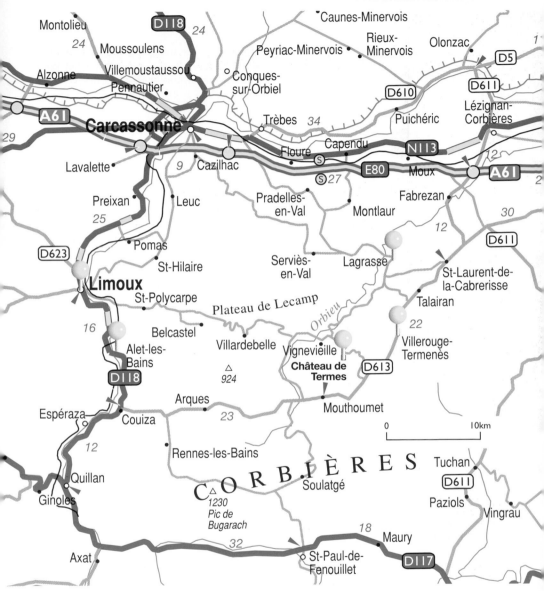

bettered. The quaint medieval centre within fortified walls has a maze
of narrow streets with several fine houses dating from around the 14th
century when the inhabitants made a good living from tanning
leather and making cloth. There is also an attractive covered market.

An 11th-century hump-backed bridge across the River Orbieu links
the town with a splendid Benedictine abbey, **Ste-Marie d'Orbie✦✦✦**,
which was founded in 799, though the present buildings date from

ⓘ **Lagrasse Tourist Information** 6
boulevard de la Promenade;
tel: 04 68 43 11 56;
www.lagrasse.com.
Open daily May–Sept;
Mon–Sat Oct–Apr.

ⓗ **Abbaye Ste-Marie d'Orbieu** € *Tel: 04 68 43 15 99. Open daily except mid-Dec–mid-Jan. Concerts take place in the abbey during the area's Fugue in Romanesque Aude music festival in July.*

◓ **Book Fair** in Sept.

the 13th to the 18th centuries. They include a simple Romanesque church, cloisters, the abbot's chapel with a decorative tiled floor in yellow, green and black, a huge dormitory with a wooden ceiling and a bell tower – with a spiral staircase worth climbing for the view over the river and town.

Accommodation in Lagrasse

Le Clos des Souquets €€ *avenue de Lagrasse, Fabrezan (11km northeast of Lagrasse on the D212); tel: 04 68 43 52 61. Closed Nov–Mar. Restaurant closed Sun.* Cosy inn with five individually decorated bedrooms, pretty gardens and pool.

Hostellerie des Corbières €€ *9 blvd de la Promenade; tel: 04 68 43 15 22. Open Feb–Nov.* Formerly the Auberge St-Hubert, this hotel on the edge of the village has been completely renovated.

LIMOUX❖❖

ⓘ **Limoux Tourist Information** 5
promenade du Tivoli; tel: 04 68 31 11 82; www.limoux.fr. Open daily.

ⓗ **Musée Petiet** € *In same building as tourist office. Open daily. Tel: 04 68 31 85 03.*

Catha-rama €€ *47 avenue Fabre d'Eglantine; tel: 04 68 31 48 42. Open daily Easter–Oct.* English commentary; also children's show, 'Au Temps des Chevaliers'.

◓ **Grand flea market** *avenue F d'Eglantine on first Sun in month (except Sept).*

For home-made conserves including fricassee and *confit de canard,* go to the Jean-Louis Garcia charcuterie, 92 rue St-Martin.

The heart of this lively town on the River Aude is its arcaded square, place de la République. A 400-year-old bridge, Pont Neuf, links the central 'grande ville' to the 'petite ville', the more modern Aragou quarter. Sections of the town's 14th-century fortified walls, built following an attack by the Black Prince, son of England's King Edward III, have survived.

Limoux has several claims to fame. First and foremost it is the production centre for Blanquette de Limoux, the world's first sparkling white wine. Another is its fricassee, a tasty pork stew served with the local white beans. And the town is notable, too, for its carnivals which take place every weekend from January to March on the place de la République, always a particularly jolly time to be there.

At **Catha-rama**❖❖, a spectacular three-screen audio-visual, you can brush up on the Cathar history and the castles in which the 'heretics' sought refuge. A small art gallery, **Musée Petiet**❖, displays 19th-century paintings by local artists, including Auguste and Léopold Petiet and Léopold's daughter Marie. The building, formerly their studio, is now shared by the tourist office.

Accommodation and food in Limoux

Hôtel Moderne & Pigeon €€ *place du Général Leclerc; tel: 04 68 31 00 25. Closed first half of Jan.* Large stately town house converted to a hotel during the 19th century and now renowned for its restaurant (€€€). Grand staircase embellished by a large stained-glass window and frescoes painted by Italian pilgrims on their way to Santiago de

Carnival on ten weekends from mid-Jan.

Compostela. The hotel's unusual name results from the amalgamation of two businesses by the present chef-owner's father.

CHATEAU DE TERMES❖❖

Château de Termes €€
Tel: 04 68 70 09 20.
Open Feb–Dec daily.

Termes castle is a crumbling ruin at the top of a wooded ridge surrounded by deep gorges. A steep track leads up to it from the bridge in the village; allow 15 minutes. Only parts of its thick walls survived its deliberate demolition in the 17th century after it had been occupied by brigands. Its position guarding the Sou valley certainly merits the climb to the top. The castle played a large part in the first stages of the Albigensian Crusade (*see pages 32–33*) when it sheltered a leading Cathar 'heretic', Ramon de Termes, but was finally taken by Simon de Montfort in 1210 after a four-month siege.

Below
Limoux Carnival

Left
Limoux Carnival

Limoux Carnival

Every weekend from January to March the centre of Limoux is filled with carnival crowds. Three times each Saturday and Sunday (starting at 1100, 1700 and 2000), costumed revellers dance solemnly around the arcades of the place de la République accompanied by brass bands, pausing for refreshment at the five bars around it.

Men, women and children take part, all wearing either colourful pierrot costumes or funny character masks with appropriate clothes. Some wave *la carabena*, a wand decorated with coloured strips of paper, while others carry sacks of coloured confetti to throw over the spectators.

The music is infectiously repetitive and the dance movements slow and precise. On the final evening a bonfire is lit in the centre of the square and everyone, both participants and spectators, dances around it.

Limoux's carnival tradition dates back to the Middle Ages when the local millers celebrated after paying their dues to the monastery of Prouille. Then instead of confetti they threw sugared almonds and flour.

VILLEROUGE-TERMENES❖

Château de Villerouge-Termenès €€ *Tel: 04 68 70 09 11; www.cathars.org. Open daily Feb–Dec.*

Château de Villerouge-Termenès❖❖❖, a square 800-year-old castle, has been completely restored. Inside you can see a vivid audio-visual about Cathar times seen through the eyes of the last *parfait*, Guilhem Bélibaste, who was burned at the stake there. The castle's restaurant serves medieval fare only (*closed Mon*).

Suggested tour

Total distance: 110km. The detour to St-Hilaire adds 4km and the detour to Alet-les-Bains adds 16km.

Time: 3 hours' driving. Allow most of a day for the main route, a full day with detours. Those with limited time should concentrate on Limoux and Lagrasse.

Links to other tours: From Limoux the D118 leads south to Couiza (*see page 102*), 15km away. From Villerouge-Termenès the D613 leads southwest to Mouthoumet (*see page 109*), 7km away. From Lagrasse the D212 leads northeast to Lézignan-Corbières (*see page 195*), 20km away.

Abbaye St-Hilaire
€ *Information tel: 04 68 69 62 76. Open daily all year. Concerts during the Fugue in Romanesque Aude music festival at end of July.*

Château du Floure
€€€ *| allée Gaston Bonheur, Floure (10km east of Carcassonne, just off the N113); tel: 04 68 79 11 29. Country mansion, partly dating back to the 12th century, with impressive formal gardens. Sixteen rooms, sun terrace, tennis and pool. Restaurant open Apr–Dec.*

Below
The Corbières hills

From Carcassonne take the D118 south beside the River Aude to LIMOUX ❶.

Detour: The birthplace of the famous sparkling white wine, Blanquette de Limoux, is the Benedictine abbey in the small village of **St-Hilaire** on the River Lauguer between Carcassonne and Limoux. To visit it, turn left off the D118 12km south of Carcassonne and go through **Pomas** (4km). Its pretty 600-year-old cloister is still in remarkably good condition, though the main attraction is the splendidly carved white marble tomb in the Romanesque church depicting St-Sernin's martyrdom. Afterwards return to the route on the D104 which winds down to Limoux (12km).

Detour: To visit **ALET-LES-BAINS** ❷, continue south beyond Limoux for a further 8km on the D118.

From Limoux the route goes east along the valley into quiet wooded countryside on the narrow D129 through **St-Polycarpe** and **Belcastel**. This winding undulating road has extensive views over distant hills. At **Villardebelle**, turn left on to the D529 where a small plaque commemorates the planting of a tree by the local priest to mark the proclamation of France's First Republic. After a 2km descent, turn right on to the even narrower D40 which goes through farmland and woods to the lonely Col de la Louviéro (599m). This is a particularly peaceful part of the Corbières and civilisation seems far away. Turn

left along the narrow Gorges du Terminèt where the **CHATEAU DE TERMES** ❸ is on the right. Continue on the D40, enjoying the wide views on both sides, until it reaches the D613 where you turn left again. Now the vineyards which produce the famous Corbières wines make their appearance. Beyond **VILLEROUGE-TERMENES** ❹ you go over the Col de Villerouge (404m) and continue through vineyards. Next turn on to the D23 to **LAGRASSE** ❺. Turn left there on to the D3 along the wide gorge of the River Alsou. Nine kilometres later, turn left again on to the D603 to **Servies-en-Val** from where the D42 makes its twisting way with glorious views back to Carcassonne.

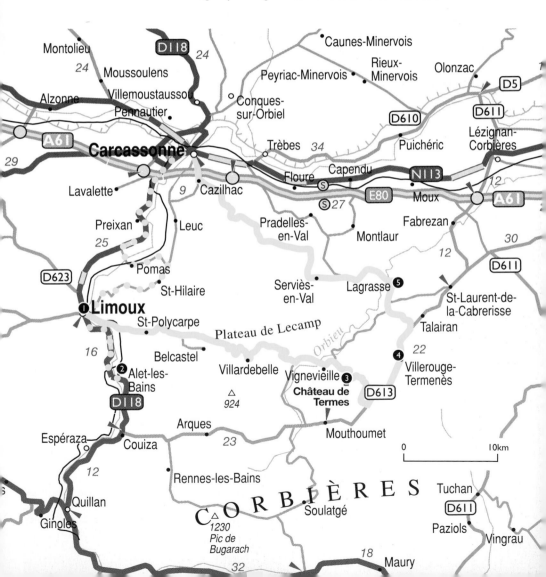

Around the Montagne Noire

Ratings

Architecture	●●●●○
Nature	●●●●○
Scenery	●●●●○
Walking	●●●●○
History	●●●○○
Outdoor activities	●●●○○
Villages	●●●○○
Art and craft	●●○○○

The Montagne Noire, the most southerly part of France's Massif Central mountains, is a rolling rural landscape with breathtaking views over green valleys bordered by steep cliffs and dotted with sleepy little towns.

The mountain acts as a dividing line between the Atlantic and Mediterranean climates. The south-facing slopes are gentle, covered in gorse, sweet chestnuts and olives and their towns have a distinctly southern feel. By contrast the northern side of the mountain, which reaches 1210m at its highest point, the Pic de Nore, is steeper and thickly wooded with pine and beech. Here the houses, built in the local grey stone, look sombre, particularly as their walls are sometimes covered in black slate as protection from the weather.

The area gets a lot of rain – and snow in winter – as it catches winds from both east and west which bring over a metre per year.

DOURGNE❖

ⓘ Dourgne Tourist Information *La Mairie; tel: 05 63 50 31 20. Open daily.*

This small village where slate is quarried has the distinction of having a convent, Abbaye Ste-Scholastique, founded in 1890 and a monastery, Abbaye St-Benoît-d'En Calcat, founded six years later. Both are run by the Benedictine order. The monastery has a large ultra-modern bookshop which also sells pottery and religious pictures. The abbeys are north of the village in Calcat on the D85.

HAUTPOUL❖❖

ⓘ Tourist Information *in Mazamet (see page 146).*

This quaint hilltop village is perched above the wooded valley of the River Arnette with Mazamet below. Its history as a fortress goes back to the 5th century but ended when Simon de Montfort stormed it during the Albigensian Crusade in the 13th century. The inhabitants

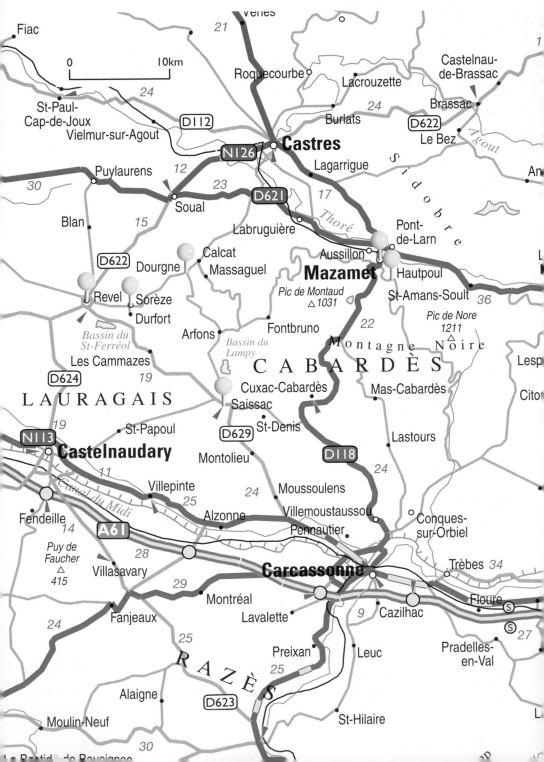

Fiac

0   10km

24

St-Paul-
Cap-de-Joux
Vielmur-sur-Agout   D112

21   Venes

Roquecourbe

Lacrouzette   Castelnau-
de-Brassac

Brassac

24   D622

Burlats   Le Bez

N126   **Castres**

Lagarrigue   S i d o b r e

12   An

Puylaurens   *23*

30   Soual   D621   *17*

Blan   *15*   Thoré   Pont-
de-Larn

Labruguière

Calcat   Aussillon

D622   Dourgne   Massaguel   **Mazamet**   Hautpoul

Revel   Sorèze   Pic de Montaud   St-Amans-Soult   *36*
△ 1031

Durfort   Fontbruno   *22*   Pic de Nore
1211

Arfons   M o n t a g n e   N o i r e

*Bassin du
St-Ferréol*   *Bassin du
Lampy*   **C A B A R D È S**

Les Cammazes   *19*   Lesp

D624   Cuxac-Cabardès   Mas-Cabardès   Cito

L A U R A G A I S   Saissac

19   D629   St-Denis   Lastours

St-Papoul   Montolieu   D118   *24*

N113   *11*

Castelnaudary   Villepinte   *24*   Moussoulens

25

Fendeille   Alzonne   Villemoustaussou   Conques-
sur-Orbiel

Canal du Midi   Pennautier

14   A61   *28*   Trèbes   *34*

*Puy de
Faucher*
△
415   Villasavary   **Carcassonne**   Floure

29   Montréal   Cazilhac   S

Fanjeaux   Lavalette   *9*   S   *27*

25   **R A Z È S**   Pradelles-
en-Val

24   *25*   Preixan   Leuc

Alaigne   St-Hilaire

Moulin-Neuf   D623

30

Maison du Bois et du Jouet €€ *Moulin de l'Oule, Val d'Hautpoul; tel: 05 63 61 42 70. Open afternoons July–Aug.*

moved down into the valley which actually proved to be more convenient for their occupation of making cloth.

The village's survival today depends largely on making wooden toys. Visitors can watch craftsmen at work in the Maison de l'Artisanat craft shop. In the valley **La Maison du Bois et du Jouet**✻✻ is a vivid modern exhibition about wood, including toys from around the world.

MAZAMET✻

Mazamet Tourist Information *rue des Casernes; tel: 05 63 61 27 07. Open daily July–Aug; Mon–Sat Sept–June. Arranges factory visits in English daily (bookings required Sept–June).*

Although there are bargain leather shops on the northeast side of the town along avenue de la

Gateway to the Montagne Noire, Mazamet is a comparatively large industrial town with a pleasant part-pedestrianised centre. It thrives on its textile industry, which was originally established in the Arnette valley after the nearby hilltop village of Hautpoul was sacked.

Today the town is known particularly for dressing imported pelts. The process of separating wool from the hide of dead animals was developed locally during the 19th century and brought considerable prosperity. Grand mansions are dotted in the wooded hillsides around the town, owned by well-to-do families whose forbears made their fortunes then. The museum in **Maison Fuzier**✻ covers the Cathars and the area's many ruined castles.

Chevalière, few of the garments they sell are locally made.

 Maison Fuzier € 2 rue Henri Gardet; tel: 05 63 98 12 80. Open May–Oct Tue–Sat.

Market Tuesday and Saturday mornings.

Accommodation in Mazamet

Le Boulevard €€ *24 boulevard Soult; tel: 05 63 61 16 08.* Long-established 14-room hotel on the edge of the town centre with traditional cooking.

Mazamet

Mazamet's tanning and textile industries took off about 150 years ago by accident after some imported sheepskins went mouldy. This made the wool drop off the hide. No need to shear sheep if you can process the wool after the animals are dead – and you have the hide to tan as well. A group of local entrepreneurs perfected the technique and proceeded to buy up skins from around the world, importing them from as far afield as Australia and Argentina. The bonus was only having to pay knock-down prices as the sheep had been slaughtered for meat or because of disease.

REVEL❖❖❖

ℹ️ **Revel Tourist Information** *le Beffroi, place Philippe VI de Vallois; tel: 34 66 67 68; www.revel-lauragais.com. Open daily June–Sept; Tue–Sat Oct–May.* Ask for the excellent town trail leaflet.

Market Sat morning brims with local produce; around Christmas this is the place to buy ducks, geese and *foie gras*.

This attractive old town, laid out in *bastide* style, is one of the most striking in the area. Dating from 1342, it has a grid of straight streets around a large square surrounded by arcades supported by pillars of wood, brick or stone. Above them the attractive old buildings have decorative wrought-iron balconies. The splendid 600-year-old market hall, each side 40m long, in the centre has a tiled roof topped by a neo-classical belfry (which replaced an earlier one in 1830). Today the town is famous for its cabinet making, particularly marquetry and lacquerwork. This developed after Alexandre Monoury, a young craftsman from Versailles, set up a studio in 1888. Locally made furniture is on sale in workshops and shops. The **Conservatoire des Métiers du Bois**❖, where marquetry is taught, is open to the public.

ⓘ **Conservatoire des Métiers du Bois €**
13 rue Jean Moulin; tel: 05 61 27 65 50. Open daily. To buy furniture, try **Espace Art & Meuble**, tel: 05 61 83 56 58, at the roundabout on the road to Castelnaudary. Open Mon–Sat.

Accommodation and food in Revel

Auberge des Mazies €€ *route de Castres (on the D622 3km northeast of the town); tel: 05 61 27 69 70; e-mail: bienvenue@mazies.com. Closed mid-Oct–mid-Nov and Jan.* Comfortably converted old farmhouse (seven rooms) with regional cooking which includes *cassoulet grillé au flambadou* and *confit de canard*.

SAISSAC**

ⓘ **Saissac Tourist Information** *in the Musée des Vieux Métiers, I place des Tours; tel: 04 68 24 47 80. Open daily July–Aug; Wed–Fri Sept and May–June.*

ⓘ **Musée des Vieux Métiers €** *I place des Tours; tel: 04 68 24 47 80. Open daily July–Aug; Wed–Fri Sept and May–June.*

Perched on a ridge above the River Vernassonne, this large grey hillside village straggles beside the ruins of its 15th-century castle. The terrace on the ramparts provides a wonderful view south over the river gorge. The **Musée des Vieux Métiers*** in la Tour Grosse, part of the old ramparts, tells the history of the village and the Montagne Noire.

Food in Saissac

Auberge de Daguet €€ *Picarel le Haut (on the D4 just north of the village); tel: 04 68 24 44 08. Open daily (reservations essential).* Deer farm with rustic dining room specialising in venison. Farm visits available daily July–Aug, weekends Sept–June.

SOREZE**

ⓘ **Sorèze Tourist Information** *rue St Martin; tel: 05 63 74 16 28; www.ville-soreze.fr. Open daily.*

ⓘ **L'Abbaye-École €** *Tel: 05 63 50 86 38. Open daily.*

Previous page
Revel's covered market

Left
The Abbey-School of Sorèze

This little town on the edge of the Haut Languedoc Regional Park is best known for **L'Abbaye-Ecole****, its abbey school, which was founded in 1638 by Benedictine monks. King Louis XVI turned it into an elite military academy in 1776 but after the French Revolution it reverted to being a school. After many ups and downs, it finally closed in 1991 but the opulent buildings, including cloisters, huge reception rooms and the church are gradually being restored and some are open to the public. One wing has been transformed into a hotel. Only the bell tower of St-Martin, the original abbey nearby, survived the Wars of Religion in the 1570s. In the town centre the rows of half-timbered houses with upper floors overhanging the narrow streets mostly date from the 17th century.

Accommodation and food in Sorèze

Hostellerie de L'Abbaye-Logis des Pères €€ *6 rue Lacordaire; tel: 05 63 50 86 38.* Fifty-two rooms in the remarkable surroundings of the town's 17th-century former abbey school. Also a restaurant in the old refectory (*closed Tue*). A further 18 simpler but equally tasteful rooms are available in the Pavillon des Hôtes annexe €.

Suggested tour

Total distance: 145km. The detour to Arfons adds 20km and the detour to Hautpoul adds 8km.

Time: 5 hours' driving. Allow at least a day for the main route, more with detours. Those with limited time should concentrate on the stretch between Revel and Fontbruno.

Above
Revel

Opposite
Sorèze

Links to other tours: From Revel the D622 leads west to St-Félix-Lauragais (*see page 170*), 10km away. From Mazamet the N112 leads northwest to Castres (*see page 184*), 17km away.

Head northwest through **Carcassonne's** industrial outskirts on the N113, forking right on to the D629 with the distant hills of the Montagne Noire to the right. Pause in **Montolieu** to look in the village church with its distinctive Stations of the Cross paintings. After crossing the River Alzeau you begin the scenic climb over rolling farmland to **SAISSAC** ❶ .

Detour: Arfons, a delightful mountain village of slate-roofed houses (10km north of Saissac on the D4), was once owned by the Knights of St John. The octagonal tower of its 17th-century church is unusual as the four sides most exposed to the weather are covered by large slate tiles. The village, in the heart of the Montagne Noire, is popular with walkers – the GR7 long-distance footpath passes through it. On the way there the D4 passes close to the **Bassin du Lampy**, a large reservoir created between 1778 and 1782 to provide more water for the Canal du Midi which needed extra supplies after the opening of the Robine branch to Narbonne. The beech woods around the Bassin are ideal for a walk in the shade. At the start of the turn off to Arfons, look out for the deer farm/restaurant (on the right) at **Picarel le Haut**, where 300 deer are reared in wooded parkland.

La Renaissance €€
St-Ferréol; tel: 05 61 83 51 50; www.hotellarenaissance.com. Open mid-Mar–mid-Nov. Seventeen-room family-run hotel scenically situated near the lake and its beach. Garden and playground.

From Saissac the D629 continues northwest past the **Barrage des Cammazes**, a dam built across the River Sor to create a reservoir to supply drinking water and irrigate the fertile Lauragais plain east of Toulouse. Beyond it the D629 passes the pretty **Bassin de St-Ferréol** lake shortly before **REVEL**.

From Revel take the D85 east to **SOREZE ❷**. **Durfort**, the neighbouring village, has revived the local tradition of copper-beating and you can call at one of the workshops making pots and pans. From Sorèze the D85 continues to **DOURGNE ❸** past a huge quarry which has made a real scar on the landscape. On the far side of Dourgne, just after passing the two monasteries at **Calcat**, turn right to go up an unnumbered road through **Massaguel** to **Fontbruno**. During World War II the Resistance was active in this hilly area, making full use of the thick cover provided by the beeches, oaks and firs of its forests. On reaching the D56, turn right briefly to see the big **Resistance memorial** which commemorates the heroism of the local men who died harassing the Germans. Turn round and follow the D56 to its junction with the D53 to go into **MAZAMET ❹**.

Detour: Leave Mazamet on the D54 and then turn right (as signed) past disused tanneries – somewhat depressing – and wind up to the hilltop village of **HAUTPOUL ❺**.

The D118 from Mazamet is a pleasingly quiet main road and very scenic, climbing through wooded hillsides. Beyond **Les Martys** the countryside opens out with views ahead to the Corbières hills. There's a southern feel to the vegetation and villages as the road runs south along the ridges back towards Carcassonne, before finally dropping down into the busy northern outskirts of the town.

Below
The Canal du Midi

Getting out of the car

Surrounded by wooded hillsides, the Bassin de St-Ferréol is the main water source for the Canal du Midi. As the water is crystal clear, it is popular for swimming in summer as well as for sailing and windsurfing. A shaded footpath goes round its banks and across the 800m-long dam. The full circuit, passing a park with waterfalls, takes about an hour to walk round. At the eastern end, there is an attractive beach with sand and children's boats. There's a large car park on the D629 near the beach.

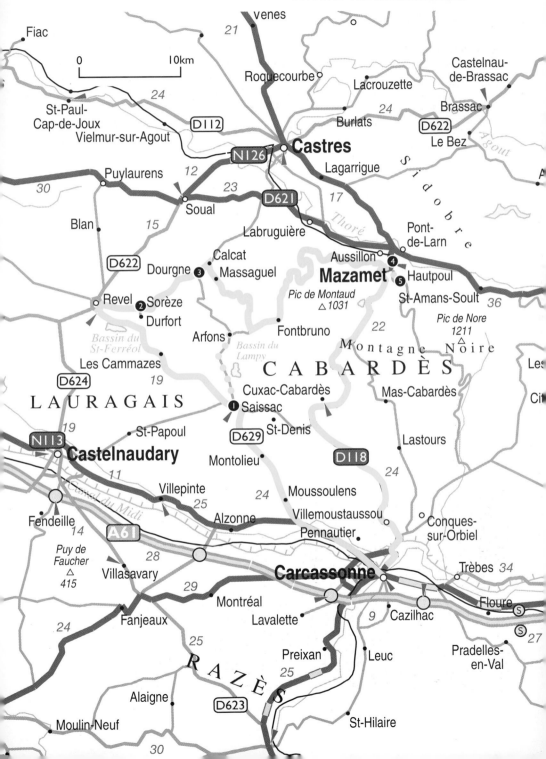

Fiac

0   10km

Venes

Roquecourbe

Lacrouzette

Castelnau-de-Brassac

24

St-Paul-Cap-de-Joux

Vielmur-sur-Agout

D112

Burlats

Brassac

D622

Le Bez

Agout

Puylaurens

12

N126

Castres

Lagarrigue

Sidobre

30

23

Soual

D621

17

Thoré

Pont-de-Larn

Blan

15

Labruguière

Aussillon

Mazamet ④

D622

Dourgne ③

Calcat

Massaguel

Mazamet

Hautpoul ⑤

Revel ② Sorèze

Durfort

Pic de Montaud
△ 1031

St-Amans-Soult

36

Bassin du St-Ferréol

Arfons

Bassin du Lampy

Fontbruno

22

Pic de Nore
1211
△

Montagne Noire

C A B A R D È S

Les

Les Cammazes

D624

19

Cuxac-Cabardès

Mas-Cabardès

Ci

L A U R A G A I S

① Saissac

St-Denis

Lastours

19

N113

St-Papoul

D629

Montolieu

D118

24

Castelnaudary

Villepinte

24

Moussoulens

Canal du Midi

11

25

Alzonne

Villemoustaussou

Conques-sur-Orbiel

Fendeille

14

A61

Pennautier

Puy de Faucher
△
415

28

Villasavary

Trèbes *34*

Carcassonne

Floure Ⓢ

29

Montréal

9

Cazilhac

Fanjeaux

Lavalette

Ⓢ

24

25

Preixan

Leuc

Pradelles-en-Val

R A Z È S

25

Alaigne

D623

Moulin-Neuf

St-Hilaire

30

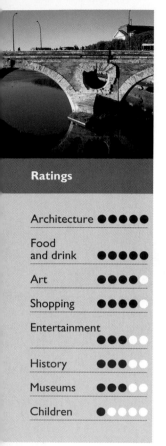

Toulouse

Ratings

Architecture ●●●●●

Food
and drink   ●●●●●

Art   ●●●●○

Shopping   ●●●●○

Entertainment
             ●●●○○

History   ●●●○○

Museums   ●●●○○

Children   ●○○○○

Thanks largely to its highly successful aircraft industry, Toulouse is a thriving modern city – France's fourth largest. Woad production (to make blue dye) made it rich in the 17th century after 200 years of skirmishing, the plague and a disastrous fire. The magnificent residences that remain from that time are built in brick, giving the city its nickname – *la ville rose*. The colourful skyline is at its most vivid in the setting sun and best seen from the left bank of the broad River Garonne which curves its way past the city centre. The Canal du Midi sweeps around it on the other side, linked to the river by the short Canal de la Brienne, so there's plenty of opportunity for waterside strolling. Months of sunshine also enable Toulousains to make the most of the terrace restaurants and the city's renowned cuisine.

Getting there and getting around

ⓘ Toulouse Tourist Information *Donjon du Capitole; tel: 05 61 11 02 22; e-mail: infos@ot-toulouse.fr; www.ot-toulouse.com. Open daily all year.*

The most straightforward routes into the city centre from the autoroute system which encircles it are from the west and north, particularly exit 30 (Ponts Jumeaux).

Airport: Toulouse-Blagnac is 10km west of the city centre. There are flights to 20 domestic airports and various European ones including London Heathrow and Gatwick. Buses run every 20 minutes to the city centre Mon–Fri (weekend frequency depends on flights) with stops at the bus station (next to the Matibau railway station), allée Jean Jaurès, places Jeanne d'Arc and Compans Caffarelli. Information can be found on the ground floor of Hall 2; *tel: 05 34 60 64 00* (Les Courriers de la Garonne shuttle bus).

Buses and the Métro services, with interchangeable zoned tickets, are run by Semvat; *tel: 05 61 41 70 70*. Carnets of ten tickets are best value. Trains are frequent on the Métro line and it is easy to use.

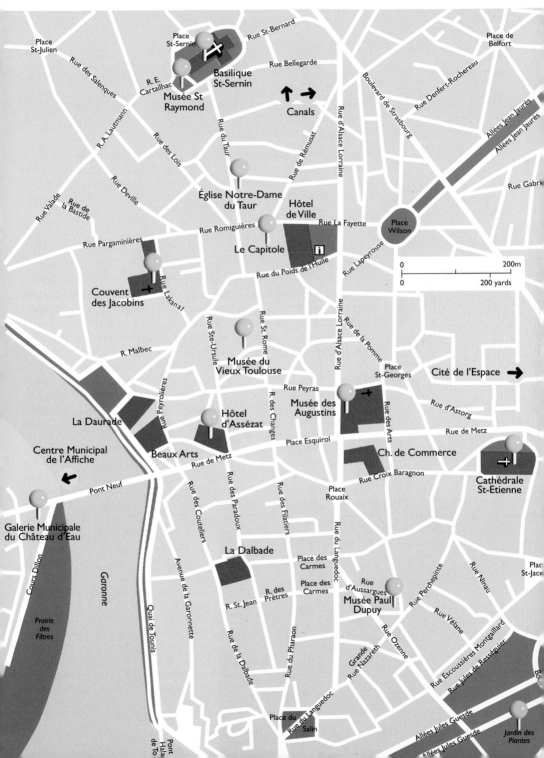

Place St-Julien

Rue des Salenques

R. A. Lautmann

Rue des Lois

Rue Deville

Rue Valade

Rue de la Bastide

Rue Pargaminières

R. E. Cartailhac

Place St-Sernin

Rue St-Bernard

Rue Bellegarde

Rue Denfert-Rochereau

Place de Belfort

Musée St Raymond

Basilique St-Sernin

Rue du Taur

Rue de Rémusat

Rue d'Alsace Lorraine

Boulevard de Strasbourg

Allées Jean Jaurès

Allées Jean Jaurès

Rue Gabri

Canals

Église Notre-Dame du Taur

Hôtel de Ville

Rue La Fayette

Place Wilson

Rue Romiguières

Le Capitole

Rue du Poids de l'Huile

Rue Lapeyrouse

0   200m
0   200 yards

Couvent des Jacobins

Rue Lakanal

Rue Ste-Ursule

Rue St. Rome

R. Malbec

Musée du Vieux Toulouse

Rue d'Alsace Lorraine

Rue de la Pomme

Place St-Georges

Cité de l'Espace

Rue Peyras

Rue Peyrolières

R. des Changes

Musée des Augustins

Rue des Arts

Rue d'Astorg

Rue de Metz

La Daurade

Hôtel d'Assézat

Place Esquirol

Ch. de Commerce

Centre Municipal de l'Affiche

Beaux Arts

Rue de Metz

Rue Croix Baragnon

Cathédrale St-Etienne

Pont Neuf

Rue des Couteliers

Rue des Paradoux

Rue des Filatiers

Place Rouaix

Galerie Municipale du Château d'Eau

Cours Dillon

Garonne

Avenue de la Garonnette

Quai de Tounis

La Dalbade

R. des Prêtres

R. St. Jean

Place des Carmes

Place des Carmes

Rue du Languedoc

Rue d'Aussargues

Musée Paul Dupuy

Rue Perchepinte

Rue Ninau

Plac St-Jac

Prairie des Filtres

Rue de la Dalbade

Rue du Pharaon

Grande Rue Nazareth

Rue Ozenne

Rue Vélane

Rue Escoussières Montgaillard

Rue Jules de Ressiguier

Pont Hala de To

Place du Salin

Rue du Languedoc

Allées Jules Guesde

Allées Jules Guesde

Jardin des Plantes

Basilique St-Sernin
place Sernin;
tel: 05 61 21 80 45.

Parking: Though the city boasts 10,000 parking spaces, on-street places in the centre are hard to find (most are pay-and-display but free Sunday) so head for an underground car park. The handiest for sightseeing and shopping are at place Victor Hugo and place du Capitole from which the main sights are all within walking distance. Or you can park free at either end of the Métro underground line which crosses the city centre.

Rail: The main railway station, Gare Matabiau, is in boulevard Pierre Sémard, just across the Canal du Midi from the centre. Facilities include car hire and showers. Four TGV trains a day connect with Paris (5 hours). Overnight Motorail services daily to and from Paris.

Cycle hire: *Holiday Bikes, 9 boulevard des Minimes; tel: 05 34 25 79 62; e-mail: contact@holiday-bikes.com*

Sights

The city's most interesting sights are compactly gathered within the centre which is encircled by grand boulevards and has the River Garonne cutting through its west side. Be prepared for a lengthy walk to see them all on foot. Allow time, too, for the distractions offered by the shops and pavement cafés on the way.

Basilique St-Sernin***
This massive Romanesque cathedral – all that remains of an 11th-century monastery on the pilgrimage route to Santiago de Compostela – is one of the most beautiful churches in France. Built in pink brick and yellow stone, it is crowned by a 65m-high octagonal bell tower which has five elegant tiers of arched windows topped by a spire. Inside, honey-coloured stone sets off a high barrel-vaulted nave and prettily vaulted galleries. After much public debate, the 'improvements' made during the 19th century by Viollet-le-Duc were removed during repairs, so the building is now back to its superb original state.

Below
St-Sernin

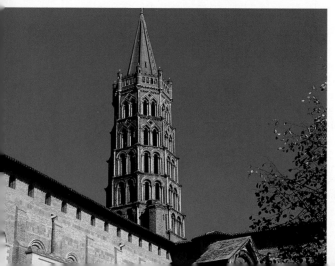

Canals**
The first section of the Canal du Midi linking the city with the Mediterranean was opened in May 1681. Ninety years later it was linked to the River Garonne by the short Canal de la Brienne. Then in 1856 its second 'leg', the Lateral Canal, was completed, extending it to the Atlantic at Bordeaux. The twin

River cruises aboard *Baladines*; tel: 05 61 80 52 28; www.bateaux-toulous-ans.com. Lunch and dinner cruises aboard restaurant-boat *Occitania*; boulevard Bonrepos; tel: 05 61 63 06 06; www.loccitania.com

Le Capitole place du Capitole; tel: 05 61 22 34 12. Interior rooms open Mon–Fri Sat–Sun by reservation only.

Cathédrale St-Etienne place St-Etienne; tel: 05 61 52 03 82. Treasury in the crypt €.

Centre Municipal de l'Affiche €€ Espace St-Cyprien, 58 allées Charles-de-Fitte; tel: 05 61 59 24 64. Open Mon–Fri all year.

Cité de l'Espace €€ avenue Jean Gonord; tel: 05 62 71 48 71; www.cite-espace.com. Open daily Feb–Aug; Tue–Sun Sept–Jan. Twenty-minute journey by Métro to Jolimont, then No 37 bus, or take exit 17 from the autoroute.

Couvent des Jacobins place des Jacobins; tel: 05 61 22 21 92. Refectory open daily.

bridges at the river basin, built in 1774, are decorated with an elaborate bas-relief in white marble by François Lucas, a local sculptor. For a walk or cycle ride along the shaded tow-path, head northwest rather than southeast where the countryside around is very flat.

Le Capitole**

The town hall, named after the *capitouls* – consuls – who once ran the city on behalf of the often absent Count of Toulouse, is an impressive symmetrical 18th-century building in pink brick and white stone with three rows of windows and a balustrade along the top. Inside, several appropriately grand rooms, Salles des Illustres, hung with paintings depicting the city's history are open to the public. Across a courtyard, the tourist office occupies part of the original keep.

Cathédrale St-Etienne**

Red brick outside, grey stone inside, the city's other cathedral took several centuries to build because of financial problems – and it shows! The mixture of styles, starting in the 11th century, combine to make an interesting if rather odd unity and it now needs more money for restoration. Pierre-Paul Riquet (*see page 199*), who built the Canal du Midi, is buried in front of the massive stone pillar which stands between the unaligned chancel and gloomy nave where tapestries tell the story of Etienne (Stephen).

Centre Municipal de l'Affiche*

Posters and postcards are the subject of this unusual modern museum. Annual exhibitions are devoted to contemporary graphic artists.

Cité de l'Espace***

This exciting space park is a showcase for the city's aviation achievements during the 20th century. Its highlights are full-scale models of the Ariane 5 rocket on its launch pad and the Mir Space Station which shows the cramped conditions for the astronauts on board. There are plenty of buttons and computer screens, so budding young scientists – and adults – can experience what it's like to launch a rocket and 'post' a satellite. There's also a planetarium.

Couvent des Jacobins***

The only decorative feature of this huge fortress-like church, built in countless thin bricks with slits for windows, is its five-tier hexagonal belfry. Founded in honour of St Dominic's visit to preach in the city in 1230, it has a massive nave with two beautiful rose windows which is a Southern Gothic masterpiece. Huge grey columns rise along each side to ribbed vaults like palm trees; indeed the most distinctive is known as the *palmier des Jacobins*. The tomb of St Thomas Aquinas, one of Toulouse University's first and most illustrious students, lies beneath the altar.

Eglise Notre-Dame du Taur *rue du Taur.*

Galerie Municipale du Château d'Eau € *1 place Laganne; tel: 05 61 77 09 40; www. galeriechateaudeau.org. Open afternoons Tue–Sat all year.*

Hôtel d'Assézat €€ *place d'Assézat; tel: 05 61 12 06 89. Open Tue–Sun all year, including Thur evenings.*

Jardin des Plantes and **Musée d'Histoire Naturelle** € *35 allées Jules Guesdes; tel: 05 62 27 48 48.*

Musée des Augustins € *21 rue de Metz; tel: 05 61 22 21 82. Open Wed–Mon all year (organ concert on Wed evenings).*

The church and its convent buildings have had a considerably more diverse use than most. Napoleon gave it to one of his artillery regiments as a barracks. The soldiers and their 300 horses made themselves nicely at home, finding the beautiful arcaded cloisters ideal as a paddock and using the chapterhouse as a smithy. In the church itself they put in an extra mezzanine floor, blocked up the windows and demolished most of the side chapels. Not surprisingly the restoration work after they left in 1864 took a lot of effort and time but finally the church was reconsecrated in 1974. The chapterhouse is used for concerts and the refectory for exhibitions.

Eglise Notre-Dame du Taur*
This old church is notable for its decorative brickwork, particularly its turret-like bell tower and façade of mitred arches in Southern Gothic style which was subsequently copied in other churches throughout the area. It stands at the place where St Sernin, who brought Christianity to the city, died a martyr's death after denouncing paganism. He is reputed to have been dragged across the city attached to a bull.

Galerie Municipale du Château d'Eau**
The city's former water tower, built in 1822 to purify the local water, was adapted in 1974 to become a photographic gallery which regularly stages special exhibitions. It has also built up a unique archive on the history of photography.

Hôtel d'Assézat***
This is one of the most impressive of about 80 grand mansions built by wealthy merchants and lawyers during the boom times of the 16th century. Designed around a large courtyard by a well-known Renaissance architect, Nicholas Bachelier, it now houses the Fondation Bemberg art collection built up by Georges Bemberg, a local industrialist. On show there since 1995, it includes works by great masters such as Tintoretto, Canaletto and Gauguin. A whole room is devoted to Pierre Bonnard's paintings.

Jardin des Plantes*
These formally laid-out gardens are an oasis of greenery with their avenues of flowerbeds and ponds. The **Musée d'Histoire Naturelle** in them is renowned for its collection of stuffed monkeys. One room is devoted to skeletons and it is fascinating to compare their shapes and sizes when you see all the bones but no skin.

Musée des Augustins**
The Musée des Augustins occupies another of Toulouse's former monasteries. The 600-year-old building itself is of interest as well as its contents. The rooms display decorative stonework, sculptures and paintings from the Middle Ages collected from various places,

Musée Paul Dupuy
€ 13 rue de la Pleau
(corner of rue Ozenne); tel:
05 61 14 65 50. Open
Wed–Mon all year.

Musée St-Raymond €
place St-Sernin; tel: 05 61
22 31 44. Open daily all
year.

**Musée du Vieux
Toulouse** € 7 rue du May;
tel: 05 62 27 11 50. Open
Mon–Sat mid-May–mid-Oct.

particularly churches, in the region. The large garden in the centre of the cloister is planted with vegetables and herbs that would have been grown in medieval abbeys. A row of gargoyles along one side of it provides a rare close-up of these decorative stone creatures which are normally at roof level serving as water spouts.

Musée Paul Dupuy⁕

This small 17th-century mansion contains an exquisite collection of antique silver, china, scientific instruments and clocks (still keeping good time) donated to the city by M Dupuy, a local collector, in 1944. One section is a reconstructed pharmacy with old-fashioned medicine bottles and jars.

Musée St-Raymond⁕⁕

One of France's most comprehensive collections of Greek, Roman and local antiquities including sculpture, stone carvings and pottery can be found in a medieval building, itself classed as a 'Monument Historique' having been built as a hospice for pilgrims at the same time as St-Sernin cathedral opposite.

Musée du Vieux Toulouse⁕

Housed in a fine 16th-century mansion, l'Hôtel Dumay, this museum tells the story of Toulouse, its personalities, institutions, crafts and customs, mainly though paintings, sculptures and pottery.

Shopping

Pharmacie de nuit
Late night chemist,
70–76 allées Jean Jaurès
(enter from rue Arnaud
Vidal); tel: 05 61 62 38 05.

The city has some memorable markets such as the one which sells food and wine in **Victor Hugo market hall** and the open-air **Marché des Boulevards** along the boulevard de Strasbourg whose stalls are colourfully piled with fruit and vegetables. Both operate daily except Monday. Place du Capitole has markets on Tuesday, Wednesday and Saturday. Bric-à-brac stalls surround St Sernin at weekends. Place St Etienne is taken over by books on Saturdays. In addition place du Parlement is the scene of a seasonal garlic market from the end of August to mid-October.

The main shopping area, including several department stores, is along rue d'Alsace Lorraine (**Galeries Lafayette** is at the northern end). The more exclusive clothes shops are off it in rue de la Pomme and rue des Arts. Crystallised violets are a local speciality; **Yves Thuriès**, 69 rue d'Alsace, claims to have the best in France.

Bricks galore

Toulouse, 'la ville rose', got its nickname from the colour of its many brick buildings though they range from beige through pink to russet and red. The scarcity of stone available in the area first prompted the Romans to make the characteristic long thin bricks out of the local clay. Originally these were made by hand, as in Italy, in wooden moulds, giving Toulouse the most Italian look of any city in France. In 1555, following a series of fires, a bye-law required all new buildings to be built in brick or stone rather than wood. As brick is light and mortar sticks to it easily, masons were able to construct churches with wide vaults that could span a single nave. This became the main feature of the Southern Gothic style of architecture.

Rugby fans can invest in the local strip on sale at **Éspace Stade Toulousain** at No 75 rue d'Alsace.

Entertainment

The city boasts ten theatres including **Halle aux Grains** (*place Dupuy; tel: 05 61 62 02 70; www.onct.mairie-toulouse.fr*), which stages opera and ballet, and **Théâtre du Capitole** (*place du Capitole; tel: 05 61 63 13 13; web: www.theatre-du-capitole.org*), the home of lighter music, particularly operetta and dance. **Stade Toulousain**, where the city's famous rugby club plays, is on an island in the River Garonne. The weekly listings magazine *Toulouse by Night* is on sale at newsagents.

In June the **Garonna** is a one-day event on the river when up to a hundred home-made rafts are raced by costumed sailors to the Pont Neuf.

The four-day **Rio Loco Festival** featuring riverside concerts is also in June, followed by **Toulouse d'Été** when music of all kinds is performed in various venues.

During October an Organ Festival highlights the importance of the town's historic organs.

Accommodation and food

A good selection of centrally situated two-star hotels in smartly renovated old buildings is to be found around place du Capitole and place Wilson. Modern hotels, with the advantage of easier parking, are along allée Jean Jaurès or further out.

Best Western Les Capitouls Jean Jaurès €€ *29 allées Jean Jaurès; tel: 05 34 41 31 21.* A friendly but businesslike hotel – not at all grand – with typically French atmosphere. Situated on the edge of the main shopping area.

Grand Hôtel de l'Opéra €€€ *1 place du Capitole; tel: 05 61 21 82 66.* The city's grandest hotel is centrally situated in a stately 17th-century building which began life as a monastery. Fifty rooms.

Hôtel des Beaux Arts €€ *1 place du Pont Neuf; tel: 05 34 45 42 42.* Overlooking the River Garonne, this is an exclusive little hotel with smart décor and attentive service. Nineteen rooms.

Hôtel St-Sernin € *2 rue St-Bernard; tel: 05 61 21 73 08.* Small, impeccably furnished hotel in a quiet street near St-Sernin cathedral. Four rooms have splendid views of its tower. Eighteen rooms.

Hôtel Sofitel €€€ *84 allée Jean Jaurès; tel: 05 61 10 23 10*. All the comforts of a large modern hotel within a 5-minute stroll of the main shops and restaurants. Non-smoking floors and parking. One hundred and nineteen rooms.

The Toulousains have a reputation for being both gourmands and gourmets. Two hundred years ago they formed the first gastronomic association in France and you can always rely on eating copiously and well. Duck, goose and fish are served in abundance and the local sausages are without equal. So, too, is the *foie gras* spiked with truffles and baked in flaky pastry. Brasserie restaurants spill out on to most of the squares. Some, particularly around place du Capitole, are ideal for watching the world go by but others, such as those around place Wilson and place St-Georges, are more intimate.

Le Bibent €€ *5 place Capitole; tel: 05 61 23 89 03*, is a *belle époque* brasserie, good for shellfish.

Le Bon Vivre € *15 place Wilson; tel: 05 61 23 07 17*, is a small friendly restaurant serving local specialities, popular with local people.

Brasserie des Beaux Arts Flo €€, *1 quai de la Dorade; tel: 05 61 21 12 12*. Bustling Parisian-style brasserie with efficient service, plush bench seats and gilded mirrors. Strong on oysters and seafood, as well as local dishes.

Café Garona €€ *quai de la Daurade; tel: 05 61 22 72 27*, is on a scenically moored boat near the Pont Neuf and has a comprehensive menu.

Sept Place St-Sernin €€€ *7 place St-Sernin; tel: 05 62 30 05 30*. Chic modern restaurant in a secluded setting opposite the cathedral. Its set menus are strong on seafood.

Taverne de Maître Kanter € *54 allée Jean Jaurès; tel: 05 62 73 16 16; www.tmk-toulouse.com*. Two hundred and fifty places. Open 24 hours, specialising in sea food, sauerkraut and regional dishes.

Below
L'Hôtel d'Assézat

Le Van Gogh € *21 place St-Georges; tel: 05 61 21 03 15*. Small brasserie in shaded square. Enormous salads.

Villa Tropezienne €€ *8–10 place Victor Hugo; tel: 05 61 22 58 58*. Matelot-dressed waiters scurry to serve Provençal dishes, especially fish, from a simple menu. Jolly atmosphere enhanced by photographs of sunny St-Trop.

Suggested walk

Length: 3km.

Duration: An hour just to go round, but allow a full day to see all the sights.

Aérospatiale *Usine Clément Ader, Colomiers.* Airbus/ Concorde factory visits are organised daily except Sun by Taxiway, *tel: 05 61 18 06 01*, and foreign visitors must book eight days in advance with passport details.

L'Aérothèque *rue Montmorency, Toulouse; tel: 05 61 93 93 57*; an aircraft museum next to the Airbus factory. *Visits Wed 1400–1700.*

Toulouse's canals

The Canal du Midi was first filled with water on 19 May, 1681. After being blessed by the Archbishop of Toulouse, it was inaugurated by Pierre-Paul Riquet, the pioneering engineer who had the grand idea of linking the Mediterranean at Sète with the Atlantic at Bordeaux. He set off with his two sons in a large state boat followed by 23 others for Sète.

From the terrace café at the top of **Nouvelles Galeries**, on the corner of rue Lapeyrouse and rue Alsace-Lorraine, you can survey the whole the city centre, so it makes a good starting point. Directly below is **place Wilson** with its fountains and shady park benches on one side and the **Donjon du Capitole** (for information and maps at the tourist office) on the other. Admire the bronze **Occitan cross** surrounded by signs of the zodiac on the huge traffic-free square in front of the **CAPITOLE ❶** (unless it's market day), then head for the arcade on the west side where the city's history is depicted on the ceiling in 29 colourful panels painted by Raymond Moretti in 1997.

Little seems to have changed at the **Hôtel du Balcon** at the corner with rue Romiguières since Antoine de Saint-Exupéry, author of the children's classic *Le Petit Prince*, lived there in the 1920s. Famous also as a pilot, he disappeared on a flight in 1944.

The straight narrow rue du Taur of small shops and cafés leads to **BASILIQUE ST-SERNIN ❷** which stands in the centre of a leafy square. This area on the north side of the centre was originally the clergy district. As you make your way to place du Peyrou and place Anatole France, notice that it is now dotted with university buildings. Continue along the rue de la Bastide, rue Pargaminières and rue Lakanal to the **COUVENT DES JACOBINS ❸**.

You are now in the 'merchant' district where several of the splendid Renaissance *hôtels particuliers* (mansions) built by the woad merchants are situated. Look out for **Hôtels de Bernuy** (now a school) in rue Peyrolières and **Assézat** (Fondation Bemberg gallery). There are no fewer than 84 old mansions dotted around the city centre including about ten along rue de la Dalbade, the lawyers' district. Turning along rue St Jean Piètres Carmes, you come to one of the most impressive, the **Hôtel du Vieux Raisin**.

Rue Perchepinte and rue Ferma, elegant quiet streets with antique shops, lead to **CATHEDRALE ST-ETIENNE ❹**. After you cross the busy rue de Metz, rue d'Astorg will take you to **place St-Georges** where you might want to linger at a pavement café before facing the temptations of the haute couture shops along rue de la Pomme or look for more affordable items along rue d'Alsace Lorraine.

Also worth exploring

A tour of **Aérospatiale's Clément-Ader factory**✷✷ where Airbuses are made is not just for aircraft enthusiasts. Looking down from a platform above the factory floor and seeing these huge planes taking shape is mind-boggling. You can also go into the paintshop and the unloading bay of the Super Guppy cargo plane which ferries parts around the world.

Place St-Julien

Rue des Salenques

R. E. Cartailhac

Place St-Sernin

Rue St-Bernard

Basilique St-Sernin

Rue Bellegarde

Place de Belfort

Boulevard de Strasbourg

Rue Denfert-Rochereau

Allées Jean Jaurès

Allées Jean Jaurès

R. A. Lautmann

Rue des Lois

Rue Deville

Rue du Taur

Rue d'Alsace Lorraine

Rue de Rémusat

Rue Gabriel

Boulevard Lazare Carnot

Rue Valade

Rue de la Bastide

Rue Pargaminières

Rue Romiguières

Hôtel de Ville

Rue La Fayette

Place Wilson

Couvent des Jacobins

Le Capitole

Rue du Poids de l'Huile

Rue Lapeyrouse

Rue Maurice Fonvieille

Rue Lakanal

R. Malbec

Rue Ste-Ursule

Rue St. Rome

Rue d'Alsace Lorraine

Rue de la Pomme

0   200m
0   200 yards

Rue Peyrolières

Rue des Changes

Rue Peyras

Musée des Augustins

Place St-Georges

Rue d'Astorg

La Daurade

Hôtel d'Assézat

Place Esquirol

Rue des Arts

Rue de Metz

Beaux Arts

Rue de Metz

Ch. de Commerce

Cathédrale St-Etienne

Allées t. verdier

Pont Neuf

Rue des Couteliers

Rue des Paradoux

Rue des Filatiers

Rue Croix Baragnon

Place Rouaix

Rue du Languedoc

Rue Perchepinte

Rue Ninau

Place St-Jacques

Cours Dillon

Garonne

Quai de Tounis

Avenue de la Garonnette

La Dalbade

Place des Carmes

Place des Carmes

Rue d'Aussargues

Rue Ozenne

Rue Vélane

Rue Escoussières Montgaillard

Rue Jules de Ressèguier

Prairie des Filtres

R. St. Jean

R. des Prêtres

Rue de la Dalbade

Rue du Pharaon

Rue du Languedoc

Grande Rue Nazareth

Place du Salin

Allées Jules Guesde

Allées Jules Guesde

Jardin des Plantes

Gro Ro

Boulingrin

Pont de Tou
Halage

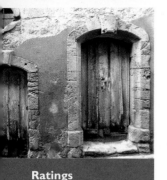

The land of milk and honey

Ratings

Canal	●●●●●
Churches	●●●●●
Architecture	●●●●○
Food	●●●●○
History	●●●●○
Restaurants	●●●○○
Scenery	●●●○○
Shopping	●●●○○

This is an easy and relaxing route to drive as the area is mainly flat. The roads are often straight and quiet, with long lines of plane trees on both sides. The Canal du Midi, however, and a few gentle hills ensure plenty of variety.

During the 16th century, the area became known as the Pays de Cocagne – the land of milk and honey – as the demand for *pastel* (woad) to make blue dye, then the fashionable colour, brought it considerable prosperity. Local farmers grew the plant in profusion, but now the rich soil is mainly devoted to vegetables.

Although Pamiers is the largest town, with good shops, the gem of the route is Mirepoix with its colourful half-timbered houses and arcades. St-Félix is another highlight, particularly in April when its Foire au Pastel turns back the clock to celebrate the great times of woad.

CASTELNAUDARY❖❖

❶ Castelnaudary Tourist Information *I place République;*
tel: 04 68 23 05 73;
www.ville-castelnaudary.fr.
Open all year.

❶ Musée du Présidial
€ I0 rue du Présidial;
tel: 04 68 23 00 42.
Open daily July–Aug.

This is very much a canal town, having thrived since the **Canal du Midi**❖❖❖ was cut through it in the 1660s. The council's decision to contribute 30,000 francs to bring it to the foot of the town proved to be a very far-sighted move.

The canal's Grand Bassin, actually more a lake than a basin, used to be a busy commercial port. Now it is used by pleasure craft and there is a constant coming and going of boats all summer. At any time of year the banks are a pleasant place to stroll, especially when the spire of Eglise St-Michel and the red tiled roofs of the houses round it are reflected in the water.

The canal's arrival enabled the town to build up pottery and brick industries. Several workshops are open to visitors and sell 'seconds'. The **Musée du Présidial**❖, in a former courthouse/prison overlooking the town, has a series of exhibitions about the area including its potteries. Among the items made in them are *cassoles*, the shallow terracotta bowls which gave their name to *cassoulet*, the town's famous

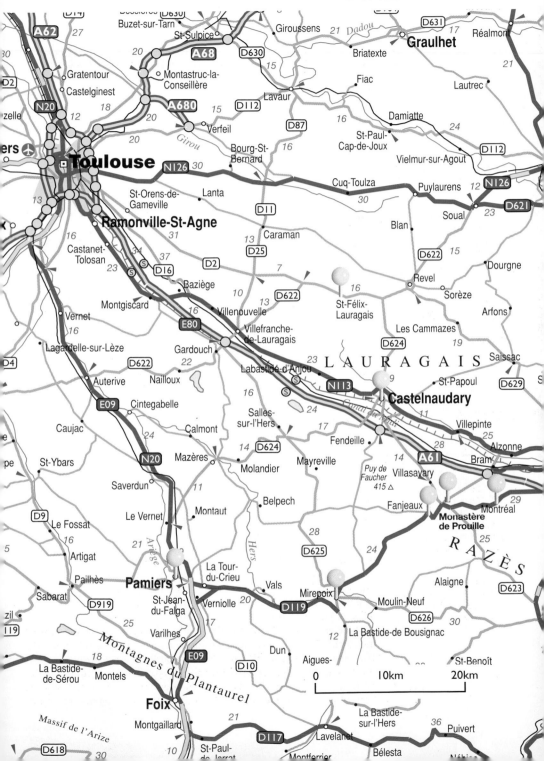

Canal du Midi holiday cruisers can be hired from **Crown Blue Line**; *tel: 04 68 94 52 72; www.crownblueline.com.* Short trips on **Le Saint-Roch** cruiser from the quai du Port, *Apr–Oct.* A website describes, in English, the facilities for enjoying the canal: *www.midicanal.com*

Moulin de Cugarel € *Open July–Aug. To organise a visit, tel: 04 68 23 15 88.*

There is a market on Mondays.

Cassoulet A website describes the delights of cassoulet, including recipes, in English at *www.cassoulet.com/anglais*

Below Mirepoix: covered arcades

thick pork and bean stew (though both Toulouse and Carcassonne also claim to have invented it). Two other local specialities, *Alleluias* and *Glorias*, are found, not in a church, but at the Pâtisserie Belloc, *48 rue du 11 Novembre.* They are small cakes flavoured with *cédrat*, a kind of grapefruit, which were named in honour of Pope Pius VII's Easter visit shortly after one of Napoleon's soldiers imported the recipe in 1800.

The town has few major sights, though the Eglise St-Michel has a 56m-high belfry, beautiful rose windows and an 18th-century organ built by the Cavaillé-Colls, a Gaillac family who were responsible for installing more than 600 instruments in the area between 1709 and 1889. The **Moulin de Cugarel**✦, a 300-year-old restored windmill complete with milling machinery, stands on a breezy hillside on the northern edge of the town overlooking flat farmland. Originally it was one of a ring of flour mills round the town powered by water from the canal.

Accommodation and food in Castelnaudary

Hôtel de France €€ *2 avenue Frédéric Mistral, Castelnaudary; tel: 04 68 23 10 18; www.cassoulet.com.* Comfortable family-run 12-room hotel well placed in town centre. Guests who enjoy the chef's award-winning *cassoulet* and other local dishes can buy them tinned to take home.

Cassoulet

Pork, mutton, sausage and haricot beans are the key ingredients of *cassoulet* which has been described as *le dieu occitan* (the Occitan God). One of the area's most famous and filling dishes, it is a thick stew whose distinctive flavour owes much to goose fat and the local pink garlic.

Traditionally prepared and served in a *cassole* (the shallow terracotta bowl glazed only on the inside from which it got its name), it is by no means straightforward to cook as several lengthy stages are involved, including soaking, boiling and frying.

Castelnaudary is generally regarded as being its birthplace, though Carcassonne and Toulouse also claim the honour. Restaurants throughout the area feature it on their menus, but it can also be enjoyed at home without effort as supermarkets and butchers sell it in tins – usually the meat and juices in one and the beans in another.

FANJEAUX❖❖

ⓘ Fanjeaux Tourist Information *place du Triel; tel: 04 68 24 75 45. Open July–mid-Sept.*

Enjoying a magnificent view of the Montagne Noire (Black Mountain) this little hilltop town of narrow streets clusters around a covered market hall and the Notre Dame de l'Assomption church. The hill was a sacred place for the Romans; hence the town's name which means Temple of Jupiter in Latin. The town also has close connections with St Dominic who founded the Dominican order. You can visit his 'bed-chamber', now a chapel but originally the saddlery of a castle which has long gone. In the church, be sure to look at the *'miracle du feu'* beam in the St-Dominic chapel. It was scorched in 1203 when Dominic de Guzman, as he then was, settled a theological dispute between Catholics and Cathars. To test their opposing views, he burned their texts. The Cathar version ended up as ashes but the Catholic one flew up intact, scorching the beam. Park your car on the edge of the old quarter and walk as the streets are very narrow.

MIREPOIX❖❖❖

ⓘ Mirepoix Tourist Information *place Maréchal Leclerc; tel: 05 61 68 83 76; www.ot-mirepoix.fr. Open daily July–Aug; Mon–Sat Sept–June.*

This attractive little town is a typical *bastide*, built in the shape of a grid around a central square which has a covered market hall with a splendid 19th-century cast-iron roof. Many of the other buildings, 500–600 years old, are half-timbered with sturdy carved beams jutting over ground-floor arcades. With its pavement cafés, the square is a pleasant spot to pass the time of day. The Cathédrale St-Maurice was built from 1327 onwards but not consecrated until 1506. Even then its

There is a market Mon and Thur mornings.

Festivals include an Easter jazz festival, medieval re-enactments in July, a puppet festival in Aug, and St-Maurice in Sept.

elegant spire had not been completed and the rib vaulting was not added until the 1860s. Southern Gothic in style, it has the widest nave in France (some say too wide for its length and height), frescoes and a series of rose windows, another late addition, high along the sides.

The town's speciality is Mirepoix sauce, made from onions, carrots and celery. The recipe was first concocted for the Duke of Lévis-Mirepoix in the 18th century.

Accommodation in Mirepoix

La Maison des Consuls €€€ *6 place des Couverts, Mirepoix; tel: 05 61 68 81 81. Open all year.* Small hotel converted from the most beautiful of the buildings which surround the town's 14th-century arcaded square. Perfect vantage point for watching the busy Monday and Thursday morning markets. No restaurant. Garage. Eight rooms, including one suite with a private terrace.

MONASTERE DE PROUILLE✢✢

St Dominic established a community of nuns here in 1206, having spotted the site from Fanjeaux. The large church in the present pink stone monastery, built in 1886, is now bare. Instead worship takes place in a modern chapel created at one end.

MONTREAL✢

Montréal Tourist Information *rue de la Mairie; tel: 04 68 76 20 05. Open Mon–Fri all year.*

France has no less than five towns called Montréal (meaning royal mount) and they have recently formed an association to foster links between each other and their rather bigger sister in Canada. This one has a collegiate church, St-Vincent, built in the austere Southern Gothic style – very big and very dark with a single nave decorated with frescoes. The church's fine 18th-century organ was built by Aristide Cavaillé-Coll, a member of the famous organ-building family.

PAMIERS✢✢

Pamiers Tourist Information *boulevard Delcassé; tel: 05 61 67 52 52; www.pamierstourisme.com. Open Mon–Sat all year.*

Markets on Tue, Thur and Sat.

The largest town on the route, this is the place to head for to go shopping, particularly as it is not at all 'touristy'. Its most distinctive features are the towers of its four monastery churches and the large red brick Cathédrale St-Antonin, which has a 49-bell carillon in its octagonal belfry which once served as a watch tower. The canal which skirts the town centre near the tourist office is one of the few hangovers from the Middle Ages when it was built for defence and to provide water for mills; it linked with the nearby River Ariège which was then navigable.

The town's role as the base of the dreaded anti-Cathar Inquisition in the 13th century is a piece of its history that today's occupants prefer to forget. Much more creditable was its bishop's grant in the 1860s to a local lad, Gabriel Fauré, which enabled him to study music in Paris and subsequently became a famous composer. *Cocos* – the white haricot beans used for making *cassoulet* – are grown on the flat farmland all around; however, the town's speciality dish is *azinat* (cabbage soup).

St-Felix-Lauragais✦✦✦

ⓘ St-Félix-Lauragais Tourist Information *place de la Mairie; tel: 05 62 18 96 99. Open daily July–Aug.*

◑ La Foire de la Cocagne at Easter evokes the time when woad brought prosperity to the area. People dress up in period costumes and take part in medieval processions. Old country crafts are demonstrated and a traditional country market sells local specialities like *foie gras*.

There is a major pottery fair during the third weekend in Sept.

This hillside village is scenically situated overlooking the Lauragais plain, the so-called Pays de Cocagne. The centre is laid out in typical 13th-century *bastide* style. Half-timbered buildings with brown brick and stone line the square which has a small market hall topped by a belfry. The 14th-century church nearby, painstakingly restored, is notable for its sculpted tableaux of the Stations of the Cross and *trompe-l'oeil* frescoes. The view from the terrace of the castle stretches from the the Montagne Noire to the Pyrenees.

Accommodation and food in St-Félix-Lauragais

Auberge du Poids Public €€ *Faubourg St-Roch; tel: 05 62 18 85 00. Closed Jan.* Named after the public weighbridge outside, this smart country hotel is considered by many to be the area's top hotel. Thirteen rooms. Michelin-starred restaurant €€€.

Woad

In the 16th century the flat countryside in the 'golden triangle' between Toulouse, Albi and Carcassonne was famous throughout Europe for its woad (which the French call *pastel*). The plant, which belongs to the mustard family and has small yellow flowers on a tall stem, was then in great demand for dyeing cloth blue, the fashionable colour of the period.

The dye was produced by letting the leaves dry in piles – *cocagnes* – and then grinding them into powder in mills. At the height of the trade, 500 mills were in operation and the area became known as the Pays de Cocagne – the 'land of milk and honey'.

Eventually woad was superseded by indigo, imported from India, though a few local people still grow it to make their own dye. It is also grown at the Château de Magrin near Lavaur, north of Albi, where a museum is devoted to its history.

Suggested tour

Total distance: 220km. The detour to St-Papoul adds 16km and the detour to Vals adds 3km.

Time: 5 hours' driving. Allow at least a day for the main route, a full day with detours. Those with limited time should concentrate on Castelnaudary (for a trip on the Canal du Midi) and Mirepoix.

Links to other tours: From St-Félix-Lauragais the D622 leads east to Revel (*see page 148*), 10km away. From Pamiers the N20 leads south to Foix (*see page 95*), 20km away.

Take the A61 autoroute southeast from Toulouse (towards Carcassonne). Turn off it at **Villefranche-de-Lauragais** and follow the D622 to **ST-FELIX-LAURAGAIS ❶** where the terrace of the castle provides a good view over the Lauragais plain (Pays de Cocagne). Today, instead of woad, the farmers have turned to more familiar crops, including the white beans which are an essential ingredient of *cassoulet*, and poultry. So many chickens are reared in the area that there is also a thriving industry in making feather duvets. Five kilometres beyond St-Félix-Lauragais, turn right on to the D624 to **CASTELNAUDARY ❷**.

Abbaye de St-Papoul €€ *Tel: 04 68 94 97 75. Open Apr–Oct daily, weekends only Nov–Mar. Closed Jan.*

Detour: The village of **St-Papoul** (8km east of Castelnaudary on the D103) boasts a 14th-century church which was elevated to the status of a cathedral in 1317 when Pope John XXII, keen to restore orthodoxy to the Catholic church in the area, installed a bishop there. Much rebuilt over the centuries, it has an attractive cloister and some fine stone carvings.

Leaving Castelnaudary, take the N113 towards Carcassonne. A fast road across farmland, it runs parallel with the Canal du Midi, railway and the A61, the 'Autoroute des Deux Mers'. After 16km, turn right on to the D4 which takes you across the canal to **Bram**, a village with an unusual layout. It is built in concentric circles around its church. Beyond Bram, cross the autoroute and turn left following the signs up the gentle climb to **MONTREAL ❸**. From there the D119 passes the **MONASTERE DE PROUILLE ❹** (on the right) just before **FANJEAUX ❺**. Continue along it across rolling farmland to **MIREPOIX ❻** and then towards Pamiers, enjoying views of the snow-topped Canigou mountain in the distance.

Detour: Ten kilometres after Mirepoix, turn right off the D119 on to the D206 to visit **Vals** (4km), a hamlet whose tiny 11th-century chapel, Ste-Marie, is – amazingly – built into a cliff. One of the oldest in the Midi, it has three tiers and a belfry. Steps in its cave-like entrance lead through a crevice to the crypt and then to the apse which is decorated with simple 12th-century frescoes of scenes from the life of Christ. From Vals, return to the D119 on the D40 (3km).

The D119 takes you to **PAMIERS ❼**, then take the N20 north (towards Toulouse) but turn right at **Le Vernet** where the D624, a long straight road bordered with plane trees, runs across flat countryside to **Mazères**. Most of this pleasant town, with its red brick parish church and market hall, dates from the 17th century (it was largely destroyed during the area's Wars of Religion). Pause in the church to admire the paintings around the altar. From Mazères, the D14 and then the D16 enable you to join the A61 autoroute just before **Villefranche-de-Lauragais** to return to Toulouse. On the way look back and enjoy the wide views over the huge fields of the plain, punctuated by villages and a lonely water tower.

Below
Fanjeaux

Getting out of the car

In Castelnaudary, it's worth considering taking a boat trip on the **Canal du Midi**. By way of introduction, there are 30-minute ones around the Grand Bassin, or you can take a 2-hour one towards Toulouse and through the la Planque lock. Like many of the roads in the area, the peaceful water is lined by plane trees which Napoleon had planted to provide shade.

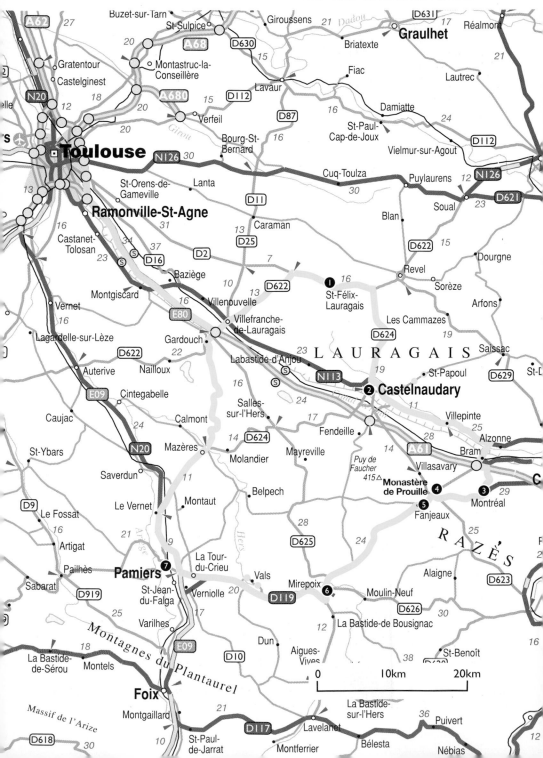

Albi

Ratings

Architecture	●●●●●
Art	●●●●●
Food and drink	●●●●○
History	●●●●○
Entertainment	●●●○○
Museums	●●●○○
Shopping	●●○○○
Children	●○○○○

Built in brick, this vivacious little city straddling the River Tarn is known as Albi la Rouge (Albi the Red), though in fact it is an attractive mixture of soft yellows and browns as well as reds. Two major features bring tourists flocking in – the fortress-like Cathédrale Ste-Cécile which dominates the skyline and the Musée Toulouse-Lautrec where you can see the world's largest collection of the famous artist's work. There is much else for visitors to discover too: how in the 13th century the city lent its name to the bloody Albigensian Crusade when Catholics wiped out Cathars in the area; how in the 16th it grew rich from woad; and how the fiery socialist Jean-Jaurès founded France's first trade union at the local glass factory in 1896. A busy calendar of events helps keep everyone entertained, including many outdoor ones in summer.

Getting there and getting around

ⓘ Tourist Information *Palais de la Berbie, place Ste-Cécile; tel: 05 63 49 48 80.* Hotel reservation service, currency exchange and a selection of publications in English. *e-mail: accueil@albitourisme.com; www.mairie-albi.fr. Open daily.*

By car, the A68 autoroute from Toulouse leads straight on to the N88 and into the city centre. From the north, you cross the Pont du 22 Août 1944 over the river to it. In high season, traffic can be heavy, particularly on both river bridges and on the one-way system around the cathedral and pedestrianised old quarter. The railway station, *place de Stalingrad* (10-minute walk from the centre) has a direct nightly service to and from Paris. Other national and international connections are via Toulouse or Montauban.

The old town quarter is small and easily walkable. Three walking tours, signed in purple, blue and yellow, lead around it. Explanatory plaques (in French) are sited at points of interest complemented by a leaflet showing the routes (available in English) from the tourist office. Street signs show their names in the old Occitan language beside their

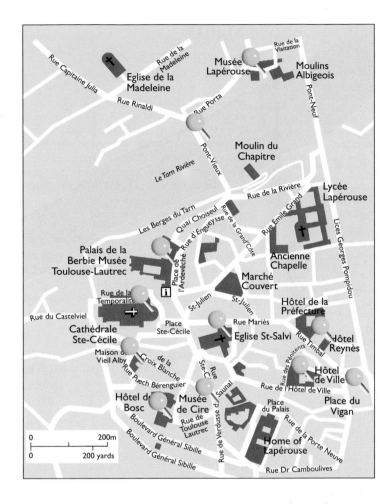

ⓘ Tarn département
Information, *Moulins Albigeois, 41 rue Porta; tel: 05 63 77 32 10.*

modern ones. A road-train operates every 45 minutes daily from the tourist office during July and August; afternoons only Saturday and Sunday. There are 35-minute boat trips on the Tarn daily every half-hour June–September.

Parking: The streets on the hill below the cathedral are the best place to try to find a space and parking is free at the bottom. There are various car parks on the edge of the old quarter to the south, including place du Vigan, Jardin National, place Jean-Jaurès and avenue Général de Gaulle, or cross the river to the Base de Loisirs de Pratgraussals park area (15 minutes' walk back to the centre).

Sights

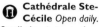

Cathédrale Ste-Cécile *Open daily. Small charge to go through the rood screen into the choir. Guided tours. Free organ recitals on Wed at 1700 and Sun at 1600 during July and Aug.*

Eglise St-Salvi *place du Cloître. Concerts are given on its 400-year-old organ which was originally installed in the cathedral.*

Hôtel de Bosc *14 rue Toulouse-Lautrec. Not open to the public.*

Hôtel Reynès *14 rue Timbal. Courtyard open daily Easter–Oct, then closed weekends.*

Hôtel de Ville *rue de l'Hôtel de Ville. Open Mon–Fri.*

Cathédrale Ste-Cécile✦✦✦

This forbidding fortress-like building is visible from miles away, as indeed it was meant to be, having been built at the end of the bloody anti-Cathar Albigensian Crusade. The idea was that no-one should be in any doubt of the power of the Catholicism and should tremble in their boots if they even thought about challenging it again. Work on it started in 1282 and took over 200 years to complete. Built in long thin pink bricks, it is a masterpiece of Southern Gothic, with a single nave, tiny windows and a huge bell tower like a castle keep. In contrast to the brickwork it had an ornate stone porch added in the early 16th century.

The interior comes as such a surprise. Beautiful frescoes, mainly royal blue and pale yellow, cover the huge vaulted roof which is 100m long and 20m wide, and also the walls of the side chapels. The work of Italian artists, they were the first Renaissance paintings to be done in France and depict scenes from the New Testament. Remarkably their vivid colours have never been retouched. Other unique treasures include a delicately sculpted limestone rood screen which looks like a lace curtain, 120 carved choir stalls and a 3500-pipe organ, France's biggest.

Église St-Salvi✦

The church of St-Salvi is dedicated to a 6th-century bishop who introduced Christianity to the area. Despite six centuries of alterations – work began in the 12th century but was constantly interrupted – the interior forms a harmonious though gloomy whole. Tour de la Gâche, its unusual three-tiered stone and brick belfry, used to double as a watchtower.

Hôtel de Bosc✦✦

This attractive creeper-covered mansion has been in the Toulouse-Lautrec family for over 300 years. The artist Henri de Toulouse-Lautrec was born there in 1864 and lived in it until leaving for Paris when he was 18.

Below
The Cathédrale Ste-Cécile

Hôtel Reynès✦

Now occupied by the Chamber of Commerce, Hôtel Reynès is one of the town's many splendid Renaissance mansions built by merchants who made their fortunes from trading in woad (or blue gold as it was nicknamed) in the prosperous 16th century. It has a small Italianate courtyard.

Hôtel de Ville✦✦

Built as a private home in the 17th century, this large mansion was later bought by the council to be the town hall. Its features include a pretty courtyard and a ceiling in the Salle des Etats Albigeois painted with the emblems of the old diocese of Albi.

Maison du Vieil Alby**

This medieval half-timbered brick house has been painstakingly restored. Like many of Albi's old buildings, it has a *solehièr* under the eaves – a room with an open balcony where woad would have been dried. Many balconies have now been glassed in.

Musée de Cire*

Albi's wax museum contains tableaux depicting the town's history through its most famous citizens including Toulouse-Lautrec, the explorer Lapérouse and Jean Jaurès. It is housed in the cellars of the fine mansion next door to the house where Lapérouse lived briefly between his marriage and early death.

Musée Lapérouse**

This museum is dedicated to the local explorer who set off on a scientific expedition in 1785 but never returned. After leaving Botany Bay he was shipwrecked in a storm on the reefs of Vanikoro. Remains from the wreck are on show, together with navigation instruments and models of the two ships which were on his final voyage.

Musée Toulouse-Lautrec***

The Musée Toulouse-Lautrec is housed in the Palais de la Berbie, originally the bishops' palace, next to the cathedral. The building's name derived from '*bisbia*', the Occitan word for bishop. Constructed in the same formidable style as the cathedral, it is more a citadel than a residence, though later additions and alterations have softened it somewhat. These include formally laid-out gardens which blaze with colour in summer and an attractive riverside promenade.

The museum is almost entirely devoted to works by Toulouse-Lautrec, the city's most famous son. The collection, donated by his family, consists of 1000 works and documents ranging from early drawings to all 31 of his well-known posters and some of his sombre last paintings. Paintings and sculptures by contemporary artists are also on show and there is an archaeological gallery.

Place du Vigan*

Place du Vigan, a large bustling square built in the 18th century, separates the medieval and modern quarters of the town. Its many pavement cafés and bars where crowds congregate on warm summer evenings should be even more popular when its pedestrianisation is completed.

Pont Vieux**

This 900-year-old bridge with six uneven brick arches is one of France's oldest. It had houses on it until 1766 when flooding swept them away.

Ⓘ Maison du Vieil Alby *corner of rue Croix-Blanche and rue Peuch-Berenguier. Tel: 05 63 54 96 38. Open Mon–Sat.*

Musée de Cire € *12 rue Toulouse-Lautrec. Open daily (afternoons only Oct–May) except Jan. Tel: 05 63 54 87 55.*

Musée Lapérouse *Moulins Albigeois, place Botany Bay, which is across the river from the town centre; the entrance is in rue Porta. Tel: 05 63 46 01 87. Open Wed–Mon. Free.*

Musée Toulouse-Lautrec €€ *Palais de la Berbie, next to the Cathedral; tel. 05 63 49 48 70. Open Wed–Mon. Guided tours June–Sept. Special exhibitions during summer.*

You get a classic view of the cathedral from it and also from its newer twin just upstream which is named after the day, 22-Août (22 August), when Albi was liberated from the Germans in 1944.

Shopping

The main shopping street, the pedestrianised rue Mariès, leads off place Ste-Cécile. There are no large stores in the town centre. Hypermarkets on the outskirts include **Géant Casino** (on the road to Millau) and two **Leclercs** (on the roads to Toulouse and to Rodez).

Confidences du Terroir, *1 place Ste-Cécile*, has a wide selection of local specialities including Gaillac wines produced in the neighbouring vineyards which are little known outside the area. Local wines are sold by the litre at **La Petite Cave** (just across Pont Vieux). In *pâtisseries* look out for little aniseed-flavoured cakes called *jeannots* and *gimblettes*.

The town's covered market at place Lapérouse is open every morning except Mon. On Saturday mornings there are also food markets at place Fernand Pelloutier and boulevard de Strasbourg, and a flea market in the Halle du Castelvieil.

Entertainment

Throughout the summer months, there is plenty of informal entertainment on the streets. Tickets for events are sold at the tourist office, including the **Jazz festival** during May and June which has outdoor concerts as well as groups performing in bars.

Theatre festival, early July.

Grand Prix, first weekend in September.

Toulouse-Lautrec

Born in 1864, Henri de Toulouse-Lautrec enormously enjoyed riding as a child, like his mother, and the family frequently visited their estate at Celeyran. While there, he also began to sketch and paint. Sadly when he was 14, he fell from a chair at his home, the Hôtel du Bosc, damaging one of his legs. A similar accident the following year left him permanently disabled when his legs failed to grow properly, compounding genetic problems arising from the fact that his parents were cousins.

Increasingly unable to join in outdoor activities – a cause of much frustration to him – he enjoyed cooking and came up with a range of recipes. Some of these are now featured by Albi restaurants on their menus.

Henri left home at 18 for the seedy bohemian lifestyle of Montmartre where he painted the singers, dancers and prostitutes who were his neighbours, becoming friends with many of them. His best money-spinners were the posters he began to design in the late 1880s. But ten years on, his health had severely deteriorated, mainly due to alcohol, and he died at another family residence, the Château de Malromé in the Gironde, when he was only 36.

La Légende de Gaucelmn is a multimedia show staged outdoors in the Théâtre du Verdure behind the cathedral about the history of the area, particularly the Cathars; Fri, Sat and Sun in August.

Base de Loisirs de Pratgraussals *tel: 05 63 60 64 06*, a large park on the north bank of the Tarn, has picnic areas, tennis courts, adventure playgrounds and a mountain bike area.

Accommodation and food

Grand Hôtel d'Orléans €€ *1 place Stalingrad; tel: 05 63 54 16 56; www.hotel-orleans-albi.com*. Friendly rather than grand, this comfortably updated turn-of-the-century hotel has always been run by the same family. Eight of the 56 rooms are family-size. Breakfast terrace beside outdoor pool. Quietly situated opposite the station with parking.

Hôtel Chiffre €€ *50 rue Séré-de Rivières; tel: 05 63 48 58 48; www.hotelchiffre.com*. This old coaching inn with stables, over 100 years old, has been been thoroughly modernised. Now smart décor complements impressive facilities (such as air conditioning and twin washbasins) in the 35 bedrooms. Situated in a quiet street in the town centre, it has plenty of parking space.

Hôtel George V € *29 avenue Maréchal-Joffre; tel: 05 63 54 24 16; www.hotelgeorgesv.com*. Small hotel near the railway station with outdoor breakfast terrace.

Viel-Alby €€ *25 rue Toulouse-Lautrec; tel: 05 63 54 14 69*. A charming small hotel (nine rooms) run by the Sicard family in the centre of the old quarter. Its restaurant – the Sicard son is chef – features a wide range of local dishes including Albi's special starter, *salade de radis au foie de porc salé* (radishes with salted liver).

Below
Albi's Pont Vieux

Le Clos Sainte-Cécile € *rue du Castelvieil; tel: 05 63 38 19 74. Open Thur–Mon*. Local cuisine served in a former school beside the cathedral. Large garden.

Le Goulu € *1 place Stalingrad (in the Grand Hôtel d'Orléans); tel: 05 63 54 16 56. Closed Sat midday and Sun*. Classic restaurant featuring local dishes at moderate prices.

La Table du Sommelier €€ *20 rue Porta; tel: 05 63 46 20 10. Open Tue–Sat*. Rustic-style wine bar and bistro owned by one of the region's leading wine experts, with some tables outdoors in summer.

Suggested walk

Length: 2km.

Duration: 45 minutes just to walk round, but allow at least half a day to visit the cathedral and the Toulouse-Lautrec museum.

The **CATHEDRALE ST-CECILE** ❶ is the obvious place to start as the oldest part of the town radiates from its square on the south bank of the **River Tarn**. Also explore the adjoining citadel, the ramparts, and **Palais de la Berbie** which houses the **MUSEE TOULOUSE-LAUTREC** ❷ inside; the tourist office also occupies a corner of it on the square.

Rue Mariès leads from the square past an interesting selection of small shops. Appropriately the street is named after Jean-François Mariès, a local town planner who succeeded in overruling suggestions that the cathedral should be pulled down when plans were afoot to completely re-design the town centre after the French Revolution. Instead he had wide boulevards built around the old quarter – a much better idea.

The **HOTEL REYNES** ❸ is situated in rue Timbal, where the 16th-century half-timbered **Maison Enjalbert** is also noteworthy. Now a pharmacy, it has criss-cross timberwork on its façade. Continue to the **Jardin National** where you can stroll amid beautifully laid-out gardens with fountains. Head back, via the quaint old **Patus Cremat** district, which has recently escaped developers' bulldozers, to the **Palais de Justice**, formerly a Carmelite convent, which has a small cloister. Then continue on to rue de l'Hôtel de Ville which used to be the city's most prestigious street. The mansions at Nos 13, 14 and 17, and the **HOTEL DE VILLE** ❹ itself at 16, are very impressive. At the top of rue Toulouse-Lautrec, No 14 is the attractive creeper-covered **HOTEL DE BOSC** ❺ where the artist was born and lived until he was 18. The former home of the explorer Lapérouse is next door and then the **MUSEE DE CIRE** ❻. Narrow cobbled streets take you back to the pretty **MAISON DU VIEL ALBY** ❼ and then on to **EGLISE ST-SALVI** ❽, whose cloister tucked behind the shops of rue Mariès is a quiet haven.

For the best view of the old town and its red rooftops, cross the **PONT VIEUX** ❾ to the north bank. This is a particularly worthwhile stroll at sunset when swallows dip over the water and the bricks of the mighty cathedral seem to glow.

Also worth exploring

The walled town of Cordes-sur-Ciel, huddled around a hilltop 25km northwest of Albi, is reached on the D600 which leads along a high ridge overlooking the vineyards of Gaillac. Protected by three lines of ramparts

Cordes-sur-Ciel Tourist Information *Maison Fonpeyrouse; tel: 05 63 56 00 52; www.cordes-sur-ciel.org. Open daily July–Aug; Mon–Sat Sept–June.*

Cordes-sur-Ciel There are two car parks at the bottom of the town and another at the top for anyone unable to negotiate the steep cobbled climb up.

Arts and crafts Over 50 artists and craftsmen live and work in Cordes-sur-Ciel and the tourist office website lists those who accept visitors to their studios and workshops. They range from painters, sculptors and potters to glass-blowers, jewellery designers, makers of musical instruments and many other crafts.

and scarcely changed in 800 years, it is as scenic from a distance as when you explore it on foot. Steep cobbled streets wind past cottages trailing flowers, leading to flights of steps. These go up through stone arched gateways into the heart of the town, a large tree-shaded square surrounded by cafés which is taken over by a market on Saturdays.

The long straight Grande Rue Haute is lined with grand houses built by the Cathar nobility when they had to take refuge in Cordes during the 13th and 14th centuries. Now many artists have studios in the quaint narrow streets but the influx of tourists has inevitably encouraged plenty of souvenir shops too.

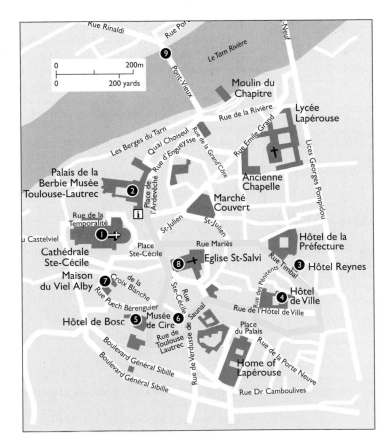

The Tarn Valley

Ratings

Rivers	●●●●●
Scenery	●●●●●
Villages	●●●●○
Art	●●●○○
Geology	●●●○○
Outdoor activities	●●●○○
Shopping	●●●○○
Historical sights	●●○○○

Why is the Tarn Gorge in the Cévennes so much more famous than the Tarn Valley, a few miles downstream? The answer is that the gorge is so dramatic, yet the Valley is certainly as beautiful. From Brousse-le-Château to Albi, the river meanders gently between its wooded hillsides and charming villages.

This route then runs south through the valley of the Rance to the Monts de Lacaune where the scenery becomes mountainous with grey stone villages and thick forests.

By way of contrast, Castres offers worthwhile sightseeing and smart shopping in congenial riverside surroundings. Réalmont is also a tempting place to pause, particularly on market days.

Bear in mind however that the route is comparatively long and has stretches that twist around hillsides as well as the fast final stretch from Castres to Albi, so allow plenty of time.

AMBIALET✧✧✧

ℹ Ambialet Tourist Information *le Bourg; tel: 05 63 55 39 14; www.si-ambialet.fr. Open daily July–Aug.*

🅗 Notre-Dame de l'Oder Although you can drive up to it and the priory, an attractive walk marked by the Stations of the Cross leads to them from the car park (and adjoining picnic tables) by the river in the village.

The village of Ambialet is distinctive mainly for its unusual position in a noose-shaped loop of the River Tarn, with a hydroelectric station (disguised as a small mansion) at the neck which is only 23m across. **Notre-Dame de l'Oder✧✧**, an 11th-century church which is all the more beautiful for its simple undecorated interior, looks down over it from a high clifftop. The church is part of a Benedictine priory which still functions. The small village church, Eglise St Gilles, also dates back to the 11th century.

Accommodation and food in Ambialet

Hôtel du Pont €€ *Ambialet; tel: 05 63 55 32 07.* Twenty-room hotel above river beside bridge with lovely view. Restaurant serves local fare.

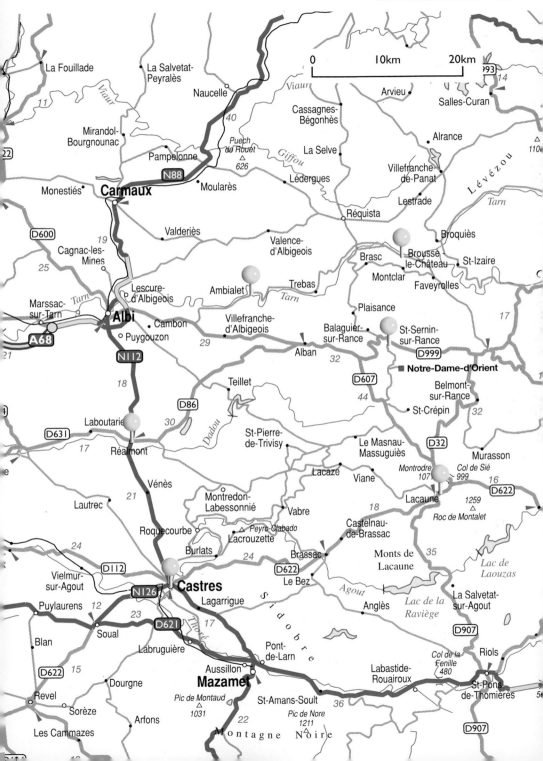

0   10km   20km

La Fouillade
La Salvetat-Peyralès
Naucelle
Arvieu
Salles-Curan
Viaur
Cassagnes-Bégonhès
Alrance
Mirandol-Bourgnounac
Pampelonne
Puech de Rouet 626
La Selve
Villefranche-de-Panat
Lévézou
Monestiés
Carmaux
Moularès
Lédergues
Lestrade
Tarn
Réquista
Broquiès
D600
Valderiès
Valence-d'Albigeois
Brasc
Brousse-le-Château
St-Izaire
Cagnac-les-Mines
25
Brousse-le-Château
Montclar
Faveyrolles
Lescure-d'Albigeois
Ambialet
Trebas
Plaisance
17
Marssac-sur-Tarn
Tarn
Albi
Cambon
Villefranche-d'Albigeois
Balaguier-sur-Rance
St-Sernin-sur-Rance
A68
Puygouzon
Alban
32
D999
21
N112
18
Teillet
44
Belmont-sur-Rance
D607
St-Crépin
32
D86
St-Pierre-de-Trivisy
Le Masnau-Massuguiès
D32
Murasson
Laboutarie
30
Col de Sié 999
16
D631
Réalmont
Lacaze
Montrodre 1071
D622
17
Vénès
Viane
Lacaune
1259
Lautrec
21
Montredon-Labessonnié
Vabre
18
Roc de Montalet
Roquecourbe
Peyro-Clabado
Castelnau-de-Brassac
Vielmur-sur-Agout
24
Burlats
24
Brassac
Monts de Lacaune
35
Lac de Laouzas
D112
Castres
D622
Le Bez
Puylaurens
12
Lagarrigue
Sidobre
Anglès
Lac de la Ravière
La Salvetat-sur-Agout
N126
Soual
23
D621
17
Agout
D907
Blan
Thoré
Pont-de-Larn
Col de la Fenille 480
Riols
D622
15
Labruguière
Labastide-Rouairoux
St-Pons-de-Thomières
Dourgne
Aussillon
Revel
Mazamet
St-Amans-Soult
36
D907
Sorèze
Pic de Montaud 1031
22
Pic de Nore 1211
Arfons
Les Cammazes
Montagne Noire
Notre-Dame-d'Orient
N88
40
Viaur
11
22
19
D600
29
Dadou
Giffou
Tarn

BROUSSE-LE-CHATEAU✦✦

🏛 Brousse-le-Château castle €
Tel: 05 65 99 45 40. Open daily Feb–Nov. Visits can include a 15-minute video on its history and the surrounding area.

Tiny alleyways bordered by old stone cottages lead steeply up to the village's partly-ruined 14th-century **castle✦✦✦** which occupies a commanding position on a ridge between the River Tarn and its small tributary, the Alrance. With its sturdy curtain walls and turrets, it is a classic example of medieval military architecture. The small church inside is prettily decorated with frescoes which have recently been restored.

Accommodation in Brousse-le-Château

Le Relays du Chasteau €€ *Brousse-le-Château; tel: 05 65 99 40 15. Closed mid-Dec–mid-Feb.* Nestling in the village street in a row of old buildings below the castle, this traditional 12-room hotel has been in the Senegas family for four generations.

CASTRES✦✦

ⓘ Castres Tourist Information 3 rue Milhau-Ducommun; tel: 05 63 62 63 62. Open daily all year. Organises guided tours.

📷 Take a 45-minute boat trip (€€) aboard the *Miredames*, a replica wooden barge, from the Pont Vieux to the Parc de Gourjade to see the waterfront at its best; June–Oct; tel: 05 63 62 41 76.

🏛 Musée Goya €€ Hôtel de Ville; tel: 05 63 71 59 27. Open daily July–Aug; Tue–Sun Sept–June.

Centre National et Musée Jean Jaurès € place Pélisson; tel: 05 63 72 01 01. Open daily July–Aug; Tue–Sun Sept–June. A Goya festival is held each July and a folklore festival in August.

Castres is well placed as a base for exploring the Sidobre hills. A sizeable industrial town, it also offers sightseeing, shopping and entertainment. The oldest part spreads along the banks of the River Agout. Along the quai des Jacobins, a row of tall clapboard houses painted white and green, once occupied by weavers and dyers, is reflected picturesquely in the water with arched doorways and overhanging balconies.

Cathédrale St-Benoît✦, on the site of a 9th-century abbey, looks rather forbidding but its interior is brightened by a huge altar supported by pillars of local red marble. There are some fine paintings in its side chapels. The Hôtel de Ville is a grand 17th-century building designed by Jules Hardouin-Mansart as the bishop's palace. On the second floor, the **Musée Goya✦✦✦** displays an outstanding collection of the artist's work, collected by a local painter, Marcel Briguiboul. Its formal gardens, laid out by the famous landscape architect, Le Nôtre, are a work of art too. One of the best examples of a *jardin à la française* (French garden), they feature a tapestry of low box hedges and tall yew trees, each neatly clipped to a different shape.

Centre National et Musée Jean Jaurès✦, is devoted to the famous French socialist politician who was born in the town in 1859. A statue of him occupies the place of honour on the main square.

Parc de Gourjad✦✦ (*tel: 05 63 72 27 06*), a leisure complex on the northeast side of town, includes indoor and outdoor pools, a skating rink, nine-hole golf course, horse riding and children's playground with a gigantic spider's web for climbing on. The town's industrial area, built up in the 17th century on textiles, but now including chemicals, meat-curing and mechanical engineering, is on the south side and does not intrude on the centre.

● **Market** Saturday morning, place Jean-Jaurès. Look out for regional specialities such as *melsat* (white sausage) and *boudin de Languedoc* (black pudding).

● Opera season at the **Théâtre Municipal** *in Castres except Aug. Reservations tel: 05 63 71 56 58.*

● **Hôtel Rivière €€** *10 quai Tourcaudières, Castres; tel: 05 63 59 04 53. Closed second half of Dec.* Fifteen rooms. Conveniently situated hotel in the town centre overlooking old tanners' houses across the river.

Right
Brousse-le-Château

LACAUNE✧

ⓘ Lacaune Tourist Information *place du Général de Gaulle; tel: 05 63 37 04 98; www.lacaune.com. Open daily July–Aug; Mon–Sat Sept–June.*

Raymond Mill € *Open by appointment through the tourist office.*

Market Sun morning and 21st of every month.

Free organ recitals in the **Église Notre-Dame** July–Aug Thur.

Grey slate roofs make this little town look rather sombre – the slate is quarried locally. Until the 1930s its small spa attracted many visitors. Tiny statues of four well-endowed men on top of the Fontaine des Pisseurs (erected in 1559) in front of the town's old open-air stone wash house demonstrate the diuretic qualities of *l'eau de Lacaune* (Lacaune water).

The charcuterie for which the Monts de Lacaune area is famous – salamis, sausages and air-dried ham – is made at several small factories around the town. Visits to some of them can be arranged through the tourist office. This industry, however, has declined in recent years as mass-production has taken over.

Another hangover from the past are seven hand-operated looms, still in working order, at the **Raymond Mill**✧, a rambling old mill run by the Raymond family from 1841 to 1992 and still fully equipped.

Accommodation and food in Lacaune

Calas €€ *4 place de la Vierge; tel: 05 63 37 03 28. Closed mid-Dec–mid-Jan.* Centrally placed old-fashioned hotel with 16 rooms, outdoor pool and gourmet restaurant.

Jean-Jaurès

You see his name everywhere in France. Almost every town in France seems to have a square or street named after him. But who was he?

The answer: a leading socialist politician and pacifist who was assassinated by a mentally ill youth in Paris in 1914. Born in Castres in 1859, he studied to be a teacher and worked in a school at Albi before becoming a philosophy lecturer at Toulouse University. When he was 26 he entered politics as the Republican member of parliament for Tarn, later becoming the Socialist member for the mining town of Carmaux. A skilful orator and writer, he argued passionately for social change, notably the introduction of accident compensation for workers and retirement pensions. He also demonstrated his independence by publicly supporting Alfred Dreyfus, the Jewish soldier whom the French High Command convicted of being a German spy in 1894, but pardoned 12 years later.

REALMONT✧✧

This is a typical *bastide* – fortified town – created in 1271 by King Philippe III with the characteristic grid layout of straight streets with a large square at the centre, place de la République. This is surrounded by arcades, some supported by sturdy wooden beams, others by stone

Left
Lacaune

Réalmont Tourist Information
8 place de la République; tel: 05 63 79 05 45. Open daily June–Sept; Mon–Sat Oct–May.

columns. Market days are definitely the liveliest time to visit as the stalls brim with the local pink garlic, poultry and other fresh produce from this essentially agricultural region.

Take time off from shopping to drop into the parish church, Notre-Dame-du-Taur, to see its splendid baroque altarpiece. On the edge of the old quarter, which was originally encircled by ramparts, the communal wash house and Fontaine de la Fréjaire, a fountain where villagers came for water until 1950 when pumps were installed, are also worth seeing.

ST-SERNIN-SUR-RANCE❖❖

St-Sernin-sur-Rance Tourist Information *avenue d'Albi; tel: 05 65 99 29 13. Open daily June–Sept; Mon–Sat Oct–May.*

Built on a rocky spur high above the Rivers Rance and Merdanson, this medieval stronghold has a jumble of old houses and a 300-year-old bridge. The film director François Truffaut put the town on the map in 1968 when he made *L'Enfant Sauvage*, based on the story of a local boy who was captured nearby on 8 January 1800 after being raised by wolves. The boy's statue stands on the place du Fort.

Accommodation and food in St-Sernin-sur-Rance

Hôtel Carayon €€ *place du Fort; tel: 05 65 98 19 19; www.hotel-carayon.com.* Sixty rooms, many with balcony overlooking garden. Large restaurant. Tennis, mini-golf and pool with slides.

The town's speciality is *gimblettes* (small doughnut-shaped caraway seed biscuits) which are sold at the Maison Nespoulous *pâtisserie (tel: 05 65 99 60 06)*. The women used to bake them on Sundays and take them to church, threaded on a stick, to be blessed.

Suggested tour

Total distance: 230km. The detour to Notre-Dame d'Orient adds 4km, the detour to St-Crépin adds 6km and the detour on to the Sidobre adds 24km.

Time: 6 hours' driving. Allow up to two days for the main route, and a full two days with detours. Those with limited time should concentrate on the Tarn Valley between Albi and Brousse-le-Château.

Links to other routes: Links: From St-Sernin-sur-Rance the D999 leads east to Roquefort (*see page 244*), 45km away. From Lacaune the D907 leads south to La Salvetat-sur-Agout (*see page 208*), 20km away. From Castres the N112 leads southeast to Mazamet (*see page 146*), 17km away.

Head east from **Albi** on the D999 (signposted Millau), which passes through the town's industrial outskirts. After 11km the scene changes welcomingly when you turn left on to the D77 as it zigzags down through old oak woods to join the D172. This takes you along the south bank of the River Tarn to **AMBIALET** ❶. Gentle wooded slopes frame the serene blue water on each side, making the valley here as scenic as any stretch on the river's varied journey from Mont Lozère, it is definitely a pleasant place for a waterside picnic. Leave Ambialet on the D700 (signposted to Couris) but fork left off it almost immediately to cross the Tarn and drive along its north bank to **Trébas**.

You will notice that this road is flat, curves only gently and occasionally goes through short tunnels. The reason is that it was part of a railway line between Millau and Albi, built by Italian prisoners during World War I. No trains ever ran on it as it was never completed.

Below
Castres: the Quai des Jacobins

Trébas, a tiny spa town with a Sunday market, claims to have the most copper-rich thermal waters in Europe. Beyond it the D172 continues along the north bank of this beautiful stretch of the Tarn to **BROUSSE-LE-CHATEAU** ❷; you cross the river and then re-cross it on your way there. From Brousse-le-Château continue east on the D902 leaving the 'railway road' where it crosses the river and disappears into a tunnel. Shortly afterwards you have to leave the Tarn too. Then, 3km later, turn sharp right just before **Faveyrolles** on to the D60 which climbs up to **Montclar**, providing increasingly splendid views over distant farmland and woods. The D552 (which becomes the D33) leads along a ridge with wide views of farmland on both sides through **Brasc**. It winds down to the wide wooded valley of the River Rance at **Plaisance**, following the river through the tiny village of **Balaguier** (which has a surprisingly large church) to **ST-SERNIN-SUR-RANCE** ❸. As you climb out of the town, be sure to look back to see the backs of its houses clinging to the hillside.

Detour: Five kilometres beyond St-Sernin-sur-Rance on the D33, the D91 on the left leads (2km) to the church of **Notre-Dame-d'Orient**, part of a Benedictine convent, which has a beautiful wooden carved and painted altarpiece from the 17th century.

Pigeon-houses

In the Tarn countryside, look out for pigeon-houses. These small windowless buildings were mostly built between the 17th and 19th centuries when pigeons were particularly valued for their ability to carry messages, their tasty meat and the fertiliser value of their droppings. The houses were often raised above the ground on pillars or arches to protect the birds from rats and other animals. As they were regarded as status symbols by the landowners, many have elaborate brick or stonework, elegant roofs and often a decorative pinnacle on top. Because pigeons prefer to live in tranquil surroundings and like to be able to watch for out predators, the houses tend to be isolated from other buildings.

St-Crépin
Musée Damien Bec
€ *Open daily; Apr–Oct afternoons only.* Local tourist offices have details of walking trails leading to standing stones.

Château du Bosc €€
Naucelle; tel: 05 65 69 20 83. Open daily all year for guided tours.

Detour: Twelve kilometres beyond St-Sernin-sur-Rance on the D33, a left turn up the D554 leads (3km) to the village of **St-Crépin** where the **Musée Damien Bec** has a section devoted to the area's menhirs. Many of these prehistoric standing stones with mysterious markings are scattered around the Monts de Lacaune hills.

After the turn to St-Crépin, continue south (now on the D607) along a panoramic ridge which climbs past farmland and woods over the Col de Sié (999m) before dropping down to **LACAUNE** ❹, a little town of grey slate roofs in the heart of the Monts de Lacaune. From there, take the D81 west which winds through beech woods (glorious in autumn) to **Lacaze**, followed by the D171 to Vabre, another small grey slate town, which has some attractive 16th- and 17th-century houses. Its isolated position surrounded by lonely hillsides is probably one of the reasons it became a hippie haunt in the 1970s. At **Vabre** join the D55 which winds through woods beside the River Agout to **Roquecourbe**.

Detour: From Roquecourbe, the D30 leads to the **Peyro Clabado** (10km). This massive precariously balanced boulder is one of many 'rocking stones' on the **Sidobre**, a wide granite plateau averaging 650m in height. Just beyond it is the **Chaos de la Resse**, a 'river' of rocks covering a real river, and the wooded **Lac du Merle**, a lake whose surface is broken by boulders.

From Roquecourbe, continue to **CASTRES** ❺, then take the N112, a fast flat road, north back through **REALMONT** ❻ to Albi.

Also worth exploring

If you're a Toulouse-Lautrec fan, **Château du Bosc**, the country house where the painter spent childhood holidays, is at Naucelle, just off the N88, 45km north of Albi. It's a small red-shuttered 19th-century castle with sturdy towers, lavishly furnished in *fin-de-siècle* Parisian style.

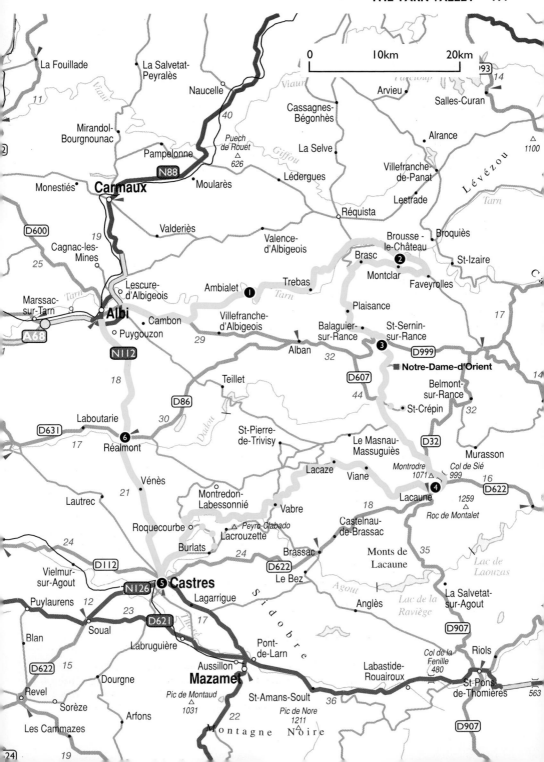

0   10km   20km

La Fouillade
La Salvetat-Peyralès
Naucelle
Arvieu
Salles-Curan
Cassagnes-Bégonhès
Mirandol-Bourgnounac
La Selve
Pampelonne
Puech de Rouet 626
Villefranche-de-Panat
Alrance
Monestiés
Carmaux
Moularès
Lédergues
Lestrade
Réquista
Brousse-le-Château
Broquiès
St-Izaire
D600
Valderiès
Valence-d'Albigeois
Brasc
Montclar
Faveyrolles
Cagnac-les-Mines
Lescure-d'Albigeois
Ambialet
Trebas
Marssac-sur-Tarn
Albi
Cambon
Villefranche-d'Albigeois
Plaisance
St-Sernin-sur-Rance
A68
Puygouzon
Balaguier-sur-Rance
N112
Alban
Notre-Dame-d'Orient
D999
Teillet
D607
Belmont-sur-Rance
D86
St-Crépin
Laboutarie
St-Pierre-de-Trivisy
Le Masnau-Massuguiès
D631
Réalmont
D32
Murasson
Vénès
Lacaze
Viane
Montrodre 1071
Col de Sié 999
Lautrec
Lacaune
D622
Montredon-Labessonnié
Vabre
1259
Roquecourbe
Peyro-Clabado
Lacrouzette
Castelnau-de-Brassac
Roc de Montalet
Burlats
Brassac
Monts de Lacaune
Lac de Laouzas
Vielmur-sur-Agout
D112
Castres
Le Bez
D622
La Salvetat-sur-Agout
Puylaurens
Lagarrigue
Anglès
Lac de la Raviège
N126
Soual
D621
Labruguière
Pont-de-Larn
D907
Blan
Aussillon
Riols
D622
Dourgne
Mazamet
St-Amans-Soult
Labastide-Rouairoux
Col de la Fenille 480
St-Pons-de-Thomières
Revel
Pic de Montaud 1031
Pic de Nore 1211
Sorèze
Arfons
Montagne Noire
D907
Les Cammazes

The Minervois and its vineyards

Ratings

Museums	●●●●●
Vineyards	●●●●●
Caves	●●●●○
Churches	●●●●○
History	●●●●○
Villages	●●●●○
Scenery	●●●○○
Canals	●●○○○

The Romans knew the flat countryside around Narbonne well – and left some fascinating traces of their occupation. It was they who first planted the Minervois vineyards on the sunny dry slopes which rise gently from it towards the hills of the Haut Languedoc. Today 61 villages produce the highly drinkable red, white and rosé Minervois wines – and the quality is improving all the time. With frequent opportunities to sample them, this is a route on which it pays not to be the driver.

South of the rugged hills which are covered in *garrigue* and vines, the River Aude and the Canal du Midi, often distinctively bordered by plane trees, follow peaceful courses across a flat band of countryside planted with yet more vines. The museums along the route help explain the area's history and wine making from Roman times.

CAPESTANG❖❖

ⓘ Capestang Tourist Information *5 boulevard Pasteur; tel: 04 67 93 34 23. Open Mon–Sat.*

🏛 Tower € *Visits by arrangement with tourist office.*

This little canal-side town has an imposing Gothic church, Collégiale St-Etienne. It had the same architect as the cathedral at Narbonne (*see page 112*) but neither was completed as he committed suicide. Climb its **tower**❖❖ for a splendid view of the Aude plain as far as Narbonne.

Food in Capestang

Le Pourquoi Pas? €€ *pont de Malviès; tel: 04 67 93 39 43. Open daily all year.* Tiny restaurant in former stables on a lonely stretch of the Canal du Midi west of the village. Run by an English couple, Steve and Kirsty Fawcett, it is one of the best for miles. Reservations essential.

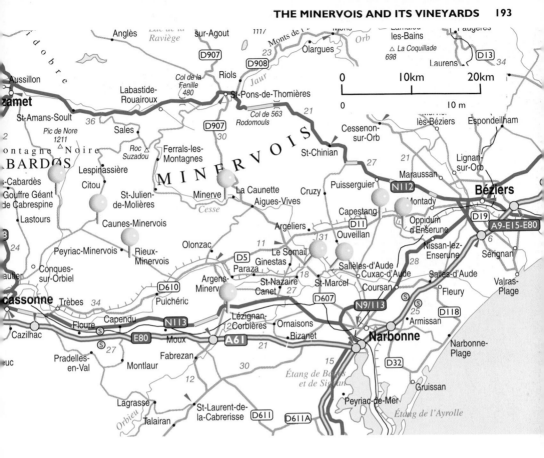

CAUNES-MINERVOIS✦✦✦

🛈 **Abbaye de Caunes-Minervois**
€€ *tel: 04 68 78 09 44. Open daily all year.* Has tourist information.

A striking modern pillar-like sculpture in the famous local red and white mottled marble (which was quarried nearby until the 1980s) welcomes you to this quaint village on the edge of the Montagne Noire. Narrow streets with some fine medieval and Renaissance mansions – *hôtels particuliers* – slope up to the honey-coloured stone **Abbaye de Caunes-Minervois✦✦**, around which the village developed over 1200 years ago. Parts of the Romanesque abbey church, resplendent with lots of the red marble, date from the 11th century. The other abbey buildings include a basement, now converted into a wine cellar, and newly restored cloister.

Accommodation in Caunes-Minervois

Hôtel d'Alibert €€ *rue Saint Genes; tel: 04 68 78 00 54. Closed Nov–Mar.* Small eight-room hotel in one of the town's historic mansions on the tiny square in the centre.

GOUFFRE GEANT DE CABRESPINE❖❖❖

ⓘ Gouffre Géant de Cabrespine €€
Tel: 04 68 26 14 22;
www.grottes-de-france.com.
Open daily Mar–Nov. Tours
last 45 minutes.

This huge cave in the Montagne Noire is known as Les Balcons du Diable (the 'balconies of the devil'). Inside, you walk along a balcony to view its various chambers – the largest is a phenomenal 250m high – and its intricate crystal formations.

LEZIGNAN-CORBIERES❖

ⓘ Lézignan-Corbières Tourist Information 9 cours de la République; tel: 04 68 27 05 42. Open daily July–Aug; Mon–Sat Sept–June.

ⓘ Musée de la Vigne et du Vin € 3 rue Turgot; tel: 04 68 27 07 57. Open daily.

You don't need to be a wine buff to enjoy the large **Musée de la Vigne et du Vin**❖❖❖, a large wine museum which now occupies an old winery and its stables near the railway station. It has an enormous collection, haphazardly displayed, of everything involved in growing vines and making and selling wine, including a huge vat for treading the grapes and a defumigating contraption which was pulled by a team of oxen. Don't be put off by the building's scruffy exterior as the exhibits are fascinating and the curator – from the fourth generation of the winery's owners – extremely knowledgeable.

MINERVE❖❖❖

ⓘ Minerve Tourist Information rue des Martyrs; tel: 04 68 91 81 43; Open Tue–Sun Apr–Sept.. Guided tours include **St-Etienne church**, which is closed otherwise.

Ⓟ Access to the village by car is for residents only; there are car parks before the bridge.

ⓘ Musée Hurepel € 5 rue Martyrs; tel: 04 68 91 12 26. Open Apr–Oct daily.

For its dramatic setting and poignant history, this small village is the jewel of the Minervois – and justifiably thronged by visitors all summer. Its sandy-coloured old houses with red roofs cluster along a rocky ledge with deep river gorges on either side. The main access is over a triple-arched bridge from which narrow streets lead up to the chimney-like tower of its ruined castle past the 900-year-old St-Etienne church whose white marble altar dates from the 5th century. Several of the handful of shops, cafés and caves offer tastings of Minervois wines.

A Cathar stronghold during the Albigensian Crusade, the village held out for five weeks in 1210 in searing summer heat when besieged by Simon de Montfort and 7000 men. After running out of water when de Montfort managed to destroy the only well, Puits St-Rustique, in the ramparts at the bottom of the village, the Cathar villagers finally gave in. Threatened with slaughter or Catholicism, about 180 stood by their faith and were burned alive. Their courage is commemorated by a memorial stone on place de la Mairie. The story of the Crusade is portrayed by miniature tableaux in the **Musée Hurepel**❖.

Left
Capestang's Gothic church

OPPIDUM D'ENSERUNE✦✦✦

Oppidum d'Ensérune *tel: 04 67 37 01 23. Open daily July–Aug; Tue–Sun Sept–June. Free.* **Museum** €€.

Standing on a hillock surrounded by flat countryside just outside the village of Nissan-lez-Ensérune, the pre-Roman site of Oppidum d'Ensérune enjoys distant views as far as the Canigou Mountain to the west and the Cévennes to the north. Today it resembles an abandoned garden, as the remains of its ancient columns and walls are mixed with cypress trees and pines. Excavations in 1915 revealed that the hill was inhabited from the 6th century BC until the 1st century AD. The earliest settlement was probably destroyed by Hannibal around 300 BC when 10,000 people may have been living there. It was rebuilt by the Romans in 118 BC when they settled in Narbonne. Pottery, coins, jewellery and even an egg (found intact in one of the graves) are on show in a small **museum**✦.

RIEUX-MINERVOIS✦✦✦

Rieux-Minervois Tourist Information *place de l'Eglise; tel: 04 68 78 13 98. Open daily all year.* Ask for the free leaflet about the church.

There is a very good reason to pause in this small town as a wonderful surprise awaits you inside Eglise Ste-Marie, part of a row of unprepossessing houses, though recognisable as a church from its sturdy bell tower. The interior is a 14-sided polygon surrounding a circular sanctuary whose dome is supported by seven arches made up of three pillars and four columns with carved capitals. It's unusual and a real gem.

SALLELES D'AUDE✧

**❶ Sallèles d'Aude
Tourist Information**
*2 quai de Lorraine;
tel: 04 68 46 81 46.
Open Mon–Sat July–Sept..*

❷ Amphoralis €€
*allée des Potiers (off
the D1626 beside the canal
1km north of town);
tel: 04 68 46 89 48.
Open daily all year.*

**Musée du Vieux
Sallèles €€** *5 avenue
Marcellin Albert; tel: 04 68
46 93 40. Open afternoons
daily May–Sept.*

The reason for going to this small town is to visit its two museums. **Amphoralis (Musée des Potiers Gallo-Romains)✧✧✧**, a striking modern construction, has been built over an old Roman pottery where amphorae – huge storage pots – and domestic items were made. The amphorae, each holding six gallons, were used to transport wine across Europe to the edges of the Roman Empire, a reminder that Languedoc has been an important wine-producing area for many centuries. The other museum, **Musée du Vieux Sallèles✧**, has three sections, covering old crafts, vines/wines and everyday life from the late 19th century to the end of the German occupation in 1945.

Food in Sallèles d'Aude

Les Ecluses € *20 grand'rue; tel: 04 68 46 94 47. Closed Tue.* This small homely restaurant, renowned for its cuisine, is popular with British people living in the area as it is run by a French–English couple.

LE SOMAIL✧✧

Left
The Oppidum d'Ensérune

Right
Le Somail's hat museum

Bargemen used to stop overnight at this delightful old canal-side village where their old stables and inn provide reminders of a slower age. Two recent unusual additions are a large second-hand bookshop,

Musée de la Chapellerie €€
3 rue Bergerie, Le Somail;
tel: 04 68 46 19 26.
Open daily June–Oct,
afternoons only Nov–May.

Below
The Canal du Midi

Le Trouve-Tout du Livre* (*tel: 04 68 46 21 64*), and **Le Musée de la Chapellerie**, a hat museum displaying 6500 examples dating back to the 1850s. Collected by Antoine Ramoneda, whose family worked in Limoux's hat-making industry for six generations, they include everything from wedding bonnets and bishops' mitres to soldiers' helmets from a succession of wars.

(Ⓠ) Canal holiday boat hire: Minervois Cruisers; *38 chemin des Patiasses, Le Somail; tel: 04 68 46 28 52; www.minervoiscruisers.com.* Bookings (in UK): *tel: 01926 81184. Canal open Apr–Oct.*

Canal du Midi

The 240km-long canal between **Sète** and **Toulouse**, designated by UNESCO as a World Heritage Site, was the brainchild of a prosperous salt-tax inspector, Pierre-Paul Riquet. In 1667 he persuaded Louis XIV to support his ambitious idea of linking the Mediterranean and the Atlantic to enable boats to avoid the long voyage around Gibraltar which was notorious for pirates. Some 15,000 labourers worked on the canal's wandering course but by the time it was completed, after 14 years, Riquet himself was bankrupt. Fed by a complicated system of smaller canals and reservoirs and punctuated by locks, aqueducts and tunnels, it remains a remarkable engineering achievement, enhanced by the elegance of its many bridges and the long lines of trees on its banks. Boats can be hired at several places along the canal.

Suggested tour

Total distance: 170km. The detour to Sallèles d'Aude adds 6km, the detour to Lézignan-Corbières adds 10km and the detour to the Gouffre Géant de Cabrespine cave adds 20km.

Time: 4 hours' driving. Allow a day for the main route, more with detours. Those with limited time should concentrate on the stretch between Caunes-Minervois and Minerve.

Links to other tours: From Caunes-Minervois the D620 leads to Carcassonne (*see page 128*), 20km away. From Sales the D920 leads to St-Pons-de-Thomières (*see page 207*), 25km away. From Capestang the D16 leads to Puisserguier (*see page 206*), 5km away, and the D11 leads to Béziers (*see page 202*), 15km away. From Lézignan-Corbières the D611 and D212 lead to Lagrasse (*see page 136*), 20km away.

Leave Narbonne northwest on the D607 across the flat countryside to **St-Marcel**.

Detour: From St-Marcel, the D1118 leads to **SALLELES D'AUDE ❶** (3km) passing its ruined abbey and crossing the **Canal du Midi** on the way to the **Amphoralis** which is to the left beyond the village centre.

From St-Marcel, continue on the D607 and cross the Canal du Midi again in the picturesque hamlet of **LE SOMAIL ❷**. Then take the D207 through **St-Nazaire** to join the D124 which goes through **Paraze** beside the canal to **Argens-Minervois**.

Detour: At Argens-Minervois, cross the canal and River Aude to join the D611 which goes to **LEZIGNAN-CORBIERES ❸** (5km).

From Argens-Minervois the D124 continues between the canal and river to **Olonzac**. Despite being the 'capital' of the Minervois, this

Above
Minerve

small town has a rather neglected feel, particularly in the maze of narrow streets in the centre. However, it has a pleasant municipal park with ducks and swans on a pond. Leave on the D610 (towards Carcassonnne), but turn right off it after 5km on to the D11 to go to **RIEUX-MINERVOIS** ❹ and then towards **CAUNES-MINERVOIS** ❺. Immaculately straight lines of vines cover almost every inch of the flat landscape.

Detour: Six kilometres after Rieux-Minervois, turn left on to the D620 and then right on to the D111 to visit the **GOUFFRE GEANT DE CABRESPINE** ❻ cave (10km).

North from Caunes-Minervois the scenery changes as you wriggle along the D620 beside the River Argent-Double. The vineyards are now replaced by apple, cherry and peach orchards as the road climbs through **Citou**, below its castle ruins, and **Lespinassière**, whose square castle tower is a landmark high on the edge of its steep terrace. Approaching **Sales** the road continues to climb through forests over the Col de Salette (886m) where you come to a sad reminder of World War II. From the road a short flight of steps leads down to the Stèle de la Résistance, a memorial to two local men killed there by the Germans in July 1944.

At Sales, turn right on to the D920 which soon passes the **Roc de Suzadou** (720m) viewpoint. The rock itself, jutting out above the

 La Bastide de Cabezac €€
Bize-Minervois (just north of D5); tel: 04 68 46 66 10. Twelve-room hotel in a renovated 18th-century *relais de poste* between Béziers and Carcassonne. Swimming pool. Disabled access.

Hôtel du Parc € *18 avenue Hompes, Olonzac; tel: 04 68 91 14 55. Small, very French hotel above a busy bar. Next door to a large school and opposite a pleasant park.*

Hôtel du Résidence €€ *35 avenue de la Cave, Nissan-lez-Ensérune; tel: 04 67 37 00 63. Closed mid-Dec–mid-Jan. Comfortable family-run hotel with 17 rooms, garden and garage.*

L'Auberge de Ferrals € *Ferrals-les-Montagnes; tel: 04 67 97 18 00. Closed Wed Oct–Mar. Small roadside restaurant in remote village on the D12.*

countryside, is a good spot for a picnic – and fun for children to clamber over. After 5km, turn right again on to the D12 through **Ferrals-les-Montagnes**, dropping down all the time. Just after **St-Julien-de-Molières**, turn left on to the D182 which runs above the **Canyon de la Cesse** (on the left), a deep winding ravine of white rocks below a plateau topped by brush and heather. Don't expect to see the river in this extraordinary canyon as it runs for several miles underground except after winter storms. Just before **MINERVE ❼** are two natural bridges, the 30m-high **Grand Pont** and 15m-high **Petit Pont**, created as the river carved its way through the white cliffs. To visit the village you have to park on the edge and walk. The landscape all around is wild and barren and on the the plateaux of sweet-smelling *garrigue* you can find dolmens, Bronze Age burial chambers made of huge stone blocks whose entrances mysteriously face east or south. Continuing down the Cesse valley, the D907 takes you past the village of **La Caunette** whose pale limestone buildings almost merge with the enormous cliff behind it. Arriving at the D5 (which becomes the D11), turn left to **CAPESTANG ❽** and **OPPIDUM D'ENSERUNE ❾**. From there, return to Narbonne through **Coursan** (whose large Gothic church has a Romanesque bell tower) on the D37 and then the N9 which has long straight stretches lined with plane trees to provide shade in the heat of summer.

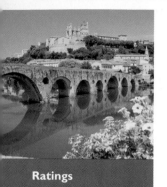

Roman Languedoc

Ratings

Scenery	●●●●●
Churches	●●●●○
History	●●●●○
Walking	●●●●○
Wine	●●●●○
Museums	●●●○○
Shopping	●●●○○
Villages	●●○○○

The quiet wooded hillsides of the Monts de l'Espinouse, where this route takes you, are another world compared with the busy streets of Béziers where it begins. In between it crosses that characteristic feature of the Languedoc plain, a seemingly endless patchwork of neatly planted vineyards. Along the way you have the choice of shopping, drinking or walking – or why not indulge in all three?

Plenty of roadside *caves* offer the opportunity to sample and buy wine. On reaching the Haut Languedoc Regional Park, shortly before St-Pons-de-Thomières, you will be tempted to leave your car and head into the hills along one of the many marked footpaths. Here the lush Monts de l'Espinouse have gloriously wide views dotted with lakes, waterfalls and prehistoric standing stones. For shopping, Béziers is well endowed with hypermarkets, but be prepared for its congested traffic in summer.

BEZIERS✦✦✦

ⓘ Béziers Tourist Information
29 avenue Saint Saëns;
tel: 04 67 76 84 00;
www.beziers-tourisme.fr.
Open daily July–Aug;
Mon–Sat Sept–June.

ⓜ Château de Raussac
route de Murviel, Béziers;
tel: 04 67 49 07 60.
Open Tue–Sat all year.
Ceramics artist Christine Viennet's workshop and collections on display; wine cellar visit and tasting.

Surrounded by vineyards, this lively town enjoys an attractive hillside setting above the River Orb and Canal du Midi. Its centrepiece is allée Paul Riquet, an acacia-shaded promenade created in honour of the famous engineer who built the canal in the 1660s. People gather there to gossip, stroll and browse amongst the stalls selling flowers and bric-à-brac. The top end slopes up to the town's grand 150-year-old theatre. At the other end is Plateau des Poêtes, a park with ornate sculptures and a small lake surrounded by trees.

Narrow streets punctuated by intimate squares lead to the fortress-like **Cathédrale de St-Nazaire✦✦✦**, a landmark for miles around. It was rebuilt in its original distinctive Romanesque style with a beautiful rose window after being burned down, when thousands of people had taken refuge inside, during the start of the Albigensian Crusade in 1209. Its 14th-century cloister leads into formal gardens, the Jardin de l'Evêché. The views down across the countryside from the cathedral's wide terrace are superb. You can see over the River Orb to the Oppidum d'Ensérune, with the Canigou mountain in the distance.

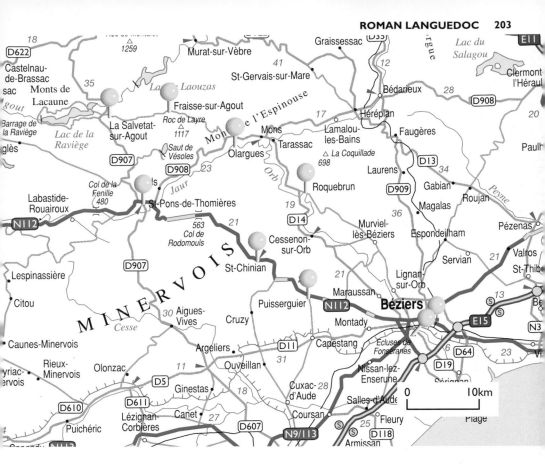

ⓘ Cathédrale de St-Nazaire €€
Open daily.

Musée du Biterrois €
rampe du 96ème, Caserne Saint-Jacques; tel: 04 67 36 81 61. Open Tue–Sat all year.

Musée des Beaux Arts €
1 rue de Bonsi; tel: 04 67 28 38 78. Open Tue–Sat all year. The Fine Arts Museum comprises two mansions, Hôtel Fabregat and Hôtel Fayet near the cathedral. They hold works by Flemish and German masters.

The **Musée du Biterrois**** (also called St-Jacques) in the former Royal Barracks covers the town's history from Roman times. Its exhibits include milestones that once lined the Via Domitia and the Trésor de Béziers, three silver platters from the 2nd, 3rd and 5th centuries, discovered in a local vineyard in 1983. It also has sections devoted to the building of the Canal du Midi and to local wines.

Today the town's highly successful rugby team, ASB, keeps it prominently on the European map. Bullfights are another sporting love.

Accommodation and food in Béziers

Imperator €€ *28 allée Paul Riquet; tel: 04 67 49 02 25; www.hotel-imperator.fr.* Centrally located 45-room hotel in 200-year-old mansion overlooking the lively allée Paul Riquet promenade, but with garden and garage. No restaurant.

Château de Lignan €€€ *Lignan-sur-Orb (7km northwest of Béziers on the D19); tel: 04 67 37 91 47.* Handsome, white three-storey mansion whose 15-acre grounds beside the River Orb include several 300-year-old trees.

Languedoc music festival in July.

Feria including street entertainment and bullfights in August.

Forty-nine rooms. Piano bar, swimming pool and whirlpool. Top-class restaurant specialising in seafood and regional cuisine such as baked pigeon.

Le Cep d'Or € *rue Viennet; tel: 04 67 49 28 09.* Tucked away in an old narrow street, this small restaurant offers a *tapas* plate of 18 different starters, though they might prevent you doing justice to its delicious *pâtisserie.*

ECLUSES DE FONSERANES◆◆◆

On the southwest edge of Béziers, just beyond the railway, this staircase of seven locks is one of the most remarkable features of the Canal du Midi, lifting the water 21.5m uphill. Boats pass through in convoy under the guidance of a lock-keeper, alternating the direction each hour. A parallel hydraulic lift-slope was built in 1983 but has never worked properly.

Below
Béziers by night

FRAISSE-SUR-AGOUT✧

Fraisse-sur-Agout Tourist Information *route de la Salvetat; tel: 04 67 97 53 81. Open daily May–Oct; Mon–Fri Nov–Apr.*

Nestled on the leafy banks of the River Agout, which fishermen rank highly, this mountain village got its name from the tall ash trees which have bordered it for centuries (*fraïsse* is the Occitan word for ash). Here, trout with mushrooms is a local speciality. During World War II the villagers were heavily involved with Resistance fighters based in the nearby Château de les Syères.

OLARGUES✧✧✧

Olargues Tourist Information *avenue de la Gare; tel: 04 67 97 71 26; www.olargues.org. Open daily July–Aug; Mon–Sat Sept–June.*

Olargues, one of the prettiest villages in the area, perches above the River Jaur on a rocky outcrop with a mountain ridge, Le Caroux, as its backdrop. The best view of it is from the quaint 800-year-old humpback bridge, Pont du Diable, over the river. A medieval bell tower, all that remains of its 11th-century fort, looks down on the red rooftops

ⓘ Musée d'Art et Traditions Populaires € *rue de la Place Escalier de la Commanderie. Open afternoons all year.*

of the old houses. Through a stone gateway opposite the tourist office, steep narrow streets lead past the 17th-century church up to the tower which enjoys a spectacular view down to the bridge and river with the mountains beyond. The **Musée d'Art et Traditions Populaires⁺** in the old Commandery building traces the village's history.

PUISSERGUIER⁺⁺

ⓘ Puisserguier Tourist Information *7 boulevard Victor Hugo; tel: 04 67 93 85 27; www.puisserguier.com. Open Mon–Sat all year.*

It's easy to hurry along the modern main street of this little town without realising that its medieval centre is only a few steps away. Be sure to park your car and turn up the narrow rue de la République to the intimate place de l'Eglise which is surrounded by a 12th-century castle, a Romanesque church and other ancient buildings, some now occupied by small shops.

ROQUEBRUN⁺⁺

ⓘ Roquebrun Tourist Information *rue du Barry; tel: 04 67 89 79 97; www.tourisme.roquebrun. free.fr. Open daily July–Aug; Mon–Sat Sept–June. Guided tours available.*

ⓘ Jardin Méditerranéen €€ *Tel: 04 67 89 55 29. Open daily mid-Feb–Nov. Guided tours (1 hour) available. Stout shoes recommended.*

Beneath its distinctive old tower, this little town spreads down a sunny hillside to the River Orb. Known as the 'little Nice of the Hérault' because of its luxuriant vegetation, it benefits from a microclimate thanks to its sheltered position and 300 days of sunshine a year. The exotic **Jardin Méditerranéen⁺⁺** features 200 varieties of cactus on riverside terraces. Canoeing is a popular pursuit on the river as it is navigable for 37km, including 11km of rapids.

ST-CHINIAN⁺

ⓘ St-Chinian Tourist Information *1 grand rue; tel: 04 67 38 02 67; www.ot-saint-chinian.com. Open daily July–Aug; Mon–Tue and Thur–Fri Sept–June.*

Surrounded by the vineyards, St-Chinian is a busy wine town with a long shaded square. Shepherds used to bring their wool to be spun in its mills here, but now it is notable for its **Cave des Vignerons⁺⁺** (*tel: 04 67 38 28 48*) where you can sample and buy the wines produced by the 20 villages which belong to the St-Chinian Appellation d'Origine Contrôlée.

St-Pons-de-Thomieres*

ℹ️ **St-Pons-de-Thomières Tourist Information** *place du Foirail; tel: 04 67 97 06 65; www.saint-pons-thomieres. com. Open daily July–Aug, Mon–Fri Sept–June.* Also information on the Parc Naturel Régional du Haut-Languedoc including maps and trail leaflets: *www.parc-haut-languedoc.fr*

🏛️ **Musée Municipal de Préhistoire €€** *rue du Barry; tel: 04 67 97 22 61. Open Fri and Sun.*

⛰️ **Pig festival** in Feb **and Chestnut festival** in Oct.

This old mountain town grew up around a Benedictine abbey founded in 936 by Count Raymond Pons of Toulouse. It stood on the site of the present cathedral which dates back to the 12th century and is richly decorated with sculptures, including a huge red and white marble altar. Though an impressive building, it was originally very much bigger as the choir used to stretch over the car park which is now in front of it. This was destroyed by Protestants in 1567, which accounts for the irregular layout and subsequent additions.

Being situated at the head of the Jaur valley in the centre of the Haut Languedoc Regional Park, the town is a good base for enjoying the great outdoors, whether by walking, riding or mountain-biking. A network of footpaths and trails radiate from it into the hills. The landscape all around is dotted with caves and prehistoric megaliths and menhirs. They include some of the oldest in Europe as the **Musée Municipal de Préhistoire**** shows.

Accommodation and food in St-Pons-de-Thomières

Auberge du Cabarétou € *Col du Cabarétou, route de Salvetat (on the D90, 10 km north of the town); tel: 04 67 97 02 31. Closed mid-Jan–mid-Feb.* A 250-year-old post house with 11 rooms at the Col de Cabarétou (947m) with fantastic views to the sea and Pyrenees, especially at sunrise.

Below St-Chinian

Les Bergeries de Pondérach €€ *route de Narbonne, St-Pons-de-Thomières; tel: 04 67 97 02 57. Closed mid-Nov–mid-Mar.* A 300-year-old farmhouse on the edge of the town with seven rooms and large garden. The restaurant features local produce such as chicken from the Montagne Noire and lamb from the Cévennes.

LA SALVETAT-SUR-AGOUT❖❖

ⓘ La Salvetat-sur-Agout Tourist Information *place des Archers; tel: 04 67 97 64 44; www.lasalvetatot.com. Open daily all year.*

Below
La Salvetat-sur-Agout

Built on a promontory high above two rivers, the Vèbre and Agout, this little town, a maze of hilly narrow streets, traces its roots back to the Knights Templar who founded 'new towns' in the 11th and 12th centuries to increase the value of their land. The 11th-century Chapelle St-Etienne de Cavall, below the town near the 800-year-old three-arch bridge, was a stop on the Via Tolosana, one of four routes which pilgrims used on their way to Spain.

The Albigensian Crusade

Although named after Albi, this fierce crusade to stamp out Catharism started in Béziers. In 1209 the French King, Philippe Auguste, saw it as his chance to subjugate the powerful Counts of Toulouse who were tolerating this new creed which had spread throughout the Languedoc. The King was supported by Pope Innocent III who was also keen to see the 'heresy' stamped out.

In Béziers the Roman Catholics stood loyally beside the comparatively few Cathars when the crusaders arrived from the north down the Rhône valley and started to rout them out. Many fled for shelter to the cathedral and the Madeleine church where they burned to death when the buildings were set on fire. Afterwards the papal legate proudly reported that they had 'only killed 20,000'.

Initially the Crusade was led by Simon de Montfort, but he was killed laying siege – for the second time – to Toulouse. The final bloody slaughter took place in Montségur in 1244, though 80 more years were to pass before the Inquisition succeeded in stamping out Catharism completely.

Suggested tour

Total distance: 145km. The detour to the Saut de Vésoles waterfall adds 10km and the detour to the Lac de la Raviège adds 24km.

Time: 4 hours' driving. Allow at least a day for the main route, more with detours. Those with limited time should concentrate on the stretch between St-Pons-de-Thomiéres and Olargues for scenery or the stretch between Béziers and St-Chinian for wine and shopping.

Links to other tours: From Béziers the D11 leads west to Capestang (*see page 192*), 15km away, the N112 leads east to Agde (*see page 270*), 23km away, and the N9 leads northeast to Pézenas (*see page 276*), 22km away. From Puisserguier, the D16 leads south to Capestang (*see page 192*), 5km away. From St-Pons-de-Thomières the D920 leads southwest to Salses (*see page 122*), 25km away. From La Salvetat-sur-Agout the D907 leads north to Lacaune (*see page 187*), 20km away.

Before leaving **BEZIERS ❶**, pause at the **ECLUSES DE FONSERANES ❷** on the **Canal du Midi,** reached along a track on the southern edge of the town. In summer the queues of boats going up and down this staircase of locks are always entertaining to watch. The flat N112 then takes you northwest towards **PUISSERGUIER ❸** through the St-Chinian vineyards which stretch along the gently rounded ridges

Above
The soil in the Somail area is ideally suited to chestnuts

making the most of the abundant sunshine. The reddish soil is poor, almost rocky, and seems to glow in the setting sun. After **ST-CHINIAN** ❹ you soon leave the vineyards behind as the road climbs into wooded hills, snaking up the Défilé de l'Llouvre to **ST-PONS-DE-THOMIERES** ❺ in the heart of the **Haut Languedoc Regional Park**. The D907 winds up picturesquely out of the town with pretty views back over its rooftops before it climbs over the Col de Cabarétou (947m). This has a splendid view over the sea to the southeast and of the Somail hills stretching away to the north. The Somail area, which rises to 1000m above the Jaur valley, is the lushest and most fertile part of the Monts de l'Espinouse. The hillsides are mainly covered with chestnut and beech trees, though these sometimes give way to expanses of moorland patched with heather.

Detour: To see the 200m-high **Saut de Vésoles** waterfall, a noted beauty spot, turn right at the Col de Cabarétou on to the D169 and then, after 4km, right again for a further 1km. The water tumbles over massive granite boulders to the River Jaur. The D907 then winds down to **LA SALVETAT-SUR-AGOUT** ❻ .

Detour: From La Salvetat-sur-Agout a pleasant 24km drive, mostly in woods, on the D14, leads round the **Lac de la Raviège** reservoir, part of the River Agout. The road crosses the dam at the far end and passes **Les Bouldouires**, a beach popular for swimming and water sports.

Leave La Salvetat-sur-Agout on the D14 which follows the river through gently rolling countryside to **FRAISSE-SUR-AGOUT** ❼ .

Roc Fourcat €
Mons la Triviale, near Tarrasac; tel: 04 67 97 71 83. Open all year. Simple eight-room family-run hotel beside the River Orb with scenic terrace.

The D14 climbs over the Col de Fontfroide (972m) where a roadside memorial commemorates the Resistance and De Gaulle's leadership of the Free French in World War II. An urn beneath it contains the ashes of concentration camp victims.

Ahead the road zigzags dramatically over the Espinouse hills before dropping down into **OLARGUES** ❽ . Follow the D908 (towards Clermont l'Herault), turning sharp right after 8km on to the D14 over the decorative white suspension bridge built in 1928 at **Tarassac** to go to **ROQUEBRUN** ❾ . As the road wriggles along the wooded Gorges de l'Orb beneath rocky ridges, the scenery becomes distinctly 'southern'. There are red-roofed villages and increasing numbers of vineyards as it flattens out on the way back through **Cessenon-sur-Orb** to Béziers.

Getting out of the car

To stretch your legs, a gentle hour's walk is marked out from the church in Fraisse-sur-Agout. It leads beside the River Agout, showing how the force of the water is used to create hydroelectricity through simple examples such as driving a musical wheel and a piston. Nearby there are picnic tables on a pretty island shaded by ash trees.

Montpellier

Food
and drink ●●●●○

Shopping ●●●●○

Architecture ●●●○○

Enterainment
●●●○○

History ●●●○○

Museums ●●●○○

Art ●●○○○

Children ●○○○○

The citizens of Montpellier have a reputation for being sociable and good-tempered, perhaps because they have the benefit of the place de la Comédie. This enormous square, surrounded by cafés and restaurants, is a popular spot for chatting over the local Languedoc wine. A high proportion of those who gravitate there each evening are young as the city has a student population of nearly 50,000. It is also swelled by an influx of visitors throughout the hot summer months.

Montpellier first made its mark on the world through its medical school which was founded over 1000 years ago and is still the most prestigious in France. This has also led to the development of a strong research base, particularly in biochemistry. Today the city prides itself on being forward-looking, epitomised by the construction during the 1980s of Antigone, a daring post-modern housing development in pseudo-classical style.

Getting there and getting around

ℹ️ **Languedoc-Roussillon regional information office** *20 rue de la République; tel: 04 67 22 81 00; e-mail: contact.crtlr@sunfrance.com; www.cr-languedocroussillon.fr/ tourisme. Open Mon–Fri.*

Airport: Montpellier Méditerranée is 8km southeast of the city centre on the D21 or D66. Information: *tel: 04 67 20 85 00*. Facilities include car hire, hotel reservations, restaurants, nursery and local products shop. As you come in to land, watch out for the view over the lagoon, Etang de Mauguio, home to 4000 flamingos. Buses to the city centre run every 30 to 50 minutes (depending on time and day). Journey time 15 minutes.

Railway station: *rue Jules Ferry. Reservations: tel: 36 35.*

By car: Leave the A9, which skirts the south side of the city, from the north at Sortie Est and take the D66, avenue Pierre Mendès-France, to the centre. From the south, leave at Sortie Sud and at the Rond-Point des Prés d'Arènes take avenue de Maurin. Driving in the centre can be a nightmare. As well as being busy, it is difficult to negotiate, as much

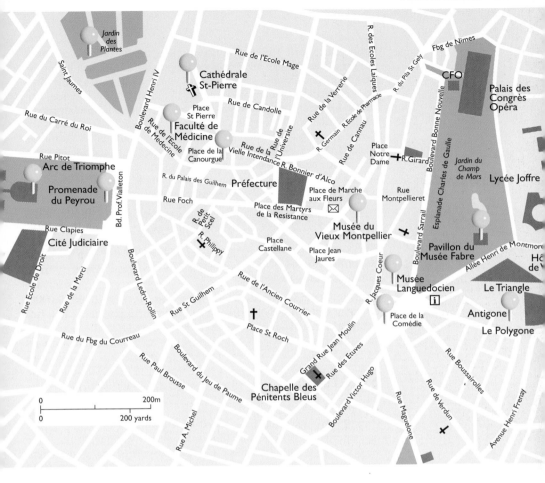

Map labels:

Jardin des Plantes

Saint Jaumes

Rue de l'Ecole Mage

R. des Ecoles Laïques

Fbg de Nîmes

R. du Pila St Gely

CFO

Palais des Congrès Opéra

Rue du Carré du Roi

Boulevard Henri IV

Cathédrale St-Pierre

Rue de Candolle

Rue de la Verrerie

Rue de l'Ecole de Médecine

Place St Pierre

Faculté de Médicine

Place de la Canourgue

Rue de la Vielle Intendance

Rue de l'Université

R. Germain

R. Ecole de Pharmacie

Rue de Cannau

Boulevard Bonne Nouvelle

Esplanade Charles de Gaulle

Jardin du Champ de Mars

Lycée Joffre

Rue Pitot

Arc de Triomphe

Place Notre Dame

R. Girard

Promenade du Peyrou

Bd. Prof. Vialleton

R. du Palais des Guilhem

Préfecture

R. Bonnier d'Alco

Place de Marche aux Fleurs

Rue Montpellieret

Boulevard Sarrail

Jardin du Champ de Mars

Pavillon du Musée Fabre

Allée Henri de Montmore

Rue Clapies

Rue Foch

Place des Martyrs de la Resistance

Musée du Vieux Montpellier

Hô de V

Cité Judiciaire

R. de Petit Scel

R. Philippy

Place Castellane

Place Jean Jaures

R. Jacques Coeur

Musée Languedocien

Le Triangle

Rue Ecole de Droit

Rue de la Merci

Boulevard Ledru-Rollin

Rue St Guilhem

Rue de l'Ancien Courrier

Place de la Comédie

Antigone

Le Polygone

Rue du Fbg du Courreau

Boulevard du Jeu de Paume

Place St Roch

Grand Rue Jean Moulin

Rue des Etuves

Rue Boussairolles

Rue Paul Brousse

Rue A. Michel

Chapelle des Pénitents Bleus

Boulevard Victor Hugo

Rue Maguelone

Rue de Verdun

Avenue Henri Frenay

0 — 200m
0 — 200 yards

ⓘ Montpellier Tourist Information *30 allée Jean de Lattre de Tassigny, Esplanade Comédie; tel: 04 67 60 60 60; e-mail: contact@ot-montpellier.fr; www.ot-montpellier.fr. Open daily all year. Tourist Information kiosks also open in summer at the railway station, rue Jules Ferry, and on the eastern approach to the city with coach parking at Moulin de l'Evêque, 78 avenue du Pirée.*

of the central area, signposted Centre Historique or L'Ecusson, is pedestrianised. Moreover the new Antigone area which stretches like a spur off the east side of the centre is both difficult to locate and worse to get into, especially from the south and west, due to its one-way streets and restricted entry. The important thing to bear in mind is that boulevard d'Antigone and boulevard de L'Aéroport International run along the north side of it and allée du Nouveau Monde, avenue S Champlain and avenue Jacques Cartier along the south side. They are linked by rue Léon Blum.

Parking: Though there are parking meters on the streets around the Centre Historique, the underground car park at place de la Comédie allows more time for sightseeing. There are also several car parks around the Antigone, but be warned, to get to them, you have to crack the one-way almost-bus-only street layout which even the locals find difficult.

Public transport: The Centre Historique is easily walkable from the Antigone area through the Polygone shopping mall, though it's not so straightforward finding your way back again. **Le Tramway**, the city's latest pride and joy, runs east–west over 15km, with distinctive deep blue air-conditioned trams (*www.tam-way.com*). **Petibus** is a minibus service on a circular route every six minutes Monday–Saturday around the Centre Historique and out to the Antigone. Normal buses go further afield; **TAM** *tel: 04 67 22 87 87*. Single-journey fares include changes. Services to the local beaches including Carnon Plage, la Grande Motte and Palavas-les-Flots depart from the bus station in rue Jules Ferry, which is linked by escalators to the railway station in place Auguste-Gibert.

There are taxi ranks beside place de la Comédie and outside the train station, 24-hour call: *tel: 04 67 20 35 20* or *04 67 10 00 00*.

Bikes can be hired from TAM Velo, 27 rue Maguelone (near railway station); *tel: 04 67 92 92 67*. A deposit of €150 per bike and identity card or passport are required.

Guided tours in French start from the tourist office, Wed, Sat and Sun Oct–May and twice daily in summer. From the esplanade Charles de Gaulle, the Petit Train (road train) sets off on a tour of the town every 45 mins from 1400.

Sights

Antigone**

Only the French could have dared to sanction such a startling new quarter only a few steps away from the Centre Historique. As the name suggests, this is Classical Greece and Rome re-created in a post-modern development of apartments, offices, hotels and shops. It was conceived in 1980 by a Catalan architect, Ricardo Bofill, to provide housing on a site vacated by the army. Whether you get to it on foot through the Polygone shopping mall or approach it from the side, it always comes as a surprise. The tall beige buildings, pseudo-classical with columns, arches and pediments, face wide, circular, symmetrically tiled piazzas. Avenues of trees, window boxes and giant pots trailing with geraniums add softness, but the area, which is pedestrian-only, has yet to really come alive, probably because *le tout Montpellier* is out gossiping on the place de la Comédie.

Arc de Triomphe*

This grand triumphal arch at the Porte de Peyrou was erected in honour of Louis XIV in 1691. Bas-reliefs around it depict the major events during his reign, including the building of the Canal du Midi, the capture of Naumur and, something that he might with hindsight prefer history to forget, the revocation of the Edict of Nantes which made Protestantism illegal.

Musée Atger *rue de l'Ecole de Médecine; tel: 04 67 66 27 77. Open Mon, Wed, Fri. Closed Aug and Christmas. Free.*

Musée de la Pharmacie *15 avenue Charles Flahault; tel: 04 67 54 80 62. Open Tue and Fri. Free.*

Jardin des Plantes *boulevard Henri IV; tel: 04 67 63 43 22; www.mediterraneangarden society.org. Open daily. Free.*

Pavillon du Musée Fabre €€ *esplanade Charles de Gaulle; tel: 04 67 66 13 46. Open daily all year.*

Cathédrale St-Pierre✦✦

The city's cathedral was started in the 14th century but not completed until the 19th. Its most striking feature is an immense Gothic porch with two large pillars, though they are somewhat out of proportion to the rest of the building.

Faculté de Médecine✦✦

The city's medical school occupies former abbey buildings, much enlarged and renovated. It was founded in 1220 and claims to be the oldest in the world. Rabelais, the 16th-century French satirist, was one of its most famous graduates. Its **Musée Atger**✦ displays over 500 drawings collected by Jean-François Atger in the 18th century. Other university faculties also have specialist museums, including **Musée de la Pharmacie** in avenue Charles Flahault.

Jardin des Plantes✦✦

France's oldest botanical garden was planted in 1593 to enable the medical school students to study medicinal plants. A *phillyrea latifolia* tree dating from that time is among its treasures. Statues of eminent botanists grace paths leading to an orangery, conservatories and ponds.

Pavillon du Musée Fabre✦✦

Facing the Esplanade, the city's main art gallery, the Musée Fabre✦✦, occupies a fine mansion which was a Jesuit college in the 15th and 16th centuries, but it is closed for renovation until 2006. Meanwhile temporary exhibitions are being staged at its Pavillon.

Below
Montpellier's Antigone District

Musée Languedocien**

Housed in a carefully restored 15th-century mansion, the Musée Languedocien displays prehistoric objects and classical artefacts from ancient Rome, Greece and Egypt.

Musée du Vieux Montpellier**

The museum of old Montpellier in the Hôtel de Varenne conjures up images of the city as it used to be, through pictures, old maps and furniture. On its top floor, the small **Musée du Fougau***, run by volunteers, displays traditional costumes, old sewing machines and local crafts.

Place de la Canourgue*

Surrounded by grand mansions, this handsome square was once the centre of the city. Its fountain with a unicorn was built in the 1760s to distribute water around the town from the nearby St Clément aqueduct.

Place de la Comédie***

This enormous square laid out in the 18th century is the heart of the city, despite being on the edge of the Centre Historique. The Comédie theatre with its fancy stucco façade, built in 1889, is at one end. In the centre is the ornately sculpted Fontaine des Trois-Graces depicting – as you might not expect from its name – three male bathers. The square is known locally as l'Oeuf, after its egg-shaped central roundabout which traffic used to race around until it was pedestrianised.

Promenade du Peyrou**

The Promenade's two tiers of terraces were built at the beginning of the 18th century at the city's highest point. Their purpose was to provide a suitably impressive setting for a commemorative equestrian statue of Louis XIV which was eventually placed there in 1718. Due to several misadventures, including toppling off a boat into the River Garonne, it had taken 20 years to arrive, and was then destroyed

---

Ⓘ Crypt Notre Dame des Tables € *place Jean Jaurès; tel: 04 67 54 33 16. A new museum using audio-visual technology to uncover the city's past. Free for visitors on a guided tour from the Office de Tourisme.*

Musée Languedocien €€ *7 rue Jacques-Coeur; tel: 04 67 52 93 03. Open Mon–Sat.*

Musée du Vieux Montpellier *Hôtel de Varenne, 2 place Pétrarque; tel: 04 67 66 02 94. Open Tue–Sat. Free.*

Musée du Fougau *Hôtel de Varennes, 2 place Pétrarque; tel: 04 67 66 02 94. Open Wed and Thur.*

Above
Montpellier's place de la Comédie

during the Revolution. The present statue is a 150-year-old replica. In the 1760s the Promenade acquired the splendid Château d'Eau, a water tower which is truly a mini-castle with pillars, arches and carved pediments. It was built for the St-Clément Aqueduct which is itself a grand affair, inspired by the Roman Pont du Gard.

From the top terrace you get a splendid view over the city and countryside with the sea and foothills of the Cévennes in the distance.

Shopping

The old streets in the Centre Historique are delightful for shopping, thanks to the many small boutiques which have opened in the ground floors of the ancient buildings. Those in rue de l'Ancien Courrier occupy a former abbey and have vaulted ceilings. Their wares are equally appealing, as in **Bernice**, a hat shop for men and women at *7 rue Jean Moulin*; **Droguerie J Estoul**, an old-fashioned pharmacy on place Castellane; and **Pomme de Reinette**, *33 rue de l'Aiguillerie*, which is crammed with toys old and new. The modern **Polygone** shopping mall is filled with chain stores as well as **Galeries Lafayette** and **Inno**. Everywhere closes at 1830, except **Monoprix** on place de la Comédie which stays open until 2100. There's a daily covered food market at place Castellane and an open-air market on the Plan Cabannes along boulevard Gambetta. On Saturdays a flea market occupies the arches of the old aqueduct along the boulevard des Arceaux.

Entertainment

Because of the city's warm climate and large number of students, much of its evening entertainment consists simply of strolling the old streets, sitting at cafés and watching street performers such as buskers and jugglers. Place de la Comédie, which has the distinction of being the largest traffic-free square in France, gets packed out on summer evenings.

Entertainment of a more formal kind is provided by ten theatres, notably opera at **l'Opéra-Comédie**, *place de la Comédie*, and **Opéra Berlioz** in the Corum building. Box office for both: *tel: 04 67 60 19 99; www.opera-montpellier.com*

For multiplex cinemas, head east from the town centre along avenue Pierre Mendès-France.

Nightclubs include **Zénith** *Domaine de Grammont, avenue Albert-Einstein; tel: 04 67 64 50 00.*

Annual events include: **Spring Theatre Festival**, le Printemps des Comédiens; *tel: 04 67 63 66 67*, and **Dance Festival**; *tel: 04 67 60 83 60*, both in June. **Festival de Radio France et de Montpellier** is a three-week music festival in mid-July featuring young performers, including free jazz concerts. The tourist office website has up-to-date details at *www.ot-montpellier.fr*

Accommodation and food

There are hotels in all price ranges. Several are situated in the streets around the railway station such as rue de la République, rue de Verdun and rue Maguelone. The newest are in the Antigone area.

Hôtel du Palais € *3 rue du Palais des Guilhem; tel: 04 67 60 47 38*, is an inexpensive small hotel in the heart of the Centre Historique.

La Maison Blanche €€ *1796 avenue de la Pompignane; tel: 04 99 58 20 70; www.hotel-maison-blanche.com*, is the most elegant of the city's hotels, yet surprisingly affordable. It stands in lush gardens on the edge, handily placed for the airport.

New Hôtel du Midi €€ *22 boulevard Victor-Hugo; tel: 04 67 92 69 61; e-mail: montpelliermidi@new-hotel.com.* Though occupying a grand 19th-century building (only steps from the place de la Comédie), it has smart new rooms, all air conditioned.

Sofitel-Antigone €€€ *1 rue des Pertuisanes; tel: 04 67 99 72 72; www.sofitel-montpellier.com,* is modern in design and facilities. Well placed between the Polygone and Antigone, it is next door to an underground garage. The rooftop terrace with a restaurant and pool has one of the best views in town.

As a university town, Montpellier abounds in inexpensive good-quality eating places as well as smart establishments. You are never far away from a restaurant or café in the old squares and streets of the Centre Historique. They come in all price ranges and their ancient surroundings make them very atmospheric.

Les Bains €€ *6 rue Richelieu; tel: 04 67 60 70 87. Closed Sun.* Occupies a leafy courtyard and has small arcaded rooms which functioned for 200 years as public baths until they closed in 1963. A *salon-de-thé* in the afternoons, it becomes a fashionable restaurant serving local specialities at moderate prices in the evenings.

Café du Théâtre € *3 place de la Comédie; tel: 04 67 66 06 55*, offers an inexpensive *plat-du-jour* (dish of the day) as well as snacks. Its best feature is its prime position for watching the world go by. *Open daily to 0200.*

Le César Antigone €€ *17 place du Nombre d'Or; tel: 04 67 64 87 87*, is a classic French brasserie, one of several specialist restaurants in the Antigone area.

La Diligence €€ *2 place Pétrarque; tel: 04 67 66 12 21; www.la-diligence.com*, is a smart little restaurant in a vaulted building, typical of the many atmospheric eateries which lurk in the narrow streets of the Centre Historique.

Maison de la Lozère € *27 rue de L'Aiguillerie; tel: 04 67 66 46 36*, serves specialities of the Lozère region such as *aligot* (potato mashed with cheese) and herb sausages. You can also buy them in its small vaulted shop.

Suggested walk

Length: 2.5km.

Duration: 1 hour.

After lingering at a café on the **PLACE DE LA COMEDIE** ❶, stroll under the plane trees along the **Esplanade Charles-de-Gaulle**. This wide promenade, laid out in the 18th century, is bordered by flowerbeds and fountains. It leads to the **Corum** building, a bunker-like 1980s addition in concrete and pink granite (from Finland) which houses the Opéra Berlioz, a conference centre and exhibition rooms. From the terrace, open daily, the dazzling white spire of the **Eglise Ste-Anne** stands out in the distance over the rooftops.

Rue Girard and rue des Augustins on the west side lead immediately into a different world, the **Centre Historique**. Locals call it *lou clapas* (the rubble) but it is signposted **L'Ecusson** because of its coat-of-arms shape formed by the boulevards which surrounded its maze of old narrow streets. The whole area, with its many old churches and Renaissance *hôtels particuliers* (mansions) built in cream stone, is a delight – the true spirit of Montpellier.

Making your way towards the **CATHEDRALE** ❷, perhaps down the hilly rue de l'Université and turning along rue de Candolle, you will see informative plaques on the most important of the 17th- and 18th-century mansions with their decorative stonework and wrought-iron balustrades. A glimpse through any of the sturdy wooden doorways which happen to be open is likely to reveal an intimate courtyard. The

Les Folies Montpelliéraines

Scattered in the countryside around Montpellier, anything from 3 to 16km from the city centre, are its *folies*. These are not the buildings usually referred to as 'follies', but elegant family mansions. Indeed the rest of France would call them *châteaux*. They were built in the 18th century by local aristocrats and wealthy bourgeois citizens, particularly bankers, as country houses where they could retreat during the hot summer months. Most have pretty gardens adorned with statuettes and fountains. At least 30 are still surrounded by their original vineyards though the city's suburbs have encroached on some. A number can be visited, including several now owned by the city such as **Château d'O** and **Château la Mosson** (details from the tourist office). Others are still private homes whose owners often act as hosts to visitors. Moderate entry charges provide much-needed funds towards their upkeep.

area was rebuilt after the destruction of virtually all the earlier buildings during various religious wars. Interesting little shops and restaurants now occupy many of the ground floors.

Place St-Pierre, with the cathedral and **FACULTE DE MEDICINE** ❸ beside it, is one of many small squares where you can while away the time in a café or restaurant. From the square, narrow streets and cobbled alleys lead uphill past **PLACE DE LA CANOURGUE** ❹ to the **ARC DE TRIOMPHE** ❺ on the edge of the Centre Historique. The Promenade du Peyrou is across the busy boulevard Prof Valleton.

Turning back along the broad rue Foch, a right turn into rue du Petit Scel takes you to the oldest part of the city, the **Ancien Courrier** district. Rue de l'Ancien-Courrier, which leads back towards place de la Comédie, is particularly worth strolling along because of its interesting old façades and courtyards.

Also worth exploring

Château de Flaugergues €€
1744, avenue Albert Einstein; tel: 04 99 52 66 37; www.flaugergues.com. Open daily July–Aug; Mon–Sat Sept–June.

Château de Flaugergues✱✱✱ and **Château d'Assas**✱✱ are two very different examples of the *folies* (see box) in the countryside around Montpellier. **Flaugergues**, a 15-minute drive east from the city centre, is one of the oldest. An unassuming, early 18th-century mansion in cream stone set in a symmetrical French garden beside informal gardens and woodland, it is the home of the de Colbert family. Count Henri de Colbert, his wife Brigitte or one of their children show visitors round. Vineyards which were first cultivated by the Romans surround it. Inside, the walls of the extravagant staircase, which occupies a quarter of the entire interior, are covered in Brussels

Château d'Assas
€€ *Assas; tel: 04 67 59 61 60; www.chateau-assas.com. Open daily by appointment.*

tapestries and family portraits. The lived-in rooms contain a variety of family treasures including some fine antique furniture. The count's highly regarded wines are on sale in the winery's cellars in an adjoining courtyard.

The castle-like **Château d'Assas**, built in 1715, is 12km north of the city in Assas off the D109. It is the home of Madame Demangel and her musician son who may be around to play one of the old pianofortes collected by Madame's late mother. Another of its treasures is a small decoratively painted domestic organ *positif* dating from 1737. Concerts are sometimes staged there and the château's vineyards produce red, white and rosé *appellation d'origine contrôlée* wines which can be bought in the village at Vignerons du Pic, *285 avenue de Ste-Croix; tel: 04 67 59 62 55; www.vigneronsdupic.com. Open Mon–Sat.*

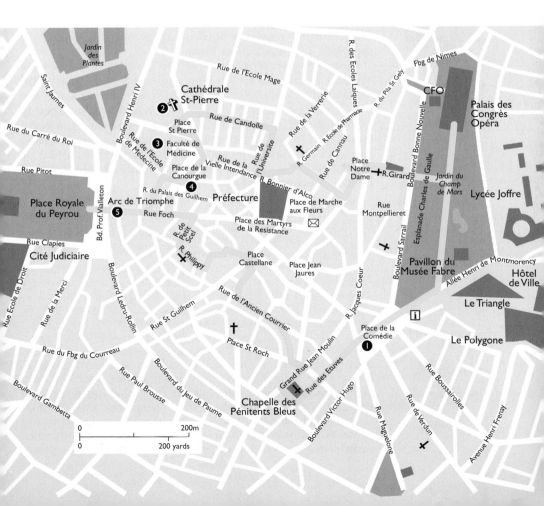

Grottes and cirques

Ratings

Caves	●●●●●
Geology	●●●●●
Scenery	●●●●○
Villages	●●●●○
Food	●●●○○
Historical sights	●●●○○
Children	●●○○○
Outdoor activities	●●○○○

The word *cirque* (natural amphitheatre of rocks) will have a new significance after you travel this route up the valley of the River Hérault. It includes two very different *cirques*. The deep wide bowl at Navacelles is surely one of the most spectacular pieces of countryside in France, whereas the cluster of massive eroded dolomite rocks at Mourèze is more like a crowded ghost town.

The route also visits some of the caves (*grottes*) that lie under the rugged white limestone hills and plateaux. Patched with yellow gorse, these hills are divided up by the surprisingly green waters of the Hérault and its tributaries.

Rural as the countryside feels once you leave the main roads, it is by no means remote, particularly now that the new A75 autoroute speeds motorists through it, and it is punctuated with small towns where pavement cafés spill out invitingly onto shaded squares.

ANIANE⋄⋄

ⓘ Aniane Tourist Information
Chapelle des Pénitents;
tel: 04 67 57 01 42.
Open daily July–Aug.

The roots of this busy little town go back to 792 when St Benoît founded a Bendictine monastery here. Many of the tall old houses along the straight narrow streets in the old quarter have fancy stonework and wrought-iron balconies, a reminder of the town's importance in the Middle Ages when it was on the ancient salt route north from the Mediterranean lagoons.

CIRQUE DE NAVACELLES⋄⋄⋄

This 280m-deep basin in the mountains, 1.5km across, is one of the most spectacular natural wonders that Europe has to offer, especially for motorists. The road winds down the sides, looking like a thin thread on the grey limestone hillsides which are patched with scrubby bushes and yellow gorse. The River Vis meanders

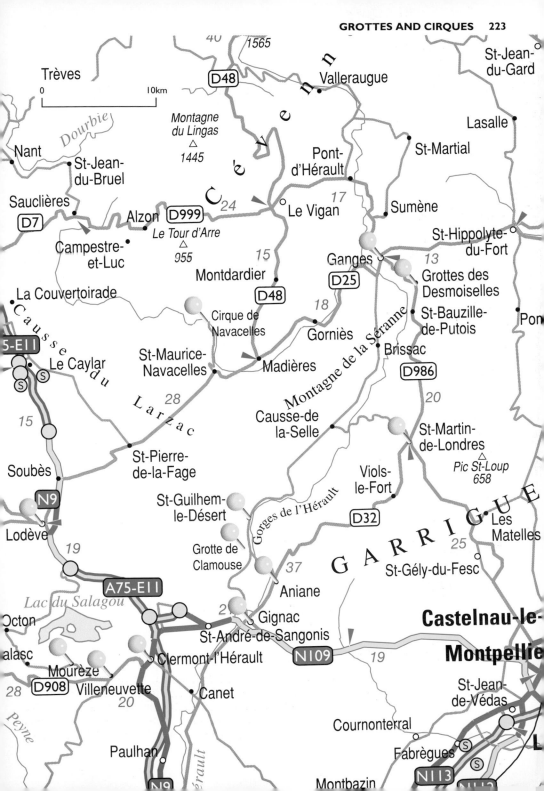

through the *cirque*, crossed by a single-arched bridge in the tiny village of St-Maurice-Navacelles which nestles almost at the bottom. Stop here for refreshment and to take in the awesome surroundings.

CLERMONT L'HERAULT**

ℹ Clermont l'Hérault Tourist Information 9 *rue Doyen René Goss; tel: 04 67 96 23 86. Open daily July–Aug; Mon–Sat Sept–June.*

🛒 There is a market on Wednesday mornings.

Huilerie Coopérative *avenue Président Wilson; tel: 04 67 96 10 36*, sells olive oil made on the premises from olives supplied by over 200 local producers.

Clermont l'Hérault is overlooked by the ruins of its huge 10th-century castle whose ramparts and towers provide splendid views of the surrounding countryside. Eglise St-Paul, which was fortified in the 15th century to help defend the town during the Hundred Years' War, has a beautiful blue and red rose window, the best in the Midi, but unfortunately it is partially obscured by the organ pipes.

Accommodation and food in Clermont l'Hérault

Hôtel du Terminus €€ *11 allée Roger Salengro; tel: 04 67 88 45 00.* Former railway hotel on quiet leafy avenue in town centre, now smartly modernised with 22 rooms, including some in a rear annexe.

L'Arlequin € *place St Paul; tel: 04 67 96 37 47. Closed Mon.* Small two-floor restaurant with sun-trap terrace beside the massive Eglise St-Paul, run by a former embassy chef.

GANGES*

ℹ Ganges Tourist Information *plan de l'Ormeau tel: 04 67 73 00 56; www.ot-cevennesmediterranee.com. Open daily July–Aug; Mon–Sat Sept–June.*

Set beside the River Hérault below a bowl of wooded mountains, Ganges made its fortune during the reign of Louis XIV when silk stockings were in vogue. Several factories still make high-class hosiery though nylon has replaced both artificial and real silk. A walking trail leads round the points of interest in the centre and through the *chemins de traverses*, a network of covered alleys (like Lyon's more famous *traboules*) which now look disappointingly scruffy. The murder of the Marquise de Ganges by her brother-in-law in 1667 shook the French aristocracy and gave the town a place in literary history as it inspired the Marquis de Sade to write a 500-page novel based on it.

GIGNAC*

ℹ Gignac Tourist Information *place du Général Claparède (Hôtel de Laurès); tel: 04 67 57 58 83. Open Mon–Sat all year.*

The fortress-like tower of Notre-Dame-de-Grâce church overlooks the River Hérault and the town's pleasant waterside promenade and marina. Canoeing is popular on the river and details of canoe or kayak hire can be obtained from the tourist office.

GROTTE DE CLAMOUSE✦✦✦

Grotte de Clamouse €€€
route de St-Guilhem-le-Désert, St-Jean-de-Fos; tel: 04 67 57 71 05; www.clamouse.com. Open daily Feb–Oct; Sun–Fri Nov–Jan for 45-minute guided tours.

Although this beautiful cave with outstanding crystal formations was not explored until the exceptionally dry summer of 1945, the poignant story of the local family whose son worked as a shepherd on the plateau above is much older. One day he discovered that a carved stick he had thrown into a swallow hole (fissure) above it had emerged far below from a spring where his mother collected water. Afterwards he regularly sent things to his parents down the hole. But, alas, one day she found his body there; he had fallen into it and drowned. Its name means 'howling' in the local dialect.

GROTTE DES DESMOISELLES✦✦✦

Grotte des Desmoiselles €€ in the village of St-Bauzille de Putois; tel: 04 67 73 70 02; www.desmoiselles.com. One-hour guided tours daily all year.

Walkways lead around this enormous cave (120m long, 80m wide and 50m high) discovered in 1770 and explored by E-A Martel in 1884. The high natural columns inside give it a church-like quality. One of the most extraordinary formations is a virgin and child stalagmite.

LODEVE✦✦

Lodève Tourist Information 7 place de la République; tel: 04 67 88 86 44; www.lodeve.com. Open daily all year.

Gobelins workshops €€
avenue du Gééraln de Gaulle; tel: 04 67 96 40 40, arrange 1-hour guided tours on Tue, Wed and Thur by appointment.

Musée Cardinal-de-Fleury €€
square Georges Auric, Lodève; tel: 04 67 88 86 10. Open Tue–Sat.

The scenically positioned town of Lodève lies at the foot of hills where the rivers Lergue and Soulondres meet. It flourished in the 13th century thanks to wool from the sheep reared in the hills to the north. One of its bishops had developed the cloth trade, having installed a mill to make paper from rags. Though the industry closed down in 1960, Gobelins tapestries are now made there, mainly copies of antique designs for official buildings. Uranium mining is another new industry and the local deposits amount to a quarter of France's reserves. The Cathédrale St-Fulcran is an imposing Gothic building with a splendid rose window. **Musée Cardinal-de-Fleury✦✦**, once the cardinal's palace, covers the town's history since Roman times and also palaeontology including huge fossilised dinosaur footprints.

Food in Lodève

Le Petit Sommelier € 3 place de la République; tel: 04 67 44 05 39. Old lace-curtained restaurant whose menus offer a wide choice of local specialities.

MOUREZE*

The main reason for visiting this smart little village of pink pastel houses is its extraordinary **Cirque***, a 2km-wide amphitheatre covered in huge eroded boulders, some the size of buildings, with bushes and sandy paths in between. It is a 5-minute walk (signed) from the main street. The ruins of an old castle perch above it at the top of a sheer cliff.

ST-GUILHEM-LE-DESERT***

ⓘ St-Guilhem-le-Désert Tourist Information 2 rue de la Font du Portal; tel: 04 67 57 44 33; www.st-guilhem-le-desert.com. Open daily all year. Guided walks.

ⓘ L'Abbaye de Gellone has guided visits every afternoon June–Sept.

This medieval village, spread up the narrow Verdus gorge between green hillsides, deserves the many visitors it attracts. Small houses in beige stone, now with craft and souvenir shops occupying their ground floors, line the two narrow lanes leading up to its 11th-century monastery church, **l'Abbaye de Gellone**. This massive building is rather plain and austere inside, apart from a striking marble altar and decorative organ. Its main treasure is a fragment of Christ's Cross given to Guilhem by his lifelong friend Charlemagne. He had been one of Charlemagne's most devoted warriors but left his service around 800 to build the monastery and become a monk. His relics, housed in the crypt, are carried with the fragment of the Cross in procession through the streets in May.

Accommodation in St-Guilhem-le-Désert

Hostellerie St-Benoît €€ route St-Guilhem (towards Aniane); tel: 04 67 57 71 63. Closed Dec–Feb. Thirty-room hotel with garden, pool and children's playground, on the edge of the village.

ST-MARTIN-DE-LONDRES***

ⓘ Tourist Information place de la Mairie; tel: 04 67 55 09 59; www.tourismed.com. Open daily July–Aug; mornings Mon–Sat Sept–June.

With its arcaded triangular square and 17th-century mansions, St-Martin-de-Londres (no connection with London) is an attractive but surprisingly un-touristy little town. The monks of St-Guilhem-le-Désert built the simple Romanesque church with its arcaded tower in the 12th century, though the interior has been considerably modified since.

Villeneuvette❖❖❖

ⓘ Villeneuvette Tourist Information Mairie
tel: 04 67 96 06 00. Open Mon–Fri all year. Guided visits by appointment. Park in the car park in front of the entrance as only residents' cars are allowed inside.

☾ Hôtel de la Source
€€ Maision de Manufacture; tel: 04 67 96 05 07; www.hoteldelasource.com. Closed Jan–Feb and second half of Nov. Well-appointed family-run hotel with 13 rooms in former factory houses. Large garden, pool, tennis, children's playground.

In 1677 Louis XIV decreed that this small cloth factory 3km southwest of Clermont l'Hérault, could become a 'Manufacture Royale' of flags. With royal subsidies and his chancellor Colbert ensuring that high standards were maintained, it thrived and the workforce rose to 800. Many of them lived on the site in a 'model' village of terrace houses built for them around a small cobbled square. Since the factory closed in 1954 other residents have moved in and the village is now being preserved as an example of industrial heritage.

Suggested tour

Total distance: 135km plus 30km each way between Montpellier and Gignac. The detour to St-Martin-de-Londres adds 24km and the detour to the Cirque de Navacelles adds 21km.

Time: 5 hours' driving. Allow at least a day for the main route, two with detours. Those with limited time should concentrate on St-Guilhem-le-Désert and the Cirque de Navacelles.

Links to other tours: From Ganges the D999 leads northwest to Le Vigan (see page 236), 17km away. From Lodève the N9 leads north to La Couvertoirade (see page 241), 26km away. From Clermont l'Hérault the N9 leads south to Pézenas (see page 276), 20km away.

Starting from **GIGNAC ❶** (38km west of Montpellier on the N109), head north on the D32 to **ANIANE ❷**. On the far side of Aniane, turn left on to the D27 which shortly passes the **Pont du Diable** where St Guilhem is said to have thrown the Devil into the River Hérault. Built by Benedictine monks in the 11th century, it is believed to be France's oldest bridge, though widened later. From it you get a good view up the narrow **Gorges de l'Hérault** where the river flows below steep white cliffs. The **GROTTE DE CLAMOUSE ❸** is on the left just after the bridge. The D4 then continues up the gorge to the village of **ST-GUILHEM-LE-DESERT ❹**.

Detour: To visit **ST-MARTIN-DE-LONDRES ❺**, turn right off the D4 at Causse-de-la-Selle on to the D122 (12km).

Beyond Causse-de-la-Selle the D4 drops back down to the River Hérault on its way to **Brissac**. Ruined ramparts stand guard over this ancient village framed by the 500m-high Roc Blanc. Its park, laid out at the foot of the village in the 17th century, is a pleasant spot to stroll and savour the rugged scenery. From Brissac, take the D108 which crosses the Hérault into **St-Bauzille-de-Putois**. Turn left on to the D986 (towards Ganges), but soon afterwards take the side road on the right to the **GROTTE DES DEMOISELLES ❻** at the foot of towering

Château de Madières €€€
Madières; tel: 04 67 73 84 03. Restaurant closed Nov–Mar. A 12-room hotel in 14th-century hillside building overlooking the River Vis gorge. Vaulted dining room, fitness room, table tennis, 12-acre grounds with heated outdoor pool.

La Calade € *place de l'Eglise, Octon; tel: 04 67 96 19 21; www.lacalade.com. Closed Jan–Feb.* Thick stone walls give this old house near the Lac du Salagou plenty of character. Seven rooms, large terrace restaurant.

Auberge les Norias €€
254 avenue des Deux Ponts, Cazilhac, near Ganges; tel: 04 67 73 55 90. Closed second half of Nov. Smart 11-room hotel in former spinning mill beside River Hérault. The owner-chef provides gourmet cuisine. Flower-decked outdoor restaurant in summer.

white cliffs. From there go to **GANGES** ❼ which lies in a bowl of wooded hills. Leave it on the D25 which runs southwest through **Gorniès** where the scenery becomes wild and rugged across the lonely Montagne de la Séranne. Then beyond **Madières** the road drops steeply down to **St-Maurice-Navacelles**.

Detour: From St-Maurice-Navacelles, the D130 climbs steeply north along a ridge, with beautiful views across the Larzac plain, to the spectacular **CIRQUE DE NAVACELLES** ❽, 8km away. The drive down to the floor of the Cirque and up out again extends for 7km.

Continue southwest from St-Maurice-Navacelles on the D25 to join the N9 into **LODEVE** ❾. Leave the town on the N9, turning off it after 5km at Junction 54 to take the D148 past the **Lac du Salagou** to **Octon** and **Salasc**. This is literally red earth country – La Ruffe – as the soil is an amazingly dark-rust colour (due to high amounts of bauxite). Next the D8 takes you through a valley of rocks to **MOUREZE** ❿ and its *cirque* on the way to Clermont l'Hérault. Fork right just beyond Mourèze (keeping the river on your left) and then turn left on to the D908 to visit **VILLENEUVETTE** ⓫ which is on the left shortly before **CLERMONT L'HERAULT** ⓬. Beyond Clermont l'Hérault the D908 and N109 return you to **Gignac**, crossing the **Pont de Gignac** shortly before the town. This majestic 175m-long, three-arch 17th-century bridge is considered to be the best of its date in France.

Getting out of the car

At the top of St-Guilhem-le-Désert, a marked path leads along the **rue du Bout-du-Monde** (road of the end-of-the-world) through the valley and then zigzags sharply up the mountainside. You get a splendid view of the village's red roofs as well as a panorama over the white cliffs and ridges of the mountains all around which gets ever more spectacular the higher you go. Fragments of a ruined castle, the **Château du Géant**, dating from 807, are perched on a high rock. Long ago the path was part of a pilgrimage route to Spain. Beyond St-Guilhem-le-Désert the gorge widens slightly. The D4 then climbs away from the River Hérault towards **Causse-de-la-Selle**.

St-Jean-du-Bruel

Sauclières

D7

Alzon D999

Le Tour d'Arre
△
955

1445

Campestre-et-Luc

La Couvertoirade

Causse du Larzac

A75-E11

Le Caylar

S S

15

Soubès

N9

9

Lodève

19

Octon

Salasc

Mourèze
10

Villeneuvette
11

D908

28

Peyne

20

Gabian

Paulhan

N9

St-Pierre-de-la-Fage

28

St-Maurice-Navacelles

Montdardier

Cirque de Navacelles D48
8

Madières

Causse-de-la-Selle

18

Gorniès

Pont d'Hérault

24

Le Vigan

17

Sumène

15

Ganges
7

D25

Montagne de la Séranne

St-Hippolyte-du-Fort

13

Grotte des Desmoiselles
6

St-Bauzille-de-Putois

Brissac

D986

20

St-Martin-de-Londres
5

Pic St-Loup
△
658

St-Guilhem-le-Désert
4

Gorges de l'Hérault

Viols-le-Fort

D32

G A R R I G U

Les Mate

Grotte de Clamouse
3

Pont du Diable
2

37

Aniane

21

Gignac
1

St-André-de-Sangonis

Clermont-l'Hérault
12

Canet

Lac du Salagou

A75-E11

St-Gély-du-Fesc

25

Castelnau-Montpel

N109

19

St-Jean-de-Védas

Cournonterral

Fabrègues
S

Montbazin

N113

S

N112

0   10km

Hérault

16

The Corniche of the Cévennes

Ratings

National parks	●●●●●
Scenery	●●●●●
Mountains	●●●●○
History	●●●○○
Nature	●●●○○
Museums	●●●○○
Restaurants	●●●○○
Trains	●●●○○

The Corniche des Cévennes is a glorious top-of-the-world road that sweeps along the spine of the mountains. To the north, the peaks of Mont Lozère spread out like a relief map. You reach the Corniche up a hairpin-bending road, thrilling to drive, at St-Laurent-de-Trèves beneath Mont Aigoual, the highest peak in the Cévennes National Park.

But this is not a route to travel just for scenery. Little towns along it such as le Vigan, St-Jean, Anduze and St-Hippolyte all have a rich history and plenty of good restaurants serving local specialities including *pelardon* (goat's cheese), young lamb, chestnut sauces and home-made charcuterie.

In winter there is likely to be snow on the passes and you may need chains or snow tyres (look out for the warning signs), otherwise the roads are commendably good.

ANDUZE❖❖

ⓘ Anduze Tourist Information *plan de Brie; tel: 04 66 61 98 17; www.ot-anduze.fr. Open daily July–Aug; Mon–Sat Sept–June.*

Ⓜ Musée de la Musique €€ *route d'Alès; tel: 04 66 61 86 60; www.museemusique.com. Open daily June–Sept.*

This attractive medieval town of narrow streets and quaint little squares nestles at the foot of a massive white rock, near the River Gardon. It has lived through more turbulent times than most places in the area. Only the clock-tower, complete with sundial, remains from the 14th-century fortifications which were enlarged and strengthened in 1622 by the Protestant leader, the Duc de Rohan, when the town was at the heart of local resistance to Catholicism. A century later it was at the centre of the Camisard uprising (*see page 33*). Eventually it settled down and was much improved by the building of the embankment which protected it from flash floods.

Vines, orchards, mulberries, distilleries and particularly pottery have all brought it prosperity. It became famous throughout France for its giant glazed vases after some were installed in the orangery at Versailles. Today it continues to produce garden pots in all sizes and colours. The **Musée de la Musique*** provides a

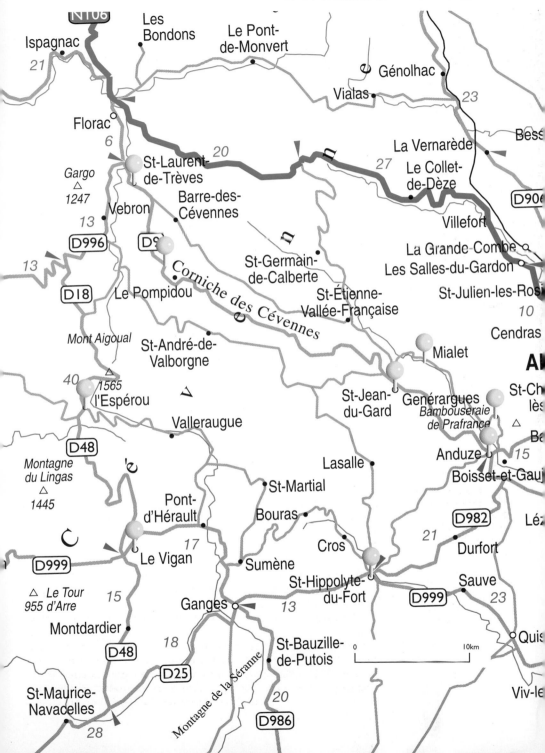

N106

Ispagnac
21

Les Bondons

Le Pont-de-Monvert

Génolhac

Vialas

23

Bess

Florac
6

St-Laurent-de-Trèves

20

La Vernarède

Le Collet-de-Dèze

D906

Gargo
△
1247

Vebron

13

Barre-des-Cévennes

27

Villefort

D996

D9

St-Germain-de-Calberte

La Grande-Combe

Les Salles-du-Gardon

13

Corniche des Cévennes

St-Étienne-Vallée-Française

St-Julien-les-Ros

D18

Le Pompidou

10

Mont Aigoual

St-André-de-Valborgne

Mialet

Cendras

40

△
1565

l'Espérou

St-Jean-du-Gard

Génargues

St-Ch
lès

AI

D48

Valleraugue

Bambouseraie de Prafrance
△

Ba

Montagne du Lingas
△
1445

Pont-d'Hérault

Lasalle

Anduze

15

Boisset-et-Gau

St-Martial

Bouras

D982

Léz

D999

Le Vigan

17

Cros

21

Durfort

△ *Le Tour*
955 d'Arre

15

Sumène

St-Hippolyte-du-Fort

Sauve

D999

23

Montdardier

Ganges

13

D48

18

St-Bauzille-de-Putois

Quis

D25

St-Maurice-Navacelles

28

Montagne de la Séranne

20

D986

Viv-le

0   10km

⬤ **Poterie de la
Madeleine** *at Tornac
(4km south on the D982);
tel: 04 66 61 63 44.
Pottery workshop and
sales counter.*

musical tour through 1400 historic instruments from around the world.

Bambouseraie de Prafrance✦✦

🏛 **Bambouseraie de
Prafrance** €€
*tel: 04 66 61 70 47;
www.bambouseraie.fr.
Open daily Mar–mid-Nov.*

The botanical garden at Générargues includes Europe's only forest of giant bamboo trees. It also has a water garden, 19th-century tropical greenhouses and an Asian village.

Corniche des Cevennes✦✦✦

Below
View from the Corniche des
Cévennes over the village of
Le Pompidou

We have King Louis XIV to thank for this remarkable road which winds along the high ridge between two rivers – both called Gardon. He had it built in haste at the beginning of the 18th century to enable his troops to penetrate the Cévennes more easily and quash the Camisard uprising. Pines, oaks, chestnuts and mulberry bushes cover the steep valley sides and the few scattered farmhouses and cottages are built on terraces to catch the sun. Their attics were once used for breeding silkworms.

L'Esperou**

ℹ **Maison de l'Aigoual** *on the D986 north of the village* has information on the Cévennes National Park and sells local produce.

L'Espérou Tourist Information
(in Valleraugue, 19km down the valley); tel: 04 67 82 25 10; www.aigoual-cevennes.com. Open daily all year. Information on the Cévennes National Park also available.

Surrounded by forests and high mountain pastures, the village of L'Espérou is an exhilarating base for walking in summer and skiing in winter. Its remote setting made it ideal as the base for the Aigoual-Cévennes resistance groups during World War II.

Accommodation and food in L'Espérou

Grand Hôtel du Parc €€ *Carrefour des Hommes de la Route; tel: 04 67 82 60 05. Closed mid-Nov–Apr.* Tranquil family-run hotel with ten rooms, sun terrace and garden. Restaurant specialises in regional dishes.

Mialet*

🏛 **Musée du Désert €€** *The Mas Soubeyran; tel: 04 66 85 02 72; www.museedudesert.com. Open daily Mar–Nov.*

The **Musée du Désert**** in this small village occupies the Mas Soubeyran, the old house where one of the leading Camisards was born. It explains the movement's history through displays which include full-size reconstructions showing how they hid and lived during the 'desert' years (1685–1787) when Protestantism was banned.

Mont Aigoual***

🏛 **Mont Aigoual observatory** *tel: 04 67 82 60 01. Open daily May–Sept.*

France's meteorological office has an **observatory*** built in 1887 at the top of this mountain (1567m) which enjoys one of the finest panoramas in Europe, extending in fine weather as far as the Mediterranean, Pyrenees and Alps. Overlooking the Gard, Hérault and Tarn valleys, the observatory is perfectly positioned to record what is happening to the wind and weather. An exhibition inside explains the history of weather forecasting and the methods used today.

St-Hippolyte-du-Fort**

ℹ **St-Hippolyte-du-Fort Tourist Information** *place des Enfants de Troupe; tel: 04 66 77 91 65; www. multimania.com/ sainthippolyte. Open Mon–Sat July–Aug; Tue–Fri Sept–June.*

This little town has an extraordinary mixture of specialities including no less than 23 decorative sundials and 13 fountains. It also makes shoes and has a silk museum, **Musée de la Soie****, which depicts the history of silk production in the Cévennes. The museum occupies the old barracks built for Louis XIV's soldiers when they constructed the Corniche des Cévennes. Visitors see how silkworms make corms of silk and how it is spun into thread then made into fabric. Silk items are on sale in its shop. The **Musée des Pompiers***, also in the barracks, displays a local businessman's collection of fire engines.

Market Tue and Fri.

Musée de la Soie
€€ *place du 8 Mai;*
tel: 04 66 77 66 47.
Open Mon–Sat all year.

Musée des Pompiers €
place du 8 Mai;
tel: 04 66 77 99 86.
Open Wed–Mon all year.

Reafforestation

In 1875 George Fabres, head warden of the French Rivers Authority and Forestry Commission, initiated a reafforestation programme in the Cévennes, having seen the devastation caused by floods once land had been stripped bare. He won considerable support by showing that the sand clogging up the port at Bordeaux had been washed down from the slopes of the Aigoual, the area's highest peak.

Up to then thousands of trees were being cut down every year to create more pastures or by glass-makers to provide charcoal for their furnaces. Sheep contributed to the problem too, by nibbling young shoots on their way between pastures. As a result, whenever rain fell very heavily – the area is subject to violent storms – torrents of water surged unchecked into the valleys.

Now, following the planting of thousands of seedlings, extensive areas have been reafforested, particularly with cedar, fir, pine and spruce, contributing greatly to both the safety and beauty of the landscape.

Fabres, a formidable man, also initiated the building of the observatory on Mont Aigoual in 1887.

Accommodation and food in St-Hippolyte-du-Fort

Auberge Cigaloise €€ *route de Nîmes; tel: 04 66 77 64 59. Closed Nov–Feb.* Ten-room family-run hotel with garden, pool and playground. Car park.

Restaurant Le Plan € *27 rue du Plan; tel: 04 66 77 91 55. Closed Wed.* Small restaurant with painted façade beside the market square. Its terrace tables are handily placed for watching *boules* games while you eat. Good value menus.

St-Jean-du-Gard❖❖

St-Jean-du-Gard Tourist Information *place Rabaut St-Etienne; tel: 04 66 85 32 11; www.otsi.st.jeandugard. free.fr. Open daily July–Aug; Mon–Sat Sept–June.*

Surrounded by orchards, St-Jean-du-Gard has a distinctly southern feel with tall houses lining narrow streets and a large riverside square shaded by plane trees. The pretty six-arch humpback bridge over the River Gardon is a reconstruction of the original built in 1754 which was swept away by floods in 1958. The **Musée des Vallées Cévenoles**❖❖, occupying a 17th-century inn, devotes one room to the local silk industry, showing how it became an important cottage industry in the area at the beginning of the 18th century. The museum also has a section devoted to chestnuts, which for centuries were ground into flour to make bread. As a result the chestnut was

Musée des Vallées Cévenoles € *95 Grand-Rue; tel: 04 66 85 10 48. Open daily Apr–Oct, Tue, Thur and Sun Nov–Mar.*

Aquarium Municipal €€€ *avenue de la Résistance; tel: 04 66 85 40 53. Open daily June–Aug; Tue–Sun Apr–May and Sept–Nov.*

There is a weekly market on Tue; night markets on Thur between July and Aug; and a **Cheese fair** *in June.*

known as the 'tree of life' until the silk industry started and mulberry cultivation became more important.

Tropical fish including piranhas and sharks (which can be fed) swim in exotic aquariums at the **Aquarium Municipal***, where there is also an artificial river and waterfall.

Accommodation in St-Jean-du-Gard

Auberge du Peras €€ *route de Nîmes; tel: 04 66 85 35 94. Closed mid-Nov–mid-Mar.* Twelve-room family-run hotel in old stone building on the edge of town with a garden and car park. Hire bicycles here.

St-Laurent-de-Treves✧✧

Grallator €€ *Tel: 04 66 49 53 01. Thirty-minute show. Open Tue–Sun June–Aug.*

The claw footprints indented in the flat rocks on the high windy headland above the village were left by dinosaurs 190 million years ago when the area was covered by a lake. The **Grallator*** opposite the tiny church is an audio-visual show on dinosaurs.

LE VIGAN***

Le Vigan Tourist Information *place du Marché; tel: 04 67 81 01 72. Open daily July–Aug; Mon–Sat Sept–June.*

Auberge le Mas Quayrol €€ *Aulas, le Vigan; tel: 04 67 81 12 38; www.masquayrol.com. Open Mar–Nov. Quality family-run hotel across the D48 on the northeast edge of le Vigan. Sixteen rooms, garden, pool and car park. Lovely view from restaurant and most rooms.*

Musée Cévenol € *rue des Calquières; tel: 04 67 81 06 86; www.musee-cevenol.com. Open Wed–Mon Apr–Oct; Wed only Nov–Mar.*

Le Vigan is a prosperous and relaxed little town enjoying a sunny position on the south-facing slopes of Mont Aigoual. Set in the lush Arre valley, its prosperity grew from spinning silk; this led to making hosiery which continues today. The **Musée Cévenol****, in an old spinning mill beside a soaring 12th-century bridge over the River Arre, provides an excellent introduction to the Cévennes, covering everything from the food and wine to traditional crafts such as basketwork, gold panning, glass-blowing and tin mining. There are life-size reconstructions of workshops and a typical cottage.

Right
Le Vigan war memorial

Suggested tour

Sentier de Barre-des-Cévennes leaflet at the information kiosk on the edge of the village.

Château du Rey
€€€ le Rey, Pont-d'Hérault; tel: 04 67 82 40 06; www.chateau-du-rey.com. Closed Oct–Apr. Much restored 13th-century castle, now a comfortable 12-room hotel. Vaulted restaurant, the Abeuradou (€€ tel: 04 67 82 49 32). Five-acre grounds with pool and helicopter pad. Fishing available.

Total distance: 175km. The detour to the Barre des Cévennes adds 6km, the detour to Mialet adds 18km and the detour to the Bambouseraie de Prafrance botanical garden at Générargues adds 6km.

Time: 5 hours' driving. Allow at least a day for the main route, more with detours. Those with limited time should concentrate on the Corniche des Cévennes.

Links to other tours: From Le Vigan the D999 leads southeast to Ganges (*see page 224*), 17km away, or west to La Couvertoirade (*see page 241*), 39km away. From L'Espérou the D986 leads northwest to Meyrueis (*see page 253*), 27km away. From St-Laurent-de-Trèves the D983 and D907 lead north to Florac (*see page 262*), 10km away. From Anduze the D910 leads northeast to Alès (*see page 260*), 16km away. From St-Hippolyte-du-Fort the D999 leads southwest to Ganges (*see page 224*), 17km away.

Starting from **LE VIGAN ❶**, take the D48 which quickly begins to twist and climb into the mountains through forests, around sheer rock faces and across ravines where water cascades down. There are two passes to cross, the Col du Minier (1373m) and then, just beyond **L'ESPEROU ❷**, the Col de la Séreyrède (1299m) where you reach the Mediterranean/Atlantic watershed. This used to be on a wide trail – the Draille du Languedoc – which shepherds used for their *transhumance* when 25,000 sheep were driven each year between their summer pastures in the mountains and winter shelter in the valley. Now they are taken to and fro by lorry. Continue north on the D18 over the Col de Prat Peyrot (1380m) where you can expect plenty of snow in winter and congestion from skiers and their cars. Shortly beyond it you pass close to the summit of **MONT AIGOUAL ❸** (1567m), signposted to the right.

Having continued north on the D18 and then the D996 (towards Florac) along the broad valley below the Causse Méjean, turn right 5km before Florac at the junction with the D983. This takes you south round hairpin bends to **ST-LAURENT-DE-TREVES ❹** and the Col du Rey (992m) just beyond it.

Detour: At the Col du Rey, turn left on to the D983 to **Barre des Cévennes** (3km). As part of the **Ecomusée de la Cévenne**, a 4km walking trail, one of five in the National Park, has been mapped out around this typical Cévenol village on a hillside halfway between valley and plateau. A descriptive leaflet covers not only its old buildings but also the landscape and local flora and fauna.

The **Train à Vapeur des Cévennes**
tel: 04 66 60 59 00; www.trainavapeur.com, runs between Anduze, Bambouseraie and St-Jean-du-Gard, daily Apr–mid-Sept, and daily except Mon mid-Sept–Oct.

The **CORNICHE DES CEVENNES ❺** begins at the Col du Rey (992m) as the D9 crosses a spectacular windswept plateau, **le Can de l'Hospitalet**. Continue south past viewpoints and over the Col des Faïsses (1026m) and the Col de Solpérière (1010m) to the small village of **le Pompidou.**

Further on, after crossing the Col l'Exil (704m) and Col de St-Pierre (597m), you reach **ST-JEAN-DU-GARD** ❻.

Detour: At St-Jean-du-Gard, turn left onto the D50 to visit **MIALET** ❼ (9km).

Detour: LA BAMBOUSERAIE DE PRAFRANCE ❽ botanical garden at **Générargues** is on the D129, 3km north of Anduze, *see below*.

Continuing southeast from St-Jean-du-Gard towards **ANDUZE** ❾, look out for the derelict spinning mill at the junction with the D57. In the 18th century the area's mulberry bushes, on which silkworms feed, became so valuable that they were nicknamed the *arbre d'or* (tree of gold).

From Anduze, the D133 leads to **ST-HIPPOLYTE-DU-FORT** ❿, then follow the D169, D153, D11 and D999 to return to le Vigan, passing through Cros, Bouras, Sumène and Pont-d'Hérault.

Getting out of the car

Views from the top of Mont Aigoual (which are best in winter) are breathtaking. On a clear day you can see across a quarter of France. But the very best time of all to be there is to see sunrise, particularly in the autumn.

The **Train à Vapeur des Cévennes**, sometimes pulled by a steam locomotive, runs on a 13km line between St-Jean-du-Gard and Anduze along the Gardon valley. The 40-minute journey provides wonderful views (some carriages are open). The train makes a stop at Générargues just before Anduze for passengers who want to visit **LA BAMBOUSERAIE DE PRAFRANCE** ❽.

Templars, plateaux and cheese

Ratings

Scenery	●●●●●
Museums	●●●●○
Villages	●●●●○
Walking	●●●●○
Food	●●●○○
Geology	●●●○○
History	●●●○○
Wildlife	●●●○○

The Causse de Larzac is one of the Cévennes' four great limestone plateaux. On these high expanses where sheep graze and birds of prey wheel overhead, little disturbs the tranquility except the wind. Side by side, literally, with this wild landscape are dramatic gorges, such as the Canyon de la Dourbie, where rivers have carved their tortuous way through the soft rock. The contrast provides a rich variety along this route. The many signposted footpaths will tempt you out of the car to savour the surroundings even more.

Although the area is less well known than many in France, the name of one of its villages – Roquefort – is famous all over the world. It has been producing its creamy blue-veined cheese for centuries. Also unique are the fortified villages of la Couvertoirade and St-Jean-d'Alcas, both interesting mini-versions of Carcassonne.

CANTOBRE❖❖❖

The name of this quaint village derives from 'quant obra' meaning 'what a masterpiece'. Its old stone houses are built into a rocky outcrop high above the Dourbie and Trévézel rivers. The walk up to the little church and cemetery at the top is well worth the effort for the beautiful view down into the valley on either side. Rock plants grow in profusion and thistles hang on most of the front doors – the local way to forecast the weather (the thistles close up when rain is imminent).

CHAOS-DE-MONTPELLIER-LE-VIEUX❖❖❖

This group of craggy stone columns spreads over 1.5 sq km among oak and pine trees north of Roque-Ste-Marguerite. It was given its name (meaning 'ruined city') by shepherds who brought their flocks up from the Languedoc plain to summer pastures there though they feared the shapes were linked with the Devil.

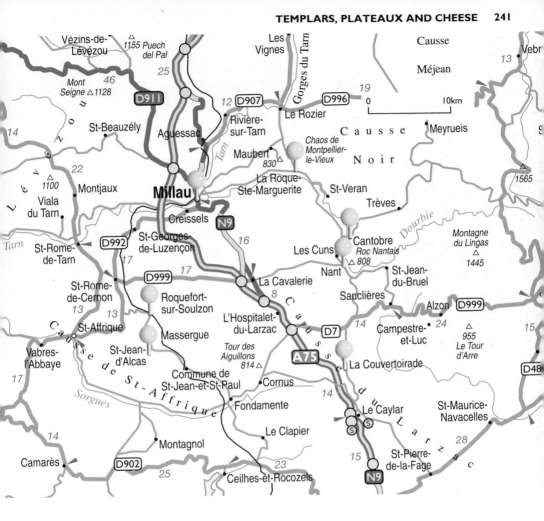

LA COUVERTOIRADE❖❖❖

ℹ **La Couvertoirade Tourist Information** *Mairie;* tel: 05 65 58 55 59; www.lacouvertoirade.com. *Open Mon–Fri all year; also daily July–Aug at the car park. Entrance to La Couvertoirade, including 20-minute video, €. Three guided visits daily in English July–Aug.*

Situated in the middle of the Causse du Larzac is la Couvertoirade, a miniature Carcassonne. Completely surrounded by high ramparts, it has a castle, church and tiny cemetery. It was built by the Templars in 1158 as a staging post for pilgrims on the old Roman road across the *causse*, though the forbidding grey stone walls were a later addition by the Knights of St John in the 15th century. Unlike Carcassonne, la Couvertoirade has never been smartened up, though a few of the buildings have been restored and craft workers have taken up residence in several of them.

The entrance is through an arched gateway beneath a square tower. In summer the narrow streets and handful of shops and cafés throng with visitors. You can walk round the ramparts and look down on the main street, rue Droite, which is lined with attractive

🏛 **Musée de la Traction Animale**
€€ *Tel: 05 65 62 26 85.*
Open all year.

little 17th-century houses. Eglise St-Christophe, the fortified church, with a tiny old cemetery next to it, formed part of the defences.

Nearby, outside the walls, the **Musée de la Traction Animale** has 60 old carriages. Most were horse-drawn but some were pulled by oxen, dogs or goats.

MILLAU❖❖❖

ℹ️ **Millau Tourist Information** *1 place du Beffroi; tel: 05 65 60 02 42; www.otmillau.fr. Open daily.* Millau has become famous for its 100km circular walk along the Gorges du Tarn, an annual competitive event, last Sat in Sept.

This little town, where the Tarn and Dourbie rivers meet, enjoys a beautiful setting in a majestic bowl of mountains. Its red roofs blend comfortably with them and the surrounding cherry orchards. The wide streets and squares, shaded by lines of plane trees, have a good selection of shops, particularly for leather gloves, bags and coats. The oldest quarter centres on the arcaded place du Maréchal-Foch which has the Romanesque Eglise Notre-Dame-de-l'Espinasse in one corner. Named after a thorn which it was reputed to possess from Christ's crown, the church attracted pilgrims from far and wide during the Middle Ages. It has a fine set of modern stained-glass windows by Claude Baillo. A curiosity on the west side of the square is a stone slab, once part of the town's stocks, with the warning '*Gara que faras*' meaning 'watch what you are doing'. The imposing **belfry**❖ in rue Droite is all that remains of the old town hall. The best way to explore the town is by following the guided walk past 18 sights marked by plaques explaining their history.

Above
La Couvertoirade

Fouilles de la Graufesenque €€
chemin de Graufesenque, across the Tarn; tel: 05 65 60 11 37. Open daily all year.

Musée de Millau €€
place Maréchal-Foch; tel: 05 65 60 01 08. Open daily June–Sept; Mon–Sat Oct–May.

Belfry *rue Droite. Open mid-June–Sept daily.*

Markets are held on Wednesdays and Fridays. Local specialities are young lamb, *trenels* (haggis of tripe), *flaune* (orange-flavoured flan made with ewes' milk) and plump cherries.

The town's prosperity dates back to 1 AD when it was called Condatomagus – the market where the rivers meet – and was one of the main pottery-making centres in the Roman empire. More than 500 potters produced shiny bright red pots of all shapes and sizes which were exported throughout Europe and the Middle East. The pottery site by the river, **Fouilles de la Graufesenque**✦✦, has recently been excavated, revealing a huge number of pots and providing important information about life in Roman times.

The vaulted cellars of the **Musée de Millau**✦✦ display a well-preserved collection of tools and pottery from the site. An equally enthralling section is devoted to fossils and dinosaur remains – including skeletons and footprints – which have been found in the area, once covered by the sea. One room is set out as a glove-making workshop with old sewing machines and patterns – another aspect of the town's past. Gloves have been made there for over 800 years ago, a by-product from the huge numbers of sheep reared on the plateaux for cheese-making. For centuries the town councillors never appeared on ceremonial occasions without gloves, though with the fall in demand for *haute couture* gloves the industry has begun to decline.

Accommodation and food in Millau

International Hotel €€ *place de la Tine; tel: 05 65 59 29 00.* A modern high-rise building, this 109-room hotel is close to the main square, with good views from the higher floors.

Restaurant La Braconne €€ *7 place Maréchal-Foch; tel: 05 65 60 30 93. Closed Mon.* In this 13th-century stone building with a vaulted ceiling, grills seasoned with local herbs are cooked in front of you on an open fire.

NANT✦✦

Nant Tourist Information *Chapelle des Pénitents; tel: 05 65 62 24 21; www.ot-nant.fr. Open daily June–Aug; Mon–Sat Sept–May.*

Hôtel des Voyageurs € *place St Jacques; tel: 05 65 62 26 88. Open Mar–Dec.* Family-owned hotel with 15 rooms and garden, just off the main square, and a restaurant, Le Ménestrel.

The Roc Nantais, a massive tower-like rock (808m), juts out dramatically from the hilltop opposite this old market town at the head of the Dourbie gorge. The town's origins date back to the 7th century when Bendictine monks drained the broad swampy valley in order to plant vineyards. The St-Pierre church, a rather austere building with an octagonal tower and spire, survives from their huge monastery. In the square the Vieille Halle, a small market hall with arches, roofed with *lauzes* (limestone slabs) typical of the area, was also part of it. A plaque on the side commemorates nine local Resistance heroes shot by the Germans in August 1944. The best view of the high 14th-century arched river bridge, Pont de la Prade, is from beside the tall cross near the square.

ROQUEFORT-SUR-SOULZON*

ⓘ Roquefort-sur-Soulzon Tourist Information *avenue de Lauras; tel: 05 65 58 56 00; www.roquefort.com. Open daily July–Aug; Mon–Fri Sept–June.*

ⓖ Caves de Roquefort Société € *avenue François Galtier; tel: 05 65 59 93 30; www.roquefort-societe.com. Open for guided tours of the cellars daily.*

Le Papillon *rue de la Fontaine; tel: 05 65 58 50 00. Open for free guided tours of the cellars daily.*

The single main street of this drab little town (though it enjoys splendid views over the Grands Causses) at the foot of the Combalou plateau always seems to be full of huge cheese lorries manoeuvring to and fro, a reminder that it is the home of the world-famous Roquefort. As early as 1407, Charles VI granted the cheese its own brand name, an *appellation d'origine*, which has been protected by law ever since. Two cheese producers, **Caves de Roquefort Société**✦✦ and **Le Papillon**✦✦, offer guided visits (including videos) to their caves which resemble the crypts of a church. Wear warm clothing!

> ## Roquefort cheese
>
> Made from unpasteurised ewes' milk, this world-famous cheese is injected with *penicillium roquefortii* mould cultivated on breadcrumbs which produces its characteristic – and tasty – blue veins. Early connoisseurs are said to have included Pliny and Charlemagne. The limestone caves under the Combalou plateau at the side of the town play a crucial role in its production as their temperature – 7–9°C (45–48°F) – and humidity remain constant all year. Air circulates through long fissures in the rock. The round cheeses are left there on oak shelves to mature for at least three months. A website in English tells the story of the cheese: www.fromages.com/usa/roqueleg.htm

ST-JEAN-D'ALCAS*

ⓘ St-Jean-d'Alcas Tourist Information *Mairie; tel: 05 65 99 14 79; July–Aug information kiosk in the fort. To book a guided tour of the village, tel: 05 65 49 26 02.*

This tiny fortified village, a mini-version of la Courvertoirade (*see page 241*), was built in the 15th century by Cistercian nuns as a safe haven during the Hundred Years' War. Symmetrically laid out – the Cistercians' abbeys were built in a similarly tidy style – and totally enclosed by ramparts, it has undergone highly commended restorations.

Suggested tour

Total distance: 115km. The detour to St-Jean-du-Bruel adds 14km, the detour to Cantobre adds 3km and the detour to the Chaos-de-Montpellier-le-Vieux adds 18km.

Time: 3 hours' driving. Allow most of a day for the main route, at least a day with detours. Those with limited time should concentrate on Millau and Roquefort-sur-Soulzon, or for scenery the Canyon de la Dourbie.

Opposite
Roquefort-sur-Soulzon

Trail starts at Roquefort-sur-Soulzon tourist office on the northern edge of the village; *allow 2–3 hours.* Wear walking shoes.

ℹ Cornus post office *tel: 05 65 99 37 39,* sells two books on Cornus and walking and cycling guides.

Links to other tours: From Millau the N9 and D907 lead northeast to Le Rozier (*see page 253*), 22km away. From Roquefort the D999 leads southwest to St-Sernin-sur-Rance (*see page 188*), 45km away. From la Couvertoirade the D55 and A75 lead south to Lodève (*see page 225*), 26km away.

Starting from **MILLAU ❶**, drive southwest through **Creissels** on the D992 and under the 2.5km-long viaduct, designed by British architect Norman Foster and opened in 2004, which soars 270m above the valley carrying the A75 autoroute past Millau. The D992 runs high above the River Tarn with wonderful views over the flat brown hills of the Causses. Then swinging south, you cross the River Cernon and accompany a scenic railway line through a wooded valley. Four kilometres beyond **St-Rome-de-Cernon**, turn left on to the D23 and climb up to **ROQUEFORT-SUR-SOULZON ❷**.

From Roquefort-sur-Soulzon the D93 makes its way around the edge of the **Causse du Larzac** through **Massergue** to **ST-JEAN-D'ALCAS ❸** where sheep graze below wooded cliffs on hillsides which merge into flat hedgeless fields – a truly rural landscape. The road continues on its quiet way to **St-Jean-et-St-Paul** and **Fondamente** where you take the D7 to **Cornus**. Pop into the post office for information on this little town which huddles at the foot of the Larzac plateau under an 80m-high cliff.

Continue on the D7 beyond Cornus and then go over the A75 autoroute towards **LA COUVERTOIRADE ❹** on the D185. On this stretch the *causse* is a wild unspoilt landscape apart from the incongruous autoroute. The rocky red soil is dotted with boulders and

Left
Millau

Right
Cornus

Château de Creissels €€ *route de St-Affrique, Creissels; tel: 05 65 60 16 59; www. chateau-de-creissels.com.* Twelfth-century château with modern extension, overlooking the village on the River Tarn. Family-run with 31 rooms, most with terrace or balcony. Restaurant **€€**; *tel: 05 65 60 31 79, in former guardroom. Open Mar–Nov.* Dinner on covered terrace in summer. Large garden.

Hôtel Midi-Papillon € *St-Jean-du-Bruel; tel: 05 65 62 26 04. Open Easter–mid-Nov.* A 19-room hotel owned and run by four generations of the Papillon family.

Relais des Gorges € *la Roque-Ste-Marguerite; tel: 05 65 62 80 62. Open all year.* Cosy ten-room hotel splendidly positioned in an isolated spot beside the River Dourbie just north of the village. Fishing nearby.

splashed with patches of yellow broom and hardy green box bushes. From la Couvertoirade the D55 leads north across the *causse* and then through soft hillsides of beech trees to **NANT** ⑤ where the **Roc Nantais** towers up on the right. This section is the 'Garden of Aveyron' where apple and plum orchards thrive in the broad river valley. Look out on the south side for the ruins of the **Château d'Algues**.

Detour: The small town of **St-Jean-du-Bruel**, 7km east of Nant on the D999, is popular as a base for exploring the area. It has an ancient humpback bridge over the River Dourbie and a 200-year-old covered market. Barrels for harvesting grapes are made in the town.

From Nant continue north along the D991 as it winds along the broad **Dourbie Valley** past the small 12th-century church at **Les Cuns** and below Cantobre.

Detour: To visit **CANTOBRE** ⑥, turn right off the D991 (5km north of Nant) on to the D145 (1.5km).

Beyond Cantobre, the Dourbie valley changes into the **Canyon de la Dourbie**, a deep but wide gorge in the limestone rocks between the **Causse du Larzac** and **Causse Noir**. The steep wooded slopes on either side are topped with cliffs where weirdly shaped pillars of rock jut out above the trees. Later you get a superb view of **St-Veran**, a tiny hamlet built into a clifftop with a tower that was once part of a castle. After crossing the River Dourbie just after St-Veran, the D991 runs along its north bank as the river turns west through **la Roque-Ste-Marguerite**. This terraced village nestles at the foot of a Romanesque chapel and the circular tower of a 17th-century castle.

Detour: This weird **CHAOS-DE-MONTPELLIER-LE-VIEUX** ⑦ area of eroded columns is a 9km drive north from La Roque-Ste-Marguerite through **Maubert**.

Left
The Chaos-de-Montpellier-
le-Vieux

After La Roque-Ste-Marguerite the route continues along the D991 beside the Dourbie, finally entering Millau across the Tarn.

Getting out of the car

The **Sentier des Echelles** is a 6km path around the **Plateau du Combalou**, a 791m-high plateau above the village of Roquefort-sur-Soulzon. The views are panoramic as you gradually climb to the top of cliffs where grassy footpaths lead past curiously shaped rock formations and a ruined chapel. The trail leads back through the village past the **Combalou caves** where Roquefort's inimitable cheese is matured.

The **Tour d'Aiguilhon**, a 815m-high viewpoint over the Larzac plateau, reached along a 1.5km footpath from Cornus, is just one of several rewarding walks in this area.

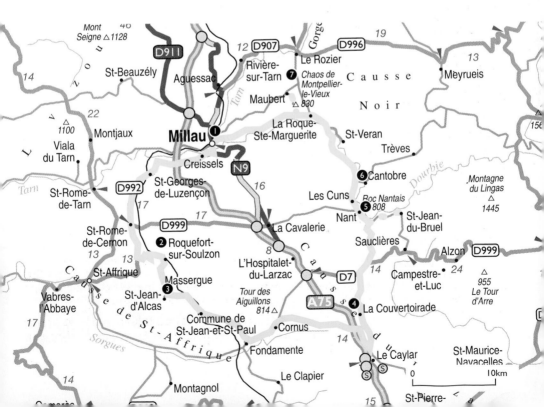

Great plateaux and gorges

This route around the Causse Méjean in the Cévennes includes one of the most famous stretches of river in France, the Gorges du Tarn. But the Tarn is not the only river to have gouged its way through the limestone to create a deep winding canyon. The Jonte's gorge, along the southern side of the Causse, is just as scenic – and less busy.

Equally spectacular in a very different way are the famous caves under the plateau, notably the Aven Armand and Grotte de Dargilan. In the sky, birds of prey wheel around, including vultures which have been successfully re-introduced to the area.

The driving is not for the faint-hearted as the roads twist tightly around cliffsides hugging the rivers or climb steeply up on to the Causse above. The little towns and villages along the way make welcome ports of call.

L'AVEN ARMAND❖❖❖

L'Aven Armand
€€€ *Meyrueis; tel: 04 66 45 61 31; www.aven-armand.com. Open daily for 45-minute guided tours mid-Mar–Nov.*

In an area which abounds in underground marvels, this is definitely one not to miss. About 11km northwest of Meyrueis, it is one of the most spectacular caves in Europe, containing a forest of colourful rocks shaped like cypress and palm trees with massive branches and delicate leaves. You view them at the end of the 200m-long entrance tunnel which opens out on to the vast cavern, 60m wide, 100m long and 45m high.

CHATEAU DE PRADES❖❖

Château de Prades
Not open to the public.

This grand castle, occupying a commanding position just above the River Tarn 6km east of Ste-Enimie, was built by the bishops of Mende in the 13th century to guard access to the Gorges and Ste-Enimie abbey just downstream. Its high vaulted rooms and imposing stone fireplaces reflect the wealth of the area at the time when vineyards covered the steep river banks.

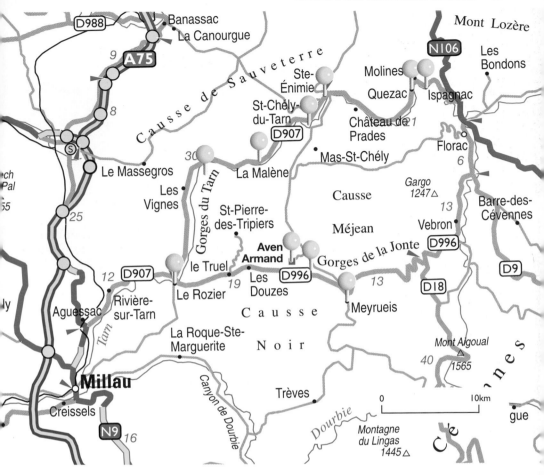

Louis Armand

When Edouard-Alfred Martel, the famous speleologist, began exploring the extraordinary underground world hidden beneath the Causse Méjean, one of his main helpers was Louis Armand, a local locksmith. Farmers told Martel about what they called *l'aven*, a deep crevice or swallow hole in the rock. When Armand climbed down it in 1897, he found it was 75m deep and had a huge chamber at the bottom. Eventually in 1927 it was opened to the public, having been named – at Martel's insistence – after Armand. Recently it has been relit with imaginative illuminations that highlight the most impressive formations.

GORGES DE LA JONTE✦✦✦

Hôtel-Restaurant de la Jonte € *les Douzes; tel: 05 65 62 60 52. Open mid-Mar–mid-Nov. Small roadside hotel facing the river in the spectacular Gorges de la Jonte. Thirty-six rooms.*

After rising on Mont Aigoual, the River Jonte is swollen by two smaller rivers, the Bétuzon and Brèze. It then cuts a deep wooded course between orange-tinged limestone cliffs for 21km from Meyrueis to le Rozier, with the road below the Causse Méjean on the north side and the Causse Noir on the south side. For some of the way, there are two levels of

cliffs, the Terrasses du Truel. As the river nears the Tarn at le Rozier, the gorge becomes increasingly narrow. All the way, the road twists on a shelf along the cliffside, mostly high above the river.

GORGES DU TARN✦✦✦

Gorges du Tarn Tourist Information *route des Gorges du Tarn, Rivière-sur-Tarn; tel: 05 65 59 74 28; www.ot-gorgesdutarn.com. Open daily July–Aug; Mon–Fri Sept–June.*

From its source on Mont Lozère, the River Tarn flows west towards the Grands Causses where it cuts its way through the limestone plateaux. The Gorges du Tarn, one of the most spectacular in France, starts past Quézac and continues for 50km to le Rozier, running between orange cliffs and steep wooded hillsides below the Causse Sauveterre (to the north) and Causse Méjean. The river is fed by 40 springs which burst from underground, tumbling into it as waterfalls. Villages are few and far between as the water level can vary dramatically and unpredictably. Those which have developed in the valley's wider stretches now thrive on tourism – canoeing, potholing and rock climbing are popular pursuits – and also industriously cultivate their orchards and vineyards.

During the French Revolution, when the nobility were being cruelly pursued, many left their homes and hid in caves in the gorge.

ISPAGNAC✦✦

Ispagnac Tourist Information *place Jules Loget; tel: 04 66 44 20 89; www.ispanac.com. Open daily July–Aug; Mon–Fri mornings Sept–June.*

Ispagnac is a go-ahead little town, popular as a touring base and offering a range of river activities. The sheltered slopes around it are covered in orchards, vineyards and strawberry fields. The delightful 11th-century church in yellow stone beside a shaded square has a fine rose window and octagonal bell tower.

La Malene✦

ⓘ Parc National des Cévennes Information Centre
tel: 04 66 48 50 77;
www.gorgesdutarn.net. Open
Mon–Sat mid-June–mid-Sept.
Out of season call the office
de tourisme at Ste-Enimie,
tel: 04 66 48 53 44.

This scenic riverside village used to be an important watering point for sheep on their way to the Sauveterre and Méjean *causses* (plateaux). From medieval times to the French Revolution, it was the seat of the powerful barons of Montesquieu whose 16th-century castle is now a hotel. The Falise de la Barre, the black stains on the cliffs above, are said to be from the smoke of a house full of walnuts when the whole village was set on fire during the Revolution.

Meyrueis✦✦

ⓘ Meyrueis Tourist Information Tour de
l'Horloge; tel: 04 66 45 60
33; www.meyrueis-office-
tourisme.com. Open daily
Easter–Nov; Sat–Sun
Dec–Easter.

☾ Château des Ayres
€€€ Meyrueis; tel: 04
66 45 60 10. Benedictine
monastery now a 21-room
hotel with garden, pool
and tennis. Restaurant
closed mid-Dec–mid-Mar.

Three small rivers, the Bétuzon, Brèze and Jonte, join together here before heading down the Gorges de la Jonte. The town is 706m high so you can enjoy clear mountain air as you stroll along the riverside promenades under plane trees or pause at a terrace bar. Its clock-tower was once part of the town's fortifications and there are several elegant Renaissance buildings lurking along the narrow streets, as well as an attractive covered market hall by the river. Just south of the town off the D986, the 15th-century **Château de Roquedois✦** (*open Tue–Sat July–Aug; tel: 04 66 45 62 81*), an imposing pink and ochre building with four round towers, houses an information centre on the Cévennes National Park; it has a detailed model of Mont Aigoual and a display of horse-drawn carriages.

Quezac✦

ⓘ Quézac Tourist Information in
Ispagnac; tel: 04 66 44 20
89; www.ispagnac.com.
Open daily July–Aug;
Mon–Fri mornings
Sept–June.

The village, situated on the left bank of the Tarn, pipes its famous mineral water from a spring on the opposite side to a large bottling plant on the edge of Ispagnac. The bridge across the Tarn was built 500 years ago at the express wish of Pope Urban V who lived in the Lozère. He wanted pilgrims to be able to come to the sanctuary he had founded on the spot where a statue of the Virgin Mary had been discovered in 1050. Pilgrims still come to the church there.

Le Rozier✦✦

ⓘ Le Rozier Tourist Information
tel: 05 65 62 60 89;
www.officedetourisme-
gorgesdutarn.com. Open
daily July–Aug; Mon–Fri
Sept–June.

Spread along the River Jonte just before it flows into the Tarn, the village is dwarfed by the cliffs of the Causse Méjean and the Causse Noir. An ancient bridge over the Jonte leads to Peyreléau, a quaint hillside village whose ruined castle, the **Château de Peyrelade✦**, which is built into the rock, occupies a commanding position above the gorges. Autumn is a particularly good time to be in

Château de Peyrelade €
Tel: 05 65 59 74 28. Open daily July–Aug; by appointment rest of year.

the area when game from the *causses* is in season. Truffles are also a local speciality.

Accommodation in le Rozier

Grand Hôtel des Voyageurs €€ *Tel: 05 65 62 60 09; www.hotelvoyageurs.com. Open Apr–Sept.* Comfortable 20-room hotel in the main street where E-A Martel stayed in 1888 while mapping nearby caves. Fully modernised. Menus include local specialities such as tripe and lamb.

ST-CHELY-DU-TARN✦✦

Son-et-lumière performances are staged in summer in front of the Chapelle du Clémaret.

Across a pretty stone bridge on the left bank of the river, this ancient hamlet and its small 12th-century chapel, Chapelle du Clémaret, nestle picturesquely where two waterfalls cascade down. Its tiny square overlooking the river still has an old walk-in communal bread oven. Narrow alleys lead off it past stone cottages.

Accommodation in St-Chély-du-Tarn

Auberge de la Cascade €€ *Tel: 04 66 48 52 82; www.aubergecascade.com. Open Mar–mid-Nov.* Old stone building with 27 rooms, modern comforts and a pool in a timeless little village in the Tarn Gorge.

STE-ENIMIE✦✦

Ste-Enimie Tourist Information *Next to the Mairie; tel: 04 66 48 53 44; www.gorgesdutarn.net. Open daily July–Aug; Mon–Sat Easter–June and Sept–Oct.*

Everyone who has driven up the twisting Gorges du Tarn arrives at this village with a certain relief. Suddenly there are shops and bars!

Ste-Enimie

Ste-Enimie was a beautiful 7th-century princess who developed leprosy after her father, the king of Merovingia, insisted she marry one of his barons. Searching desperately for a cure, she was led by an angel to the Source de Burle, a spring fed by rainwater from the Causse de Sauveterre. She jumped in and was immediately cured, but as soon as she tried to return home the leprosy returned. Recognising that her cure must be a sign from God, she set up home in a cave beside the spring and stayed in it to do good works.

Above
Le Rozier

Musée Le Vieux Logis € Tel: 04 66 31 69 20. Open daily July–Aug for guided tours; by appointment rest of year.

Petit Train des Causses leaves from car park beside the bridge and travels to Boisset farm; tel: 04 66 48 50 73. Twice daily July–Aug; by reservation rest of year.

But it's hard to believe now that such a small place, which stretches up from the river in terraces, used to be an important trading centre. The centre is a medieval grid of steep narrow streets and pale stone buildings roofed in round grey slates. In the small 12th-century chapel, colourful modern ceramics by Henri Constans tell the story of Enimie, a 6th-century saint whose discovery of the Burle spring nearby cured her of leprosy. The **Musée Le Vieux Logis**✦ shows what life used to be like in the area. From the village a 'road train', **Le Petit Train des Causses**✦✦✦, does two-hour trips around the Causse de Sauveterre July–Aug €€.

Accommodation and food in Ste-Enimie

Auberge du Moulin €€ rue de la Combe; tel: 04 66 48 53 08. Closed mid-Nov–mid-Mar. Old converted mill in pink stone by River Tarn, just across the road from the town's medieval village. Ten rooms and homely restaurant.

Château de la Caze €€€ *near Ste-Enimie; tel: 04 66 48 51 01; www.chateaudelacaze.com. Closed mid-Nov–mid-Mar.* Former castle, complete with towers, dating back to the 15th century and romantically situated on the riverbank in the Tarn gorge, 5km north of La Malène on the D907. Garden with swimming pool. Also noted for its cuisine.

Suggested tour

Total distance: 125km. The detour to the Aven Armand cave adds 22km, the detour to the Roc des Hourtous and the Roc de Serre adds 26km and the detour to St-Chély adds 1km.

Time: 4 hours' driving. Allow a day for the main route, more with detours. Those with limited time should concentrate on the Gorges de la Jonte and the Gorges du Tarn.

Below
The Gorges du Tarn

Links to other tours: At Florac this route touches the 'Heart of the Cévennes' route (*see page 264*). From Florac the D907 leads south to St-Laurent-de-Trèves (*see page 235*), 10km away. From Le Rozier the D907 leads southwest to Millau (*see page 242*) (22km away). From Meyrueis the D986 leads southeast to L'Espérou (*see page 233*), 27km away.

Climb out of **Florac** up to the **Causse Méjean** on the D16 (signposted Les Vignes). This is one of the most exciting roads in the region as it twists in steep hairpin bends around the cliffsides, providing a magnificent panorama over the Cévennes and Mont Lozère with Florac spread out below along the valley bottom. Sunset is the most dramatic time of all to drive up it. The plateau at the top, a desolate expanse of rough grass, box bushes and strangely shaped white boulders, is over 1000m high. Grazed in summer by sheep, it is dotted by the occasional farmhouse. A wide variety of birds inhabit the crags, particularly birds of prey such as kestrels, hen harriers and golden eagles. Drive across the *causse* (21km) to the junction with the D986. Turn left there to drop down towards **MEYRUEIS ❶**.

Detour: The **AVEN ARMAND** ❷ cave is signed to the right 9km after the D16/D986 junction. Take the 2km road to it.

Continue into Meyrueis where the route turns back on itself to go west along the D996 through the 21km-long **GORGES DE LA JONTE** ❸. As the gorge becomes increasingly impressive downstream, with pillars of rock jutting up on the skyline above the steep hillsides of pines and beeches, this is definitely the better way to drive along it rather than going in the other direction. Halfway along you pass through les Douzes, a pretty riverside village with a bell tower and hillside cemetery, and then come to le Truel.

Continuing the route towards **LE ROZIER** ❹, look out just after le Truel for signs to the **Belvédère des Vautours** where two viewing platforms enable you to see over both sides of the gorge. You might also catch sight of vultures wheeling over the crags of the *causses* above as protected nesting sites have led to their reintroduction to the area. At le Rozier the River Jonte flows into the Tarn which you cross to follow the D907 north along the **GORGES DU TARN** ❺. The valley widens a little at les Vignes, a starting point for rafting, and bends dramatically below the Cirque des Baumes before reaching **LA MALENE** ❻.

Detour: Across the river from La Malène a steep narrow road climbs to the Col de Rieisse (946m) on the D16 (8km). Three kilometres beyond the Col, turn right to Rieisse. Beyond it, two clifftop viewing points, the **Roc des Hourtous** (1km to the left) and the **Roc de Serre** (1km to the right), both enjoy superb views of the gorge.

Detour: Eight kilometres beyond la Malène, a bridge over the Tarn leads straight into **ST-CHELY-DU-TARN** ❼ on the opposite bank.

Twisting and turning along the Gorges du Tarn, the D907 continues to **STE-ENIMIE** ❽.

From Ste-Enimie, continue along the gorge past the **CHATEAU DE PRADES** ❾. Two kilometres after it, you will see the ruins of Castelbouc castle on a steep rock overhanging the village which huddles below it. The gorge officially ends just beyond it where the river and road bend very sharply left between the plateaux but the scenery remains similar. Continue to **Molines**, **QUEZAC** ❿ (just across the river) and **ISPAGNAC** ⓫. From there, take the N106 south, still beside the Tarn, to return to Florac.

Right
Gorges de la Jonte

Getting out of the car

To walk around the **Arcs de St-Pierre**, an area of extraordinary rock formations, turn right off the D996 at le Truel on to the unnumbered road which climbs steeply up hairpin bends towards **St-Pierre-Des-Tripiers**. After 3km the rocks are signposted off to the left. The Arcs themselves (a 10-minute walk from the road) are three big natural arches. Other dramatically eroded rocks, within a further 10-minute walk which passes the remains of a prehistoric village, include the Grande Place, an amphitheatre with a 10m-high column in the centre.

To see the **Burle spring**, take the footpath behind the Gîtes St-Vincent at the top of Ste-Enimie. The walk takes about 25 minutes each way or you can get there by driving 3km along the D986 towards Mende. Two rocks are hollowed out like chairs at the entrance to L'Hermitage de Ste-Enimie, the cave where Enimie is said to have lived. Inside is a tiny chapel. The view is magnificent, extending over both the town and the Tarn.

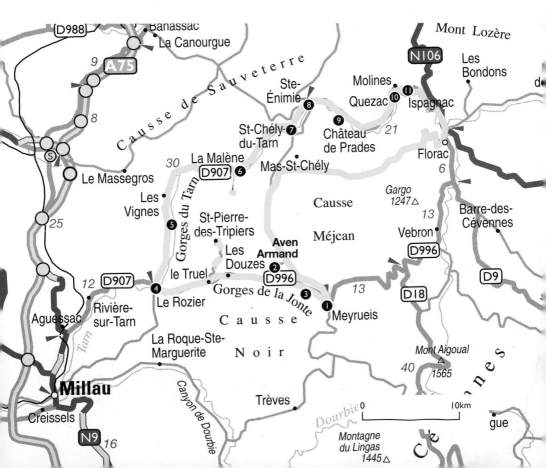

The heart of the Cévennes

Ratings

Mountains	●●●●●
National parks	●●●●●
Scenery	●●●●●
Walking	●●●●○
Geology	●●●○○
Villages	●●●○○
History	●●○○○
Museums	●●○○○

From the less-than-lovely tower blocks of Alès this route soon climbs northwest into the mountains, becoming more and more remote all the way. Along the edge of the Montagne du Bourges the road is impressively speedy, as it now bypasses most of the villages, though it would be a shame to hurry through such majestic scenery. After the route turns east, however, it twists and turns so much that there is no chance of hurrying through the villages that nestle in the rural valleys below Mont Lozère. Idyllic now as holiday retreats, many were the scene of bitter skirmishes 400 years ago between Catholics and Protestants.

Mont Lozère itself, vividly splashed with yellow gorse all summer, can only be truly discovered on foot. Fortunately its rugged hillsides are criss-crossed with ancient sheep trails which now make wonderful paths.

ALES*

🛈 **Alès Tourist Information** *place de l'Hôtel de Ville; tel: 04 66 52 32 15; www.ville-ales.fr. Open daily July–Aug; Mon–Sat Sept–June.*

🚇 **Mine-Témoin €€€** *chemin de la Cité, Ste-Marie, Rochebelle (3km west beyond the Rochebelle bridge over the River Gardon); tel: 04 66 30 45 15. Guided tours, lasting 1 hour 20 minutes. Open daily all year.*

Try to ignore the tower blocks on the outskirts of this former mining town – the last mine closed in 1986 – as you head for the centre. Its wide boulevards, close to the broad River Gardon, have the biggest selection of shops in the area. Not surprisingly, the town's main points of interest concern mining. The **Mine-Témoin****, a disused colliery with 650m of shafts hollowed out of the hillside, vividly depicts the history of mining in the region. Benedictine monks first extracted coal there in the 13th century. Wear a sweater as the temperature remains a constant 13–15°C (55–59°F).

The **Musée Minéralogique*** at the mine engineering school has one of Europe's finest collections of minerals, ranging from Australian opal to black quartz found locally. There are also fossils and an exhibition on the natural resources of the region. In complete contrast, the **Musée-Bibliothèque Pierre-André-Benoît*** in the former bishops' residence has an excellent collection of contemporary art donated by M Benoît who was a local printer and painter. It

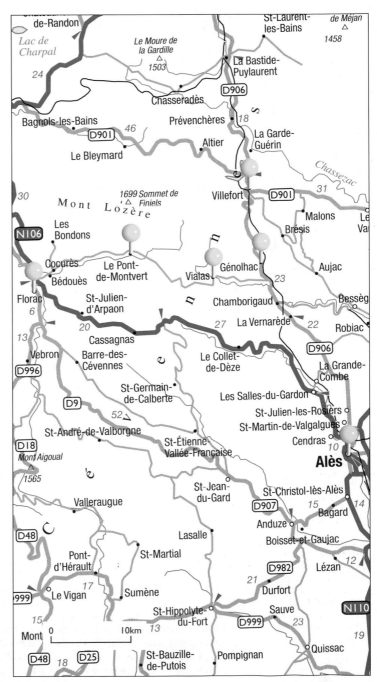

Musée Minéralogique €€

6 avenue de Clavières, attached to the Ecole des Mines. Tel: 04 66 78 51 69. Open mid-June–mid-Sept Mon–Fri; by appointment mid-Sept–mid-June.

Musée-Bibliothèque Pierre-André-Benoît €

33 montée des Lauriers, Rochebelle (take the Rochebelle bridge over the Gardon and follow the signs). Tel: 04 66 86 98 69. Open afternoons Tue–Sun.

The modern Marché de l'Abbaye market hall, open mornings Mon–Sat specialises in local produce, notably honey and mushrooms.

includes works by Picasso, Miró and Braque. The 200-year-old Cathédrale St-Jean-Baptiste is a large gloomy building in much need of restoration but with interesting frescoes.

FLORAC✧✧

Florac Tourist Information *avenue Jean Monestier;* tel: 04 66 45 01 14; *www.mescevennes.com. Open daily July–Aug; Mon–Sat Sept–June.*

Château de Florac Parc National des Cévennes information centre; tel: 04 66 49 53 01; *www.cevennes-parcnational.fr,* with Passagers du Paysage exhibition about the Park €€. *Open daily July–Aug; Mon–Fri Sept–June.*

Thur morning market.

Though well placed in the heart of the Causses as a touring or walking base, this is otherwise a rather plain little town. The **Château de Florac✧**, its much-modified 17th-century castle, is now used by the Parc National des Cévennes to house its information centre and an exhibition about the park. Previously the building was used as a prison, military hospital and then bank. An earlier castle had to be rebuilt, like much of the town, following skirmishes between local lords when the area was known as the 'land of the Gévaudan tyrants'. The town's position is interesting geologically as it is sited at the meeting point of four formations: the limestone Causse Méjean, the schist of the Cévennes, the granite of Mont Lozère and the granite/schist of Mont Aigoual. A footpath starting near the castle leads to the source of the River Pêcher which froths up from a spring on the Causse Méjean (30 minutes walk each way).

Genolhac❖❖

ⓘ Génolhac Tourist Information place du Porche; tel: 04 66 61 18 32; www.cevennes-montlozere. com. Open Mon–Sat July–Aug; Tue and Thur–Sat Sept–June.

ⓒ Hôtel du Mont Lozère €€ 13 avenue de la Libération; tel: 04 66 61 10 72. Closed Jan. Family-run, 11-room hotel with garden and garage.

This small old town of tall grey granite houses with warm red roofs has narrow streets often bridged by arches. Many of the buildings in the medieval centre were originally warehouses with living quarters above storage areas. If you wonder why some of them have stones sticking out in odd places from their otherwise plain walls, the explanation is that they were put there by the builder to show when he needed a drink. The owner would then put wine on them. Eglise St-Pierre has a *clocher-peigne*, a flat open stone belfry with two suspended bells, typical of the area. A plaque opposite the Hôtel du Mont Lozère marks the spot where a Resistance hero was gunned down by the Germans in June 1944.

Bells

The area's bell towers are called *clochers de tourmente* – storm towers – because in bad weather they were rung continuously to help travellers find their way. Otherwise their main use was to call people to mass and let farmers working in the fields know the time.

Although holidaymakers find the mountains very attractive, the towers provide a constant reminder that when the cold Tramontane wind blows from the northwest, the area can be very bleak. The local people have always had a struggle to make a living on the rocky terrain and poor soil, hence the chilling phrase 'Mont Lozère, terre de misère' (land of misery).

Left
The Château de Florac

Le Pont de Montvert❖❖

ⓘ Le Pont de Montvert Tourist Information rue du Quai; tel: 04 66 45 81 94; www. cevennes-montlozere.com. Open daily July–Sept.

ⓜ Eco-Musée du Mont Lozère € including walking trail leaflets; tel: 04 66 45 80 73; www.cevennes-parcnational.fr. Open daily Apr–Sept. Combined admission with Ferme de Troubat, an old farmhouse, 6km east of the D998 at Troubat.

The old-fashioned village of le Pont de Montvert, straddling the River Tarn and two of its tributaries, has a real mountain atmosphere and is a popular walking centre. The tower at one end of the old bridge over the Tarn once served as a tollbooth. In 1702 a Catholic abbot was flung off the bridge while trying to escape from local Protestants. His death sparked off the Camisard uprising, a bitter two-year struggle by local peasants to be allowed to worship as Protestants. The Maison du Mont Lozère, part of the **Eco-Musée du Mont Lozère❖❖**, houses an exhibition about the local landscape, its people and wildlife.

Accommodation in le Pont de Montvert

Aux Sources du Tarn € *Tel: 04 66 45 80 25; www.hotel-lozere.com.* Homely 19-room hotel beside the Tarn, popular with walkers. Advance reservations essential Dec–Feb.

VIALAS❖

ⓘ **Vialas Tourist Information** *rue du Haut; tel: 04 66 41 05 95; www.montlozere.com. Open daily July–Aug.*

Vialas, a little hamlet of stone dwellings clustered around narrow streets, has a church and sweeping views across the valley. Typical of the area, its Protestant church has a sloping *lauze*-tiled roof and a bell.

Accommodation and food in Vialas

Chantoiseau €€ *Vialas; tel: 04 66 41 00 02. Open Apr–Oct.* A 17th-century post house transformed into a charming 13-room hotel. The chef-owner features traditional Cévennes cooking such as *gratin d'agneau* (baked lamb) and chestnut tart. He is also very proud of his wine cellar which has over 1000 bottles. Swimming pool with panoramic views.

VILLEFORT❖❖

ⓘ **Villefort Tourist Information** *rue de l'Eglise; tel: 04 66 46 87 30; www.villefort.free.fr. Open daily July–Aug; Mon–Fri Sept–June.* A good day to visit is 24 June as the whole town celebrates the Fête de Ste-Jeanne with a bonfire in the square. People jump over it as it dies down.

Nestling beneath Mont Lozère in the Phalère valley, Villefort makes a good holiday base, surrounded as it is by walking trails. The Lac de Villefort reservoir on its north side is popular for watersports.

Accommodation and food in Villefort

Hôtel Balme € *place Portalet; tel: 04 66 46 80 14; www.hotelbalme. free.fre. Closed mid-Nov–mid-Feb.* Traditional and elegant 16-room hotel run by chef-owner and his wife for over 30 years. High reputation for both hospitality and food. La Clède gastronomic restaurant. Garden and garage.

Suggested tour (see map page 269)

Total distance: 200km. The detour to the Belvédère des Bouzède adds 16km and the detour to la Garde-Guérin adds 12km.

Time: 6 hours' driving. Allow most of two days for the main route, two full days with detours. Those with limited time should concentrate on the stretch from Florac to Villefort.

Links to other tours: At Florac this route touches the 'Great plateaux and gorges' route (*see page 256*). From Florac the D907 leads to St-Laurent-de-Trèves (*see page 235*), 10km away. From Alès the D910 leads to Anduze (*see page 230*), 16km away.

From **ALES** ❶ take the N106 north beside the River Gardon, bypassing the former mining town of **La Grand-Combe** which

Opposite
Villefort

contains little of interest. Beyond the Cambous dam (on the left), the road climbs along wooded mountainsides, still beside the river, over passes and past villages such as **Cassagnas** and **St-Julian d'Arpaon** to FLORAC ❷. On the far side of Florac, turn right on to the D998, a quiet winding road through peaceful countryside along the River Tarn valley. Here the scenery is pretty rather than grand. Sheep – sometimes black – graze in fields which give way to the rocky slopes and forests of Mont Lozère. Each village has its landmarks – a huge church surrounded by campsites in **Bédouès**, a sawmill in **Cocurès** and the ancient tollbooth beside the quaint stone bridge in **LE PONT-DE-MONTVERT ❸**. Now the road narrows, climbing through beech woods high above the river over the Col de la Croix de Berthel (1088m). Approaching **VIALAS ❹** the hillsides are patched with broom and heather amongst the boulders.

From Vialas you pass through forests and over the Col de Valoussière (501m) on the way to **GENOLHAC ❺**.

Detour: Turn left out of Génolhac up an unnumbered road to the spectacular 1235m-high **Belvédère des Bouzède** viewpoint (8km) where the views stretch like a relief map south over the Cévennes and east towards the Ardèche.

From Génolhac the route goes north on the D906, twisting through woods. Beyond **Concoules**, the countryside opens out and you get wide mountain views to the east on the way to **VILLEFORT ❻**.

Detour: North of Villefort the D906 continues past the town's reservoir to **La Garde-Guérin** (6km), a quaint medieval village whose narrow streets and simple stone houses seem to have changed very little over the centuries. During the Camisard uprising, it was fiercely

Left
Villefort

Stevenson's travels in the Cévennes

When Robert Louis Stevenson's book, *Travels with a Donkey in the Cévennes*, was published in 1879, it put this remote area of France on the map.

The previous year he had taken himself to le Monastier because he wanted to get away and decide on his feelings for Fanny Osbourne – whom he later married. Having bought a donkey, Modestine, he set off on 22 September to walk south via le Pont de Montvert (which reminded him of the Killiecrankie Pass in Scotland) and Florac to St-Jean-du-Gard. The 220km journey took him only 12 days.

On the way he drew small sketches in his diary (now at Yale University in America), with notes such as 'The road lay under chestnuts and though I saw a hamlet or two below me in the vale and many lone houses of the chestnut farmers, it was a very solitary march all afternoon'. Later he added background information about the Camisards to turn it into a book for which he was paid 30 francs – though he thought it worth at least 50 francs.

The R L Stevenson Association's leaflet (available from local tourist offices) has lists of places to stay and eat along the route and where to hire a mountain bike, horse – or donkey.

The Voie Régordane

The Régordane long-distance path, GR72, runs north–south along the crests of the Cévennes through la Garde Guérin, Villefort, Génolhac and Alès. It is part of an ancient route between the Auvergne and the Mediterranean which pilgrims used on their way to Rome in the Middle Ages. Originally it was probably formed by shepherds driving flocks between the valleys and the plateaux during the traditional *transhumance* in spring and autumn. In Roman times it was the only route between the Languedoc and the Auvergne. When Marseille developed as a port, it would have been busy with mule carts, but with the construction of the railways, it once again became a quiet country track.

 Hôtel Lou Cante Perdrix €€ *la Vernarède (between the D29 and the D906, 5km east of Chamborigaud); tel: 04 66 61 50 30; www.canteperdrix.fr. Closed Jan.* Fifteen-room hotel in a 200-year-old mansion with garden, pool and tennis. Bicycles for hire. The name means 'partridge field' in the local dialect.

attacked by Protestants. The ruined tower which stands guard over it provides good views over the Gorges du Chassezac – though the steps up to the tower are steep.

From Villefort the route turns east (towards la Vans) on the D901 over the Col Mas de l'Air (846m). Two kilometres beyond the Col, turn right on to the D155 through **Malons** to join the D51 at **Brésis**. This quiet rural road through trees and along stone terraces has a wonderful view of Mont Lozère with its gentle hilltops spread out above wooded slopes. Enjoy the remoteness as you continue on the narrow D51 through **Aujac**, overlooked by a hilltop castle, then wind down through the forest above the River Cèze to **Bessèges**, a distinctly industrial town. Cross the river, turning immediately right on to the D29 to **Chamborigaud**. Now the remoteness has gone but there are still good views as the D906 takes you back to Alès.

Getting out of the car

For a flavour of Mont Lozère, take the **Sentier de Gourdouse**, a rocky footpath which climbs north from Vialas into the hills below granite ridges. Listen for the sound of cowbells competing with the roar of mountain streams and look out for wild pansies and orchids.

Also worth exploring

France's second largest collection of prehistoric standing stones (after Carnac in Brittany) is on the Mont Lozère plateau north of Florac. Turn left off the D998 at Cocurès and go through Les Bondons to the junction with the D35 (9km from Cocurès). Turn left again and the stones, which include 21 menhirs and a dolmen, are signed shortly afterwards on the left.

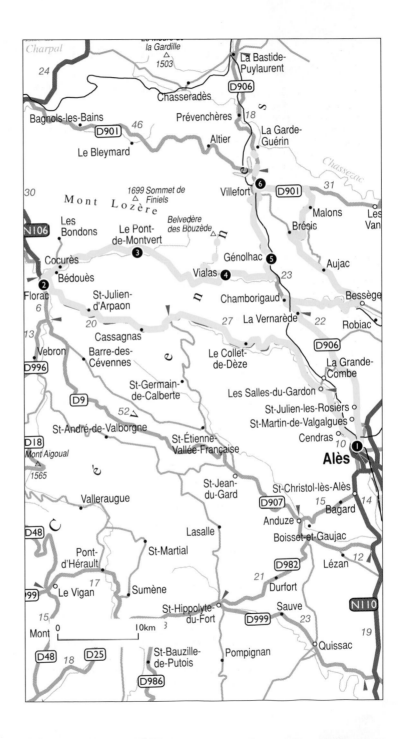

Charpal

24

Le Mont de la Gardille
△ 1503

La Bastide-Puylaurent

Chasseradès

D906

Bagnols-les-Bains

D901

46

Prévenchères

18

La Garde-Guérin

Altier

Le Bleymard

Chassezac

30

M o n t   L o z è r e

1699 Sommet de △ Finiels

Villefort **6** D901

31

N106

Les Bondons

Le Pont-de-Montvert

Belvédère des Bouzède △

Malons

Brésis

Les Van

Cocurès

3

Génolhac **5**

Aujac

Bédouès

Vialas **4**

Florac **2**

6

St-Julien-d'Arpaon

Chamborigaud

Bessège

13

20

27

La Vernarède

22

Robiac

Cassagnas

D906

Vebron

Barre-des-Cévennes

Le Collet-de-Dèze

La Grande-Combe

D996

St-Germain-de-Calberte

Les Salles-du-Gardon

D9

52 △

St-Julien-les-Rosiers

St-Martin-de-Valgalgues

St-André-de-Valborgne

St-Étienne-Vallée-Française

Cendras

10

D18

Mont Aigoual △ 1565

Alès **1**

St-Jean-du-Gard

St-Christol-lès-Alès

Valleraugue

D907

15

Bagard

14

D48

Lasalle

Anduze

Boisset-et-Gaujac

Pont-d'Hérault

St-Martial

D982

Lézan

12

99

17

Le Vigan

Sumène

21

Durfort

15

Mont

St-Hippolyte-du-Fort

D999

Sauve

23

N110

19

0   10km   3

Quissac

D48   18   D25

St-Bauzille-de-Putois

Pompignan

D986

The coastal resorts south from Montpellier

Ratings

Beaches	●●●●●
Naturism	●●●●●
Children	●●●●○
Coastal villages/ towns	●●●●○
Wildlife	●●●●○
Entertainment	●●●○○
Food	●●●○○
Outdoor activities	●●●○○

A long this route you will discover the essence of the Languedoc-Roussillon coast with its long sandy beaches and lagoons. Until the 1960s, comparately few holiday-makers went there. Sète was the only town of any importance, though Palavas, an old fishing village, had been attracting visitors from Montpellier since the railway arrived a hundred years ago.

Purpose-built resorts arrived when the French government initiated an ambitious programme of tourist development in 1963. The Cap d'Agde headland and beaches were transformed by the building of smart marinas and apartment/villa complexes stylishly laid out with gardens and promenades.

Shallow lagoons – *étangs* – lie just inland along much of the coast, separated from the sea by narrow sandbars. The calm semi-salt water of the Bassin de Thau has proved ideal for the cultivation of shellfish, while delicate pink flamingos have long been at home on the quieter lagoons around Palavas.

AGDE❖❖

ⓘ Agde Tourist Information *Espace Molière (near place Molière); tel: 04 67 94 29 68. Open daily June–Sept; Mon–Sat Oct–May.*

🏛 Cathédral St-Etienne *Open only for mass. Guided visits only, bookable at tourist office.*

The ancient little town of Agde spreads along the River Hérault just before it reaches the sea. It was once the largest port on the Languedoc coast, having first been developed by the ancient Greeks in 500 BC. However, the river silted up centuries ago and now only pleasure craft and small fishing boats line its narrow quays, overlooked by rows of former merchants' houses. Many of the buildings in the town centre are made of sombre-looking local black basalt, hence the town's nickname – 'La Ville Noire'. They include the dour 12th-century **Cathédrale St-Etienne❖** whose sturdy tower and slit windows make it look like a fortress.

The **Musée Agathois Espace Molière❖❖**, housed in a quaint 17th-century building, formerly a hospital, vividly presents the town's history through pottery, paintings, costumes and reconstructions of interiors of local houses. It also has a splendid array of ancient

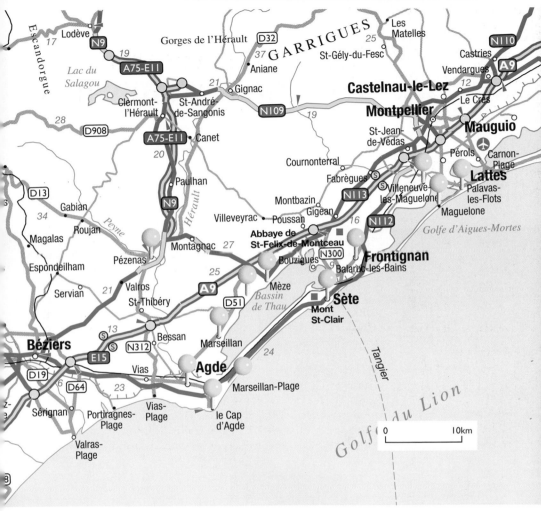

wooden shields used in jousting tournaments which are still a colourful feature of the town's summer entertainment on the river.

Agde is well-endowed with places to eat, particularly along the narrow riverside terraces where you can bask in the evening sun and watch the comings and goings on the water as you dine.

Accommodation in Agde

Hôtel Le Donjon €€ *place Jean Jaurès; tel: 04 67 94 12 32; www.hotelledonjon.com. Open all year.* Inexpensive 20-room hotel with plenty of character and a pool. In the old town centre, only steps away from the shops and restaurants.

BASSIN DE THAU✢✢

Musée de l'Étang de Thau € *Quai du Port de Pêche, Bouziques; tel: 04 67 78 33 57. Open daily all year.*

This lagoon, the largest of many along the Languedoc coast, is separated from the sea by a 20km-long sandbar, the Isthume des Onglous. The villagers on its northern shore, who used to make their living from fishing, have now turned to oyster and mussel farming. The water ripples around the poles and garlands of nets used in their cultivation. Bouziques is the main oyster centre, and the lagoon's oysters are known as *huitres de Bouziques*. An oyster fair is held here in mid-August, and the **Musée de l'Étang de Thau**✢ on the quay of Bouziques small fishing harbour traces the history of shellfish breeding.

Below
Cap d'Agde

Cap d'Agde✦✦✦

Developed in the 1960s around a headland, this purpose-built town could scarcely be more different from its ancient sister, 3km away. Broad avenues bordered by gardens of colourful oleanders lead to clusters of pink and ochre villas and apartments beside a large marina and 14km of sandy beaches.

On summer evenings, a constant flow of visitors parade up and down in front of the restaurants, bars and souvenir shops surrounding the quays. Singers and groups compete to entice customers into their bars – and the party atmosphere continues well into the night. Other revellers head for the Ile des Loisirs which offers a choice of over two dozen nightclubs, a funfair and a casino.

By day the town seems to have a club for every pursuit – tennis, golf, squash, horse riding, scrabble, bridge, snooker, etc. You can take a boat trip round the harbour, snorkel along an underwater trail or have a course of thalassotherapy. To keep children happy, **Aqualand**✦✦✦ the waterpark, has slides and a wave pool. There are beachclubs and daily children's shows too.

Cap d'Agde's famous Quartier Naturiste, Europe's largest naturist village, has accommodation for 20,000 people. It has its own shops, restaurants, marina and a hotel beside a wide beach. Day visits (nudity optional) are permitted for a small charge. The beach is excellent but you must be prepared to take all your clothes off.

Frontignan✦

Muscat, the highly-reputed local wine, is the best reason for seeking out Frontignan which is surrounded by vineyards in an otherwise industrial area between the sea and the *garrigue* – hilly scrubland. The sweet fortified wine can be tasted in various cellars.

Maguelone✦✦✦

The history of the isolated **cathedral**✦✦ at Maguelone is no less remarkable than its breathtaking location at the end of a sandbar. Remains found there have been traced back almost 2000 years. Together with a palace it was built by Bishop Arnaud in the 11th century and became very important when several popes sought refuge there during quarrels between church and state. The whole estate

Cathedral *Open daily; organ concerts on Sat evenings July–Aug. Tel: 04 67 60 69 92.*

later fell into ruin and changed hands several times during the construction of the Rhône-Sète Canal beside it. The former cathedral, whose thick walls and small windows make it seem more like a castle than a church, dates back to the 15th century. It was bought and restored in the middle of the 19th century by Frédéric Fabrège.

MARSEILLAN❖

Marseillan Noilly Prat *Free guided tours ending with a tasting. You can also buy the product. Tel: 04 67 77 75 19; www.noillyprat.com. Open daily Mar–Sept.*

Hard as it is to imagine today, Marseillan was situated on the coast in Roman times when it was an important port of call for shipping between Agde and Sète. Later drifting sand caused the Bassin de Thau to form behind a sandbar. Now it is an unassuming fishing port on the Bassin de Thau. It has achieved world-wide fame thanks to Noilly Prat, an aromatic vermouth aperitif made from the local wine. After being left to age in oak vats for a year in quayside cellars, it is transferred to open casks and left for another year. The small quantity which evaporates is said to be fit for angels. Finally it is mixed with fruit alcohol, herbs and *mistelle* (grape juice).

Right
Marseillan: the Noilly Prat cellars

Marseillan-Plage*

ⓘ Marseillan-Plage Tourist Information
avenue de la Méditérranée; tel: 04 67 21 82 43; www.marseillan.com. Open daily Apr–Sept; Mon–Sat Oct–Mar.

◊ A local festival with traditional music takes place halfway through Lent.

Côte Sud €€
18 quai Antonin Gros; tel: 04 67 01 72 42. Open daily all year. Small restaurant on the quayside, strong on fish.

This small seaside resort with the usual selection of campsites, beach shops and holiday homes is situated on a sandy beach which stretches for miles in both directions. Altogether the sandbar, backed by dunes, goes all the way from Cap d'Agde to Sète – a distance of 20km. The stretch of beach on the west side of the resort is reserved for naturists, joining up with the one at Cap d'Agde. To avoid paying to get an all-over tan on the naturist beach, park your car in one of the roads behind the dunes in Marseillan-Plage and walk there (2km).

Meze**

ⓘ Mèze Tourist Information *8 rue P.A. Massaloup, Mèze; tel: 04 67 43 93 08. Open daily July–Aug; Mon–Sat Sept–June.*

◊ Jazz festival in July.

The charming old town of Mèze, with its narrow streets, has an attractive harbour on the Bassin de Thau where fishing boats and yachts line up. Stalls along the waterfront sell freshly gathered oysters, clams and mussels. **Station de Lagunage***, the lagoon's research station *(2km west of Mèze)*, has an aquarium of tropical fish as well as displays, films and photographs about the local shellfish industry *(visits by appointment only; tel: 04 67 46 64 94)*.

Palavas-les-Flots**

ⓘ Palavas-les-Flots Tourist Information *Phare de la Méditérranée; tel: 04 67 07 73 34; www.palavaslesflots.com. Open daily Mar–Sept; Mon–Sat Oct–Feb.*

Redoute de Ballestras €€ *Tel: 04 67 68 56 41. Open daily July–Sept; Tue–Sun Oct–Nov and Feb–June; Sat–Sun Dec–Jan.*

This lively little resort, much loved by families for its 7km-long sandy beach, is on the narrow band of land between the Etang de Pérols lagoon and the sea. Unlike most resorts along the Languedoc-Roussillon coast, it is no latter-day tourist development. Having started out as a fishing community, it became popular for a day out with people from nearby Montpellier when the railway (now closed) arrived in 1872. The way they flocked in on the 'Petit Train de Palavas' with their shrimping nets and picnics was later immortalised by a local cartoonist, Albert Dubout. A collection of his work is housed in an old fort, the **Redoute de Ballestras***, which is a landmark on the edge of the Etang de Pérois. It was built in 1743 to protect local fishermen from pirates. When the threat subsided, it became a water tower until being converted into a museum to house the Dubout cartoons.

⬤ **Jousting tournaments** in July and Aug.

⬤ **Rôtisserie Palavas** €€ 5 rue de l'Eglise; tel: 04 67 68 52 12. Closed Sun July–Aug; Sun–Mon Sept–June. Seafood restaurant.

On the west side of the busy old fishing port, there is now a large marina for yachts and cruisers. Its seafood restaurants, which buy direct from the fishermen, are as popular for a night out with people from Montpellier as they are for holidaymakers. Throughout the summer, street entertainment and open-air concerts are staged. The casino is another attraction for many.

Pezenas❖❖

ℹ️ **Pézenas Tourist Information** place Gambetta; tel: 04 67 98 36 40; www.paysdepezenas.net. Open daily all year. Guided tours available.

⬤ **Musée Vulliod-St-Germain** € 3 rue Albert-Allais; tel: 04 67 98 90 59. Open Tue–Sun all year.

⬤ The town stages several colourful events during the year, including pre-Lent carnival processions.

For 250 years this small town was the seat of the governors of Languedoc. During the 16th and 17th centuries, its royal court rivalled that of Versailles. The *vielle ville* (old quarter) has not changed much since those illustrious times when aristocrats built fine mansions with ornate doorways and balconies. Leading artists and musicians of the day came to entertain the court. Molière made his name as a playwright there, putting on several plays with his own theatre company. He stayed at the Maison du Barbier Cély, now the tourist office, and staged the plays at the **Hôtel Alphonse❖** (now a private house) which is one of the best-preserved buildings from that period. It has a decorative portico and two tiers of loggias.

Musée Vulliod-St-Germain❖, in the 16th-century Hôtel de St-Germain, devotes a room to Molière memorabilia. There are Aubusson tapestries and an audio-visual on the town's history, particularly its Molière connections.

In cake shops, watch out for *petits pâtés* – little pies – the town's speciality. They look like cotton reels and are stuffed with sweet spice, glacé lemon and minced meat. Restaurants serve them for dessert.

Food in Pézenas

Côté Sud €€ *12 place du 14 Juillet; tel: 04 67 09 41 74. Closed Mon July–Aug; closed Mon and Wed Sept–June.* Small lively brasserie on the edge of the old town with imaginative menus featuring local specialities such as *petits pâtés*.

Petits pâtés de Pézenas

In 1768 Lord Clive of India spent the winter at Larzac castle near Pézenas, hoping the mild weather would be good for his health. He was accompanied by his Indian cooks who passed on the recipe for these little pies to local bakers. Several continue to make them by hand and restaurants proudly serve them for dessert. Incidentally, they're also made in Market Drayton, Lord Clive's home town in England (now 'twinned' with Pézenas) where they are known as Clive Pies.

SETE❖❖❖

Sète is the oldest and most interesting town along this part of the coast, thanks to its canalside restaurants, small speciality shops and sandy beach. It is also an important fishing and industrial port. The port was developed 300 years ago as part of the grand Canal du Midi project. This included building the town itself on the sides of Mont St-Clair, a rocky 183m-high outcrop with the sea on one side and the Bassin de Thau on the other.

Narrow streets spread steeply up the hillside from the Canal Royal where pastel-coloured Italianate buildings line the busy quays. A row of restaurants and bars makes them one of the liveliest places along the coast for eating out.

The climb up Mont St-Clair is strenuous but it is definitely more interesting to walk (at least 15 minutes) than drive. The views from the top are splendid. The complex port is laid out below you and, on a clear day, the Cévennes and Pyrenees mountains are visible in the distance. Chapelle Notre-Dame-de-la-Salette behind the terrace is delightful. This small chapel with elaborate mosaic decorations was built in 1864 on the site of a medieval hermitage and is a centre for pilgrimages; the most important are in September and October. On the way you will be tempted to linger in the *pâtisseries*, *épiceries* and other small shops, particularly in rue Gambetta and rue Jean Jaurès.

On the sea side, the formidable Fort Richelieu was built in 1744 after a two-day occupation by the English. The sailors' cemetery, Cimetière Marin, just below it is the subject of a moving poem by Paul Valéry who was born in the town and buried there in 1945. The local history museum, **Musée Paul Valéry❖**, has sections devoted to him and another local personality, the singer Georges Brassens. Below it the defences which Vauban constructed, Fort St-Pierre, have been

ⓘ **Sète Tourist Information** *60 Grand'Rue Mario Roustan; tel: 04 67 74 71 71; www.setetourisme.fr. Open daily all year.*

Traffic can be very heavy along the quays of the Canal Royal and on the hilly streets which climb from it into the town centre.

ⓜ **Musée Paul Valéry** €€ *rue Desnoyer; tel: 04 67 46 20 98. Open daily July–Aug; Wed–Mon Sept–June.*

▲ A highlight of the day is the fish auction beside the Old Port at 1500.

Above
The Canal Royal in Sète

Jousting tournaments, dating back to 1666 when the port was built, take place on the Grand Canal during the Sète Festival season in July–Aug which also includes plays, music and dancing.

transformed into the 1500-seat open-air Théâtre de la Mer where plays are staged from mid-June to mid-August.

Accommodation and food in Sète

La Conga €€ *plage de la Corniche; tel: 04 67 53 02 57. Open daily.* Small hotel in quiet location near the beach. Nineteen rooms.

La Calangue € *17 quai Gal Durand; tel: 04 67 74 28 37. Open daily.* Quayside restaurant where you can watch the world go by as you eat such Sète specialities as *tièles* (fish and tomato pies) or stuffed mussels.

Grand Hôtel €€€ *17 quai de Lattre-de-Tassigny; tel: 04 67 74 71 77. Closed second half of Dec.* Imposing old 45-room hotel with modernised facilities overlooking the canal. Garage and car park. No restaurant.

Below
Water plays a large part in life in the south

VILLENEUVE-LES-MAGUELONE❖

Mas d'Andos €
route de Mireval;
tel: 04 67 69 58 44.
Open daily July–Aug for
guided visits (40 mins) at
1700; Sun only Sept–June.

A comparatively recent addition to this ancient village is an ostrich farm, the **Mas d'Andos**❖. Visitors can see how the 500 birds are reared and buy decorative eggshells, feathers and ostrich sausage.

Accommodation in the coastal resorts area

Though there are plenty of small hotels to be found in the area, self-catering dominates the purpose-built resorts like Cap d'Agde which has a huge choice of holiday apartments and villas. The area has many campsites too; some have chalets to rent for those who do not have their own caravan or tent. Pre-erected tents can be booked through several British tour operators.

Hérault area hotel reservations: *tel: 04 67 67 71 71; www.herault-tourisme.com.*

Suggested tour

Total distance: 135km. The detour to Pézenas adds 40km.

Time: 4 hours' driving. Allow at least a day for the main route, more with detours. Those with limited time should concentrate on the stretch between Sète and Agde.

Links to other tours: From Agde the N112 leads to Béziers (*see page 202*), 23km away. From Pézenas the N9 also leads to Béziers (*see page 202*), 22km away, or to Clermont l'Herault (*see page 224*), 20km away.

This is a mainly flat route of good, well-signposted roads. However it covers peak holiday territory and is near Montpellier so the roads get very busy in high season. Leave Montpellier on the D986 to **PALAVAS-LES-FLOTS** ❶. This takes you between the Pérols and Arnel lagoons, home to hundreds of pink flamingos which stand picturesquely in groups preening themselves, foraging for fish or asleep on one leg. Those with grey/white feathers are the youngest. The shallow lagoons also attract many sea birds so you are unlikely to want to hurry along their tranquil shorelines.

Joutes Nautiques

Jousting tournaments provide colourful entertainment during summer, particularly at Sète and Agde. Two jousters dressed in splendid costumes stand facing each other on *tintaines* – small platforms – in rowing boats, one red, one blue, propelled by teams of ten oarsmen. The one who dislodges the other with his 3m-long, three-pronged lance is the winner – and of course there is much cheering and jeering whenever one or the other falls into the water.

Getting out of the car

Eucalyptus trees, cedars and pines shade the former cathedral, a small castle-like building in cream stone, at **MAGUELONE** ❷, 4km southwest from Palavas-les-Flots. You walk to it along a spit of land between the sea and L'Etang de l'Armel.

From Palavas-les-Flots, return on the D986 to join the D185 which goes past **VILLENEUVE-LES-MAGUELONE** . Interestingly a causeway road used to lead direct from Maguelone to Villeneuve-les-Maguelone until the 1700s when the Rhône-Sète Canal was built, cutting it in two. The N112 leading to Sète is not an attractive road though a visit to the Muscat cellars in **FRONTIGNAN** (just north of it; *tel: 04 67 48 93 20*) can provide a welcome distraction. Note, however that it's very easy to speed past the turning by mistake. There are two routes around **SETE** and **Mont St-Clair**, either south along the scenic corniche beside the sea or to the north across canals and past the railway station. The N112 then continues to **MARSEILLAN-PLAGE** beside the railway line along a long straight sandbar with water on both sides. The **BASSIN DE THAU** lagoon is mostly hidden behind trees, while dunes obscure the sea. The road system around **CAP**

Camping Californie Plage *Côte Ouest, Vias Plage; tel: 04 67 21 64 69;* Secluded beachside campsite under trees with swimming pool, restaurant and shop. Caravans for rent by the week; also pre-erected tents bookable in the UK through **Eurocamp**; *tel: 08703 338 338 (UK); www.eurocamp.co.uk and www.californie-plage.fr.* Open Apr–Oct.

D'AGDE (just south of the N112) is confusing and the only way to reach either the marinas or the beaches is to park and walk. Watch for signs to the various *Plages*, or for the central marina follow 'Capitainerie du Centre-Port'. The naturist village is signed 'Naturisme'. The old town of **AGDE** is 4km inland on the north side of the N112 beside the River Hérault.

Detour: To visit **PEZENAS** leave Agde on the D13 (20km).

From Agde the route goes north on the D51 through **MARSEILLAN** until it meets the N113 which goes to **MEZE** and **Bouzigues** on the way back to Montpellier. At **Poussan**, you have the option of joining the A9 autoroute to Montpellier. This is only slightly faster but enables you to skirt the south side of the city. If you continue on the

La Maison des Vins du Languedoc €€

Mas Saporta (beside the D986/D189 junction just south of Montpellier); tel: 04 67 06 88 66; www. cuisiniers-vignerons.com. Restaurant serving regional specialities with own wine cellars selling local Coteaux du Languedoc wines.

N113, it is worth taking a right-hand turn at **Gigean** up to **St-Félix-de-Montceau**, the ruins of a Benedictine abbey on a hilltop. The view is superb and the countryside smells sweetly of herbs and pines.

Also worth exploring

To take time off on the beach, a further alternative is to turn south off the D912 for **Vias Plage**. This is one of several small resorts in the area, all popular with families as they have well-equipped campsites. For walking, there is the shady tow-path of the Canal du Midi which runs parallel to the coast all the way from Portiragnes to Agde. Boat excursions on the Canal (*Tue–Sat July–Aug*), start from **Agde**, **Marseillan** and **Portiragnes**, operated by **Bateaux du Soleil**; *tel: 04 67 94 08 79*. Alternatively, you can hire a self-drive cruiser for weekend or one-week trips (*Mar–Oct only*) from **Crown Blue Line**'s base at **Port Cassafières** in **Portiragnes**; *tel: 04 67 90 91 70; www.crownblueline.com*

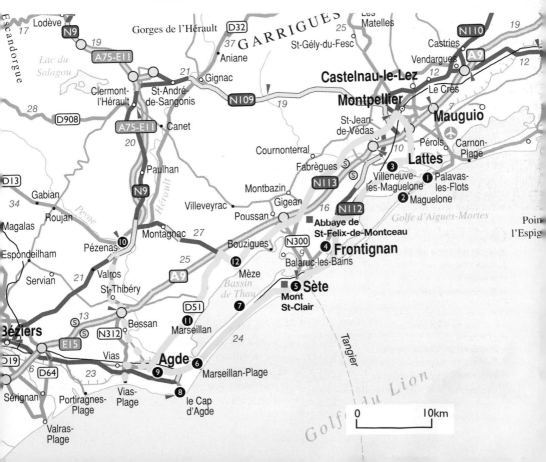

Language

Although English is spoken in most tourist locations it is courteous to attempt to speak some French. The effort is generally appreciated, and may even elicit a reply in perfect English! The following is a very brief list of some useful words and phrases, with approximate pronunciation guides. For driver's vocabulary, see page 28. The *Thomas Cook European 12-Language Phrasebook* (£4.99/$7.95) lists more than 300 travel phrases in French (and in 11 other European languages).

- **Hello/Goodbye**
  Bonjour/Au revoir *Bawngzhoor/Ohrervwahr*
- **Good evening/Goodnight**
  Bonsoir/Bonne nuit *Bawngswahr/Bon nwee*
- **Yes/No**
  Oui/Non *Wee/Nawng*
- **Please/Thank you (very much)**
  S'il vous plaît/Merci (beaucoup) *Seelvooplay/Mehrsee (bohkoo)*
- **Excuse me, can you help me please?**
  Excusez-moi, vous pouvez m'aider s'il vous plaît? *Ekskewzaymwah, voo poovay mahyday seelvooplay?*
- **Do you speak English?**
  Vous parlez anglais? *Voo pahrlay ahnglay?*
- **I'm sorry, I don't understand.**
  Pardon, je ne comprends pas. *Pahrdawng, zher ner kawngprawng pah.*
- **I am looking for the tourist information office.**
  Je cherche l'office de tourisme. *Zher shaersh lohfeece de tooreezm.*
- **Do you have a map of the town/area?**
  Avez-vous une carte de la ville/région? *Ahveh-voo ewn cart der lah veel/rehzhawng?*
- **Do you have a list of hotels?**
  Vous avez une liste d'hôtels? *Vooz ahveh ewn leesst dohtehl?*
- **Do you have any rooms free?**
  Vous avez des chambres disponibles? *Voozahveh deh shahngbr deesspohneebl?*
- **I would like to reserve a single/double room with/without bath/shower.**
  Je voudrais réserver une chambre pour une personne/pour deux personnes avec/sans salle de bain/douche. *Zher voodray rehsehrveh ewn shahngbr poor ewn pehrson/poor der pehrson avek/sawns sal der banne/doosh.*

- **I would like bed and breakfast/(room and) half board/(room and) full board.**
  Je voudrais le petit-déjeuner/la demi-pension/la pension complète. *Zher voodray ler pewtee-dehjewneh/lah dermee-pahngsyawng/lah pahngsyawng kawngplait.*
- **How much is it per night?**
  Quel est le prix pour une nuit? *Khel eh ler pree poor ewn nuwy?*
- **I would like to stay for . . . nights.**
  Je voudrais rester . . . nuits. *Zhe voodray resteh . . . newyh.*
- **Do you accept traveller's cheques/credit cards?**
  Vous acceptez les chèques de voyages/les cartes de crédit? *Voos aksepteh leh sheck der vwoyazh/leh kart der krehdee?*
- **I would like a table for two.**
  Je voudrais une table pour deux personnes. *Zher voodray ewn tabl poor der pehrson.*
- **I would like a cup of/two cups of/another coffee/tea.**
  Je voudrais une tasse de/deux tasses de/encore une tasse de café/thé. *Zher voodray ewn tahss der/der tahss der/oncaw ewn tahss der kafeh/teh.*
- **I would like a bottle/glass/two glasses of mineral water/red wine/white wine, please.**
  Je voudrais une bouteille/un verre/deux verres d'eau minérale/de vin rouge/de vin blanc, s'il vous plaît. *Zhe voodray ewn bootayy/ang vair/der vair doh mynehral/der vang roozh/der vang blahng, seelvooplay*
- **Could I have it well-cooked/ medium/rare please?**
  Je le voudrais bien cuit/à point/saignant s'il vous plaît? *Zher ler voodray beeang kwee/ah pwahng/saynyang, seelvooplay?*
- **May I have the bill, please?**
  L'addition, s'il vous plaît? *Laddyssyawng, seelvooplay?*
- **Where is the toilet (restroom), please?**
  Où sont les toilettes, s'il vous plaît? *Oo sawng leh twahlaitt, seelvooplay?*
- **How much does it/this cost?**
  Quel est le prix? *Kehl eh ler pree?*
- **A (half-)kilo of . . . please.**
  Un (demi-) kilo de . . . s'il vous plaît. *Ang (dermee)keelo der . . . seelvooplay.*

Index

Acknowledgements

Project management: Cambridge Publishing Management Ltd
Project editor: Karen Beaulah
Series design: Fox Design
Cover design: Liz Lyons Design
Layout and map work: Concept 5D/Cambridge Publishing Management Ltd
Repro and image setting: PDQ Digital Media Solutions Ltd/
                                    Cambridge Publishing Management Ltd
Printed and bound in India by: Replika Press Pvt Ltd

We would like to thank Image Select International/Chris Fairclough Colour Library for the photographs used in this book, to whom the copyright in the photograph belongs, with the exception of the following:

Front cover: Albi, Peter Adams/Getty Images
Back cover: Pont-du-Gard, Diana Mayfield/Getty Images

Gillian Thomas and John Harrison (pages 139, 140, 142, 152, 154, 156, 159, 161, 185, 197, 200); The Travel Library/Stuart Black (pages 132, 202).

Feedback form

If you enjoyed using this book, or even if you didn't, please help us improve future editions by taking part in our reader survey. Every returned form will be acknowledged, and to show our appreciation we will give you £1 off your next purchase of a Thomas Cook guidebook. Just take a few minutes to complete and return this form to us.

When did you buy this book? ....

Where did you buy it? (Please give town/city and, if possible, name of retailer)
....

When did you/do you intend to travel in Languedoc and Southwest France? ....

For how long (approx)? ....

How many people in your party? ....

Which cities, national parks and other locations did you/do you intend mainly to visit?
....
....

Did you/will you:
❏ Make all your travel arrangements independently?
❏ Travel on a fly-drive package?
Please give brief details: ....

Did you/do you intend to use this book:
❏ For planning your trip?   ❏ Both?
❏ During the trip itself?

Did you/do you intend also to purchase any of the following travel publications for your trip?
A road map/atlas (please specify) ....
Other guidebooks (please specify) ....

Have you used any other Thomas Cook guidebooks in the past? If so, which?
....
....

Please rate the following features of 'Drive Around Languedoc and Southwest France' for their value to you (circle VU for 'very useful', U for 'useful', NU for 'little or no use'):

The Travel Facts section on pages 14–23	VU	U	NU
The Driver's Guide section on pages 24–29	VU	U	NU
The Highlights on pages 40–41	VU	U	NU
The recommended driving routes throughout the book	VU	U	NU
Information on towns and cities, National Parks, etc	VU	U	NU
The maps of towns and cities, parks, etc	VU	U	NU

Please use this space to tell us about any features that in your opinion could be changed, improved, or added in future editions of the book, or any other comments you would like to make concerning the book:

....

....

....

....

....

....

....

....

Your age category: ❏ 21–30   ❏ 31–40   ❏ 41–50   ❏ over 50

Your name: Mr/Mrs/Miss/Ms ....

(First name or initials) ....

(Last name) ....

Your full address: (Please include postal or zip code)

....

....

....

....

....

Your daytime telephone number: ....

Please detach this page and send it to: The Series Editor, Drive Around Guides, Thomas Cook Publishing, PO Box 227, The Thomas Cook Business Park, 15–16 Coningsby Road, Peterborough PE3 8SB, United Kingdom.

Alternatively, you can e-mail us at: *books@thomascook.com*

We will be pleased to send you details of how to claim your discount upon receipt of this questionnaire.